Interactive, Multi-ı
Learn *Your*
Watch and Listen inside.

Visual   **Auditory**   **Kinesthetic**

This *one-of-a-kind* multi-media book gives you new learning and life skills strategies in all three learning styles –visual, auditory and kinesthetic.

Learn the way you like best!

★ Listen to the authors read each chapter aloud at http://www.HowToLearn.com/amazing-grades-audio or you can also listen on author's websites if they are listed at the bottom of their chapter.

★ Watch videos when you see the scan tags – scan them with your smart phone (get the free app you see below)

★ Read the book and take notes

QR codes in this book open to videos that are related to the chapters. Grab a QR Code Scanner and Reader free from your App Store.

Then, hold your smart phone a few inches from the QR code and it opens to the video. Or, you can just type in the url you see next to the QR code.

How To Give This Book Away

Corporations, Groups, Individuals and Companies:

Your sponsorship will give students the learning and life skills to maximize their grades and open more doors to their success.

We rely on you to donate the book. If your social responsibility or corporate sponsorship program includes programs aligned with schools, students and libraries, we have a special Give Away Package with more information. Contact the Publisher at 1-707- 837-8180 or email fasterlearning@gmail.com to discuss how to do this.

Special Thanks To Authors

Special Thanks to All Authors in *Amazing Grades*

The publisher wants to extend a very special thank you to all the authors from 13 countries around the world who donated their time, love and expertise to contribute a chapter to this worldwide goodwill book. None of the authors in this book accept royalties and their generosity to help the students of the world is deeply appreciated!

Special Thanks to All Proofreaders

Judith McCutcheon, Jerry Hollis, Deb Brauneller, Jo Lisa Byers, Shari Hippeard, Debi Mayes, Peggi Rieger, Ralph Sirvent, Barbara Carder, Lanette Perkins, Debbie Keith, Dr. Marva Dixon, Marcia Collins, Linda VandeVoort, Y. Dov Klahr, Pamela F. Quarles, Leslie Putney, Reese Lovett, Suzan Bunn, Debbie Foster, Letticia Torres, Abena Addo-Yobo, MicheleR Ricoma, Philip Saparov Donald Hill, John Winter

We dedicate this book to the students of the world and value your ability to inspire yourselves and others to greatness...

Is This Book for Me?

Check the boxes you agree with below.

☐ I want to know "how" to get better grades in even my toughest classes.

☐ I get nervous before my exams.

☐ I feel challenged by courses like algebra, pre-calculus, and higher level math and would love some strategies to make these classes easier.

☐ I feel like I know the material before my exams but sometimes can't recall it during the exam.

☐ I want guidance on how to get higher SAT and/or ACT scores.

☐ I feel like I could be better organized and wonder how to make it happen.

☐ I wish I knew how to cut my learning time and still get good grades.

☐ I struggle with a learning difference.

☐ I would love to know how to complete college in less than four years and save on tuition.

☐ I am motivated sometimes but want to know how to keep myself motivated even when I don't feel like it.

☐ I am a student who is required to learn another language and I want to know "how" to cut my learning time and get better grades in these classes.

☐ I know I'm smart but sometimes my eyes get tired when I read and I think I might skip lines.

☐ I know I'm smart but sometimes I forget what I read.

☐ I see other students reading faster, learning the material faster and getting better grades than I do. I sure wish I knew their secret.

☐ I'd love to see my teachers, friends and parents be proud of my accomplishments – and feel proud of myself too!

Praise for *Amazing Grades*

If you've ever struggled in school, I can tell you for sure I was right there with you. Just a few short years ago, I felt like a failure - reading was actually painful for me and this made my other subjects a real struggle. But today is a whole new story. I have a Master's Degree and am studying for a doctorate in clinical psychology. When I'm finished, I will have achieved my dream of becoming a psychologist. I have so many of the strategies in this book to thank because they truly worked! As a student, I really encourage you to read, watch or listen to them because they are completely life-changing!

Kathryn Langley, M.A., Doctoral Student at California School of Professional Psychology

FINALLY! ONE innovative and substantive book with specific strategies, and information on the wide range of topics that students really need without 200 pages of fluff. This is what we all want and nobody published until now. Save your time and money reading 50 plus books…it's all here… One or two chapters alone is more than worth the price of this book and what all students, including my kids, really need.

Stan DiOrio, J.D., parent, Legislative Director for Senator Rob Wright, Public Policy Advocate, Sacramento, CA

Thank you Pat! Amazing Grades is so much more than a book! It is an institution, a beacon of hope and light for everyone. You put together such a distinguished group of professionals from all over the world with a broad spectrum of teaching and learning methods, it will resonate with all students. Because I struggled with dyslexia through school, I especially appreciate the section on learning differences and recommend that every student, parent, teacher and professor read this book.

Helen LaLousis, CEO Face OFF Productions FaceOFFProductions.com

With today's emphasis on student achievement and school accountability, Amazing Grades is a much-needed resource. The fact that it includes student learning styles while appealing to students' natural proclivity for technology makes the book unique and important for every student.

Jeannine R. Studer, Ed.D., Professor of Counselor Education, The University of Tennessee

What a great piece of work! Amazing Grades gives a wide range of "what to do," if you want to improve your grades and your life. You can choose from over a 100 contributions of authors to learn about specific actions that might work for you as a student, teacher, or parent so you can realize your dreams.

Robert M. Hooper Ph.D., Director of Special Projects, Eastern Shore Psychological Services, Maryland

Amazing Grades

101 Best Ways To Improve Your Grades *Faster*

Pat Wyman, M.A. with 100 other best selling authors and experts

This is a worldwide goodwill book written by 101 authors from 13 countries around the world.

The Center for New Discoveries In Learning, Inc. – HowToLearn.com
Nevada

The Center for New Discoveries In Learning, Inc.
HowToLearn.com
6375 South Pecos Rd., Suite 216
Las Vegas, NV 89102

Second edition, 2017.

Corporate, Company, Individual Sponsorships:

For information on corporate sponsorships and how you or your company can donate this book to schools, students and libraries, contact The Center for New Discoveries in Learning, Inc. (HowToLearn.com). Email fasterlearning@gmail.com or call 1-707-837-8180.

For information on special discounts for bulk purchases, please contact The Center for New Discoveries in Learning, Inc. at 1-707-837-8180.

If you wish to book any authors in this book for a live or media event, contact us at 1-707-837-8180 or email fasterlearning@gmail.com

Manufactured in the United States of America.

10 9 8 7 6 5 4 3 2

No part of this book is intended to be construed as medical advice, diagnose or treat any condition. Please contact your health care provider if you have questions.

Special Thanks:

Cover design: Steven Peterson
Interior design: Spring Moon
Administrative Life Saver! Debra Winter
Keyboards: Jay Oliver. Listen to renowned pianist Jay Oliver's rendition of Amazing Grace. This is a song about second chances recorded especially for this book. Visit MusicMathSystem.com/amazing-grades.

ISBN-10: 1542841496

Softcover ISBN: 978-1542841498

Contents

Interactive Techniques; Learn Your Way, Scan Video with Your Smart Phone........................... i

How To Give This Book Away and Special Thanks ii

Is This Book for Me iii

Praise for *Amazing Grades* iv

Introduction for Students, Parents and Teachers:

How to Remove Learning Roadblocks... x

Part I: Life Skills

What is School For? 1

FOCUS: Get What You Want with This One Simple Change 3

How To Become a Very Confident Student in Two Simple Moves 5

How To Have the Attitude of a Winner 7

Use Internal Rewards to Achieve More 9

How To Take Charge of Your Emotions 11

How Brain Healthy Foods Relate to Higher Test Scores 13

Self-Esteem: If It Gets Lost How Do I Find It Again? 15

Smart Foods, Smart Brain = Better Grades 17

Laugh Your Way to Better Grades 19

The Big Breakthrough That Makes Learning Naturally Easy 21

Brain Matters That Make a Difference in Your Grades 23

Office Hours - A Poem 25

How Fitness Fortifies the Brain for Your Students 27

Putting Happiness First 29

How To Choose the Right College 31

Community College Facts to Help You Achieve Your Goals 33

Part II: Study Skills

Visual Skills Needed in School: Do You Have Any of These Symptoms 35

Outsmart Your Stress Before the Test 37

Motivation Magic 39

How To Use Creative Visualization to Get Better Grades 41

Balance Your Brain to Boost Your Grades 43

Goal Getting Goal Setting to Improve Your Grades Faster 47

Use Picture Mapping to Ace Your Exams 49

How Music Makes You Smarter 51

How To Use Mental Photography to Improve Test Scores 53

Memory Skills Made Easy 55

How To Get Better ACT, SAT, GRE… Test Scores 57

8 Ways to Beat Exam Anxiety Before and During Your Exams 59

How To Get Good Grades in College 61

Cracking The College Code: 5 Study Secrets Excellent Students Use 63

Your High Tech Brain and Technology 65

Tablets: The Backpack of Tomorrow to Raise Your Grades 67

How Can You Tell When You Know Something? 69

3 Ways To Make an "A": How One Student Went From Failing to 4.0 71

3 Strategies Guaranteed to Reduce Your Study Time 73

Learn More Study Less 75

Part III: Subject Area Learning Strategies

Conquer Algebra by Making Concepts Concrete 77
5 Strategies to Master Precalculus 79
Developing Your Higher Math Intuition 81
Biology Bits and Tips: How to Get to the Head of the Class 85
How To Get Better Grades in Science Courses 87
Got Chemistry? How To Master It Faster 89
Creative Critical Thinking 91
Don't Know Much About History? How to Master it Faster 93
7 Steps to Accelerate Your Language Learning 95
From Loathing to Loving Literature 97
How To Make Reading Easier in High School and College 99
How To Integrate Technology Into Your Learning for Better Grades 101
How To Use Google to Help You Get Better Grades 103
How To Prepare for the SAT Exam 105
Vocabulary Vibes: The Key to Mastering New Vocabulary 107
Best Learning Strategies for Kinesthetic Learners 109
5 Foolproof Ways to Remember What You Read... 111
Colossal Comprehension Clues: How to Understand Everything You Read ... 113
Reading in College: Overcoming Three Major Challenges 115
How To Write a Winning Essay in Three Easy Steps 117
How To Unleash Your Creative Genius When You Write 119
Easier Ways to Read Your History Text, Make it Come Alive and Get Better Grades 121
How To Turn Your Subjects into Games and Create Faster Learning 123
Use Speed Reading, CLEP, Dante and DSST to Finish College in Just One Year 125

Part IV: Learning Differences

Learning Differences: The Advantage of a Disadvantage.............................. 127
How To Advocate for Yourself if You Have Learning Differences 131
Dyslexia is Your Strength: 5 Strategies That Will Help You Get Better Grades 133
Overwhelmingly Overwhelmed: How to Tackle Studying One Night at a Time 135
Literacy Strategies for Secondary Special Needs Learners Across the Spectrum 137
Conversations About Making the Educational Experience Better for Students with ODD 139
Asperger's and Better Grades 141
SAT and ACT Strategies for Students with Learning Differences 143

Part V: Special Factors That Affect Learning

Vision is More Than 20/20 145
Smart Fats: How Omega-3s Enhance Your Brain For Better Grades 147
Conversations with a Doctor About ADHD 149
How Bullying Affects Academic Achievement 151
How To Stop Bullies in Their Tracks 153
How To Acquire English as a Second Language 155
How English Language Learners Manage Writing Anxiety in College 157
How To Handle Peer Pressure and Get Higher Grades 159
Feeling Depressed or Anxious? Here are Tips Which May Help 161

Part VI: Special Section for Teachers

How To Inspire Students to Believe They Can Achieve Their Goals and Dreams 163
How To Create an Emotionally Intelligent Classroom 165
The Tools of Success for Every Teacher 167
Two Simple Ways to Get Students Interested and Involved in Lessons 169
How To Foster High Achieving Resilient Students 171
15 Ways to Become a More Effective Teacher 173
Engage, Engage, Engage 175
Back to The Future with Mastery-Based Learning 177
How To Create Joyful Learning in the Classroom 179
Education Technology: Cutting Edge Meets the Classroom 181
Teaching Strategies for Transitioning in a Multilingual Educational Environment 183
31 Tips to Easily Integrate English Language Learners into your Classroom 185
Cultural Matters in the Classroom 187

Part VII: Special Section for Parents

A Letter from the Principal 189
Three Techniques to Help Your Child Build a Faster Better Brain 191
A Parent's Formula for Your Child's Success: Success = Engagement 193
Don't Let Your Child Be Mistakenly Labeled for ADHD 197
5 Best Behavior Strategies for ADHD 199
How To Advocate for Your Child with Special Needs 201
Why Grades are Important to Homeschoolers 203

Part VIII: Planning for the Future

Are You Prepared for Learning and Work? Assessing 21st Century Skills 205

Index 207
Resources 211

Introduction

Success means having the courage, the determination, and the will to become the person you believe you were meant to be.
- George Sheehan

Amazing Grades is the first book of its kind that includes new technology and allows you, the student, to learn in the personal style that works best for you. Use your smart phone to scan videos that are related to chapters, listen to authors reading their chapters aloud or if you prefer, read the words here and take notes.

This is a world-wide goodwill book! 101 authors and experts from 13 countries around the world collaborated to bring you unique and proven strategies that help you achieve academic success more rapidly by showing you how to remove any roadblocks that interfere with your learning as well as how to build the solid foundation you need for school and life-long learning achievement. You may want to take the quick inventory on page iii so you know whether this book is right for you before beginning.

Not only is this book designed to give you specific strategies to help you get higher grades, but it also includes life skills you will use forever. As you hold the book in your hands, you will find the chapters with life skills that help you develop into a conscious adult who knows how to think critically, solve problems, have a better memory, make good decisions, and achieve your goals. These skills prepare you to become a better person who has more to offer your family, community, state, nation and the world.

If you are in a hurry to get better grades, you may want to turn to the 'how to' success strategies in specific subject areas and they begin on page 77, successful study skills on page 35, learning differences on page 127, special factors that affect your learning on page 145 and life skills useful for every situation on page 1.

If you are a parent or teacher reading this book, please note we have included special sections just for you which provide the much-needed information that will help you support student success and give you unique tips never before seen in any one book! While I address the remainder of this chapter to students, I encourage parents and teachers to read it as it sheds some new light on specifically how students can maximize their academic and personal accomplishments!

Are You "Trying Hard" to Get Good Grades and Still Wish They Could Be Better?

When you "try really hard" and don't get the results you want, you need to know that "trying hard" does not take into account whether there are learning roadblocks in your way. Even though you may work very hard, something you might not even be aware of could be getting in the way of the success you want.

Do Parents or Teachers Ever Say You're Not Trying Hard Enough to Get Good Grades?

While they mean well, these people don't realize how the words on the printed page look to you, how your ears hear the words spoken by the teacher (maybe they are muffled or other noise in the classroom distracts you), whether or not you know 'how to learn' or how a dozen other factors affect *your* perception. Just because someone tells you to learn something does not automatically mean you know how to do it or that something undiagnosed is not interfering with the learning process.

When you are told to read a chapter in a book and that you will be tested on it later, there are built in assumptions that you heard the directions correctly, see the words on a page perfectly, understand them, know 'how to' study, have mastered all known memory strategies, and that you know how translate what you read into such items as essays. The assumptions behind instructions like this are almost frightening. It's akin to telling someone to solve a complicated physics problem before taking any type of math course to prepare them for it. Remove assumptions like this and it's much easier to see and fix learning roadblocks.

Get the Roadblocks Out of the Way and Good Grades Are Yours

If you want to get good grades faster, it's important to make sure that your learning foundation is clear and solid before adding the 'roof' to your learning house. Laying the foundation includes assessing your current learning strategies and removing the roadblocks to your success. My intention is that this introduction will help you build a great learning foundation before using the strategies in this book. Once you build it well, the sky's the limit on those "A's" you want! Let's look at the practical steps that you can use to successfully build a solid foundation for learning.

5 Steps to Build a Solid Foundation for Learning

1. Make sure you have excellent visual skills

Good reading skills make it easier to get better grades. Great reading skills speed up the process. Honestly, I believe that most people love reading when it is easy. Whenever I hear a person tell me they get tired when they read, don't like to read or quickly forget what they read, I instantly know there is a roadblock in the way to their success. Just because you can see the words on a page does not mean you can make meaning out of them. You may skip lines, miss punctuation, insert words that aren't there, omit words, get tired when you read, or do many other things that interfere with comprehension and memory.

HowToLearn.com

For example, just because you passed an eye chart screening at 20 feet away while covering one eye, this has nothing at all to do with skills you need to read a book. After all, who reads their book at 20 feet away while covering one eye? (Author's Note: As a reading specialist and expert who testifies on vision screening legislation, I believe it is crucial that students receive school vision screenings designed to evaluate both the near point skills demanded of them during reading, writing and looking at computer screens as well the distance skills needed to see the blackboard and other things like playing sports. Combining these screenings helps to identify and prevent student reading problems as well as potentially saving billions of dollars on remedial reading programs).

Be sure to take a look at, or listen to the chapters in this book by the Optometric Education Program Foundation and Dr. Kristy Remick as they provide more specifics about reading and visual skills improvement related to learning and better grades. You can also take the Eye-Q Reading Inventory ™ online at tinyurl.com/czefhzo and it will tell you whether you have the visual skills you need to be a great reader and if not, what to do about it. Solutions like vision therapy and the use of colored overlays placed over print (more info at tinyutl.com/7u36pvk) or computer screens can remove reading stress and help you read faster and easier.

2. Find out how you learn best. What is your preferred learning style?

Students learn in different ways and this is known as their personal learning style. Some students prefer to look at and read new material (visual learners), some find it easier to listen (auditory learners), and some like to interact with, touch or move around when learning (kinesthetic or tactile learners). When you know how you learn best you can take certain steps to adjust the material you need to learn your preferred learning style. If you are an auditory learner for example, listening to the mp3 chapters in this book may help you master the material more quickly.

IMPORTANT: School, with all its written tests, caters to highly visual learners. These students excel at test-taking because they turn what they read and hear into pictures in their mind, then recall those images faster during a test. Brain research supports this rapid image recall. Knowing that visual learners have an advantage school, you can get the same advantage by adding some visual learning strategies to your preferred learning style. When you read, stop every little while and make images of what you just read. Add color and motion, then, during your tests, look up, see the images and turn those images back into words.

To find out how you prefer to learn best take the Learning Styles Quiz at HowToLearn.com. There is an app that lets you email the results to your teacher and friends or place your results on social media sites to compare how you learn best with your friends and then talk about what that means in school or even in relationships. (Yes, learning styles affect relationships too).

3. Verify that your listening and speaking skills are excellent

Hearing involves what is known as receptive language (your ability to hear clearly and understand what you hear) and expressive language (your ability to produce language and communicate your message).

For example, have you ever been on the phone talking and someone else in the room tries to speak to you at the same time? How does this affect your concentration and conversation? There are technical names that relate to receptive and expressive language skills you need for good grades but my goal here is not to be a sesquipedalian. Part of those skills include things like auditory figure ground issues which means that you may miss a portion of what you hear because you can't separate one person's voice from the rest of the background noise in the classroom. The bottom line is that listening and speaking significantly affect your learning abilities and grades just as reading does.

If you feel that you're struggling at all when you're trying to listen, speak or learn then I recommend you go to an audiologist as well as a speech and language pathologist to have hearing, perception, receptive and expressive language tested. Make sure your foundation in this area is really solid and if not, take steps to make accommodations for it.

4. Accommodate learning differences

Amazing Grades contains a listing of special learning differences, such as ADHD, Dyslexia, Dysgraphia, Asperger's, ODD and others that could affect some people's ability to learn. Be sure you know that none of these differences has anything to do with your innate intelligence or ability to succeed in school and life. You will simply want to ensure that you are aware of the accommodations you are entitled to if you have learning differences so that you receive the same education everyone else does.

5. Be brain and body smart

Folks, eventually your eating habits will catch up with you. It may not seem like it today but if you really want to enhance your ability to get better grades, just know that the food you put into your mouth affects both your brain and your body. Eat a bunch of fast food and you put stress on all your organs, including your brain. Use common sense when eating. If you skip breakfast, your blood sugar plummets from hours of no nourishment and then you can't concentrate as well. The answers to better food choices are part of building a good foundation for learning and they are all listed in this book.

Why are Lifelong Learning Skills Important?

The days when the information you need is delivered in just one format and for a single purpose are long gone. *Amazing Grades* gives you video, audio and tactile strategies to get higher grades, and also includes 'how to learn' life skills – information that will help you become a lifelong learner. Your ability to learn is fundamental to your ability to grow, change and achieve your purpose in this life. It allows you to acquire new knowledge, shows you how to act consciously and teaches you to become self-sufficient. In sum, understanding how to learn is the key to achieving your highest potential.

In addition, it's currently estimated that you will change jobs a minimum of seven times in your life. Each one of these jobs will require that you learn new things. Add to this that you may need to study for a certification, learn for on-the-job changes and promotions, take professional exams or simply study to renew your driver's license. You will continue to need to learn as you may also want to maintain quality relationships, raise a child well, be truly healthy, buy a home, decide who to vote for, grow a garden, and so much more...

All of these things require that you know 'how to learn'. As a learning expert, my favorite quote is this:

Learning is not about being smart – it's about strategy
- Pat Wyman

Those who want to know how to use their innovative thinking, intuition, creativity, kindness, empathy, big picture understanding, intra and interpersonal skills in combination with the learning strategies in this book already have a significant head start on learning success.

Every Person is 'Smart' in Their Own Unique Way

I've never really cared for the word 'smart' to describe a human being. What if you're a gifted artist and yet your grades in school make it appear as if you're not "smart" in that environment? What if you inspire millions of people with your actions but still don't have a report card reflecting the kind of person you are? Smart is a relative term so it's more accurate to say that every person is "smart in their own unique way." While grades in school are simply a representation of what you can accomplish and the type of habits you are developing, you are born with innate talents and gifts that are uniquely yours. Remember, intelligence in nearly all forms can be developed.

Put School in Perspective

When you put school learning and grades in perspective, you realize that school can only measure specific types of success. Your grades alone do not determine *who you really are* because your intelligence and talents cannot be simply reduced to letters on a report card. That said, school *is* a place to develop certain habits that society believes will represent the type of person you are and can become. Your good grades indicate that you know how to organize your time, work together on a team, make tough decisions when needed, communicate well, relate parts to the whole, read, write, think, and a host of other "Bloom's Taxonomy" skills. The habits it takes to produce good grades predict, in most people's minds, whether you are prepared to enter the workforce or higher education equipped with positive and important skills that will serve you, and others, for a lifetime.

Ultimately, the best advice I can offer you is to use this book to find out ***how to get the very best grades*** and then use those grades to open more doors than you ever thought possible. Your good grades can help you get scholarships, better jobs, quality work training, and much more. Then you can head out into your life, positively confident that your excellent grades and strong life skills will pave the road to your highest and best success.

Pat Wyman, M.A., is the best selling author of several books, and the founder of HowToLearn.com with over three million visitors a year. She is a university instructor for teachers in continuing education at California State University, East Bay, frequent media guest and known as America's Most Trusted Learning Expert. Her mission is to help all students be successful and achieve their full potential. Find out how you learn best and check your visual skills by taking the free Learning Styles Quiz and Eye-Q Reading Inventory™ on her site at HowToLearn.com.

Listen to this chapter at HowToLearn.com/amazing-grades-audio

What is School For?

Education is what is left after you have forgotten everything you learned at school
-Albert Einstein

I visualize GOOD schooling like an iceberg. The visible 15% is the knowledge about the subjects that students acquire and are assessed on covered by the curriculum.

The invisible 85% is the ability to analyze, work in teams, research, experiment, plus the disposition to be continuously curious and persistent. This should be 'what's left', when the welter of facts from the curriculum is forgotten. Retention of knowledge is schooling –the development of learning and problem solving *skills* and a love of learning is education. The government mandates the former but the teacher controls whether the important 85% is acquired or not.

Of course subjects like history, math and literature are worthwhile in their own right but they become life enhancing when they are also used as vehicles to help students gain the skills to tackle the unknown problems of the future, build their deductive powers, their creative thinking, reflection and good judgment. Wouldn't that make education more relevant, inspiring and interesting to both student and teacher?

There is a Gap to be Closed

Most **'real life' learning** is focused on the present, with a specific motivating goal, i.e. I need to learn how to use Power Point today, because I need to make a presentation tomorrow. All carrot: no stick.

School learning is mostly focused on the future. Learn this today because at some future date you might need to know it and there will be an exam. Almost all stick: little carrot!

In **Real Life Learning** you are faced with a new challenge and you research it and figure it out for yourself, often through trial and error, though not necessarily on your own. It involves questioning and often discussion with others, and often copying other people's successful strategies. It engages your emotions. It involves reflection. And you control the timing and the process. In short 'real life learning' is actively creating knowledge and it's motivating. It is present orientated and students are very present orientated.

School learning is mostly broken down into bite size pieces and is offered up gradually by the teacher in pre-digested bits. It's mostly a solitary with little role for collaboration. Copying is discouraged. Your task is less to figure things out, but to memorize what others have already discovered. It has far less emotional engagement.

Questions from students are rare. (The average number of questions generated by students is one a month. The average number of questions generated by teachers is 40 per day!). And you neither control the timing or the process. In short school learning is passively consuming knowledge and it's not very motivating. It is future orientated and students are very present orientated.

Teaching in the Age of Google

Students leaving schooling today are likely to have several different careers over their lifetime. It's a world where the sum of human knowledge is available within a few key strokes on their computer. In such a world our students must leave school knowing how to be quick, efficient researchers and learners, how to independently interrogate a subject so they really understand it and how to think logically and creatively. Anything less will not equip them for exponential change and a highly competitive world.

Students may have differing abilities, but <u>every</u> student can become better at learning. They only need some simple-to-acquire techniques. The answer is to embed and demonstrate these learning and thinking techniques and habits day by day into every classroom.. And the good news is it's easy to do.

The European Union recognizes this logic and has recently funded a large project in Poland called EduScience which aims to greatly enhance the teaching of science, math and indeed all subjects at all ages in Poland. I am proud to be part of the EduScience team that includes the Polish Academy of Sciences. My contribution has been to create two books – delivered in digital form. The first, short book is for students. It trains them in 26 simple learning techniques to make their learning less stressful and more successful. It is designed to be taken home and help engage parents in the process of their children's learning.

The second book is for teachers. It shows how easy it is to embed effective learning and thinking strategies into <u>existing</u> lesson plans. The over 100 practical teaching ideas have all been proven in classrooms from Europe to Asia to North America. Any one of these ideas can be implemented to enhance a class tomorrow! The two books are companions. So students and teachers are, literally working to the same model of what makes for successful learning. They are deliberately <u>both</u> called *'Did You Ask a Good Question Today?'* (the title of both books are inspired by Nobel Prize winner for Physics, <u>Isidore Rabi</u>. He credits his success to an inquiring habit of mind stimulated early on by his mother, who would ask him that same question every day when he got in from school.) The result is a more lively, motivated and engaged class.

Ten years of independent research at the University of Newcastle in the UK show that teaching learning strategies: improves student grades; increases student motivation, increases teacher enjoyment of teaching and motivation; improves collaboration between students, teachers and parents.

I believe that we can raise the standard of education if we consciously teach learning and thinking skills <u>at the same time</u> as we teach curriculum content. Because **what** you know can easily become out of date – whereas knowing ***how to learn*** is a skill for life. And because all the major researchers in the intelligence field are sure that intelligence can be developed.

David Perkins of Project Zero at Harvard University states, "We can become more intelligent through study and practice, through *access to appropriate tools,* and through learning to make effective use of these tools." Robert Sternberg, formerly of Yale University, identifies three elements of intelligence: analytical ability, (to analyze, evaluate, judge, compare and contrast); creative ability, (to create, invent, discover, imagine); and practical ability, (to apply, utilize, implement, and activate). And he believes that these abilities can be increased through study and practice.

Lauren Resnick of the University of Pittsburgh defines intelligence as "seeking information and organizing that information so that it makes sense and can be remembered, i.e. working to figure things out until a workable solution is found." These definitions suggest that we can actually help our students to become more intelligent by helping them acquire thinking and learning strategies. <u>Every</u> student can get better at learning and thinking and thereby be better equipped for the 21st century.

Colin Rose is the international best selling author of hundreds of books and programs including Accelerated Learning, *Did You Ask A Good Question Today?,* and co-author of *Accelerated Learning for The 21st Century.* He is founder of AcceleratedLearning.com, fellow of The Royal Society of Arts, founding member of UK Campaign for Learning, member of the British Association for the Advancement of Science and a senior member of the Royal Society of Medicine.

Listen to this chapter at HowToLearn.com/amazing-grades-audio

FOCUS: Get What You Want with This One Simple Change

Do you hate taking two days to do something you could do in an hour and see no point in wasting your precious time on things that have no purpose? I know I do!

Well what if I could tell you a secret that would super charge everything you do and make your life seem easier and show you how to use it to get better grades? Would that be useful to you? You probably already know how to create the right environment for studying and already learned the value of a good study technique –that's where your teachers come in and the value of a book like this. Even concentration can be practiced until you find a way to get really good at it.

This Secret Is All About How You Focus

The great thing about focus is that whether you realize it or not, you already do it all the time! If you do it well, it can be a very powerful tool, but if you don't, it will really slow you down. Imagine if I asked you to choose a light to pinpoint a distant object at and said you could either use a flashlight with a wide, fuzzy, yellow beam or a sharp, crisp laser. Which would you choose? Of course you'd pick the laser, because you can point it right at the object and its beam will stay clear and precise. The flashlight might give a general direction and rough outline, but you'll light up lots of other irrelevant stuff too.

tinyurl.com/7s4vf6b

Next, I'm going to give you the choice of either facing the object, or standing with your back to it. Now which will you pick?

It sounds obvious doesn't it and yet, when it comes to getting the best grades more easily, by using the power of your focus, you may well be facing entirely the wrong way and using a blurry old torch!

When it comes to good focus, the key thing to get right is the <u>direction</u> and you'll be pleased to know there are only two to choose from! You can either focus on moving closer to the things you want, or away from the things you don't want. Both will work to a degree, but only one will work really well.

If your focus is on avoiding what you don't want – like bad grades, getting told off or the prospect of a job you won't enjoy –you'll picture precisely that in your mind and it's the fear of getting what you don't want that will make you work.

You'll waste time and energy trying to avoid these negative things. When your grades pick up a bit, you'll feel less like studying because the thing you are afraid of will seem further away and less likely. This usually means your results will go down again, until you get close to trouble and then, the fear will kick back in and you'll work harder again. It's a bit of a yo-yo effect. The problem is that you will always be focusing on those negative things and if you don't work hard enough at the right time, it might be too late for your grades.

If however, you pick the smart option and choose to focus towards what you really do want, you'll be more motivated and more excited the closer you get to the thing you're after. In other words, as your grades get better, you'll work even harder because you know you're getting closer to what you want! It's like a magnet pulling you on. Isn't that cool! You'll do better and you'll enjoy it too!

To work out which way you're focusing right now, ask yourself why you want good grades and write down your answers. If you get a list that says mainly things like, 'So I don't have to…' 'To get away from/

avoid…' and 'Not to…' then you're focusing on moving away from things.

If your list is mostly, 'So I can…' 'To be able to…' and 'To have…' then you are more likely focusing towards positive things. Changing the direction of your focus, if you need to, is easy!

Begin by thinking of as many great reasons as you can for getting the best possible grades. Write down all the things you will <u>do</u>, <u>have</u> and <u>be</u> when you get them.

Then, imagine your perfect future. The kind of life that you will be able to have when you get the grades you want.

In your head make a little movie of the moment that you get that thing you really want, the best thing that good grades will get you. Imagine it so clearly that you can already feel those great feelings. Listen to the sounds around you in that moment and picture what you'll see. Maybe proud faces at your graduation, or the great house or fancy car you'll buy; or the wonderful gifts you'll be able to give, thanks to that dream job. There is no right answer - whatever makes you want to work hard and do your best, is perfect.

Make a dream board with pictures of the things you'll get; things that excite you and make you want that life already and put it somewhere you can see it every day – perhaps near where you study.

Write a short paragraph describing yourself and your future. Talk about the great things you will have because you worked hard at school and write it as though you already have it all. Make it sound as exciting as you can and read out loud every day.

The more you want it and think about it, the more desire to have it you will create and your focus will become laser sharp.

Like running a race, you wouldn't set off with your back to the finish line would you! Keep your eyes firmly on the prize! In any area of your life being clear about exactly what you want and making sure you are focusing on the positive and moving towards it, will always increase your chances of success.

Remember, your education is a gift that you prepare now to unwrap later, so grab the best that you can. You have to go to school, so make the most of it and get the best grades you can. The harder you work at school, the more choices you will have later in life and only you will lose out by not doing your very best. Use that laser and light up your perfect future!

Amanda Ball, BA (Hons) is the author of the bestselling personal development series *The Self Help Bible* at theselfhelpbible.com. She is also a master Practitioner of NLP, Hypnosis and Time Line Therapy™.

Listen to this chapter at http://www.theselfhelpbible.com/learning

How To Become a Very Confident Student in Two Simple Steps

What does a person who has no confidence or self-belief look like? How do they stand? How do they walk and talk? Yes, that right – their shoulders will be slumped forward and they will shuffle along with their eyes fixed firmly on the ground. If you were to talk to them they would respond mumbling words that are vague and indistinct.

What does a person who is brimming with confidence and self-belief look like? How do they stand? How do they walk and talk? You're got it! They stand upright with their shoulders pulled back. They walk purposefully looking people in the eye, smiling, and saying, "Hello."

The mind and body, you see, are intimately connected – how you *think* and *feel* effects your *posture* and your *posture* affects the way you *think* and *feel*.

If you want to feel negative and pessimistic about yourself then slouch around with your head hanging down. However, if you want to feel really, really confident and positive about yourself then stand upright with your shoulders back, breathe slowly but deeply and *smile*. You will soon be feeling a lot better about yourself - I guarantee it!

Confidence is a *state of mind* and you can create that state of mind whenever you want.

For example, try this simple exercise:

★   Imagine that your body is like that of a string puppet with strings attached to your head and shoulders.

★   Stand upright in a relaxed and comfortable manner. Imagine your puppet strings are being tugged up and as they are being pulled up you find your back and shoulders becoming straighter and more upright.

★   Now imagine that your puppet strings are being relaxed and as the strings drop your shoulders gently drop too. You find yourself slumped forward gazing at the ground and as you slump forward you start to feel really, really low.

★   Now imagine that your puppet strings are being pulled up gently, and as they are being pulled up you find you're back starting to become straighter and your shoulders start to move back too. Your face is now upright and you find yourself looking clearly at the world around you. Your posture is now upright and you are feeling positive, optimistic and really, really good about yourself.

This simple, but powerful exercise shows how easy it is to create a posture that makes you feel really, really good about yourself, and you can create that feeling whenever you want simply by adopting the right posture. I have included another exercise similar to the one above. It shows you how to adopt a really confident posture.

Whenever you find yourself feeling worried, anxious or scared, whenever you know that confidence is the state of mind you want and need, such as just before you take an exam, for example then get yourself into 'confidence mode' by adopting a confident posture and your state of mind will immediately improve. Here is the exercise. It's simple to use but very effective.

Boost your Confidence now!

1. Stand upright looking forward.

Imagine a time when you were feeling *really, really confident*. What were you doing when you were feeling this wonderful feeling of confidence? Concentrate on this image of you feeling *really, really confident*. Concentrate on what it is you are doing. Imagine this really confident you, is standing right in front of you right now facing the same way you are.

2. Now, imagine stepping forward into the image of this really, really confident you.

As you do so see the world through their eyes, hear the world through their ears and *feel, really feel* their confidence. Notice how they stand, how they breathe and how they look. What are they doing? Make the colors you can see even *brighter*, make the sounds you can now hear *clearer* and *sharper*. Take those wonderful feelings and make them *stronger* – that's right, make them stronger. Turn up your feelings like you were turning up the volume on a TV or radio.

3. Every time you feel the need to feel confident create an image in your mind of the confident person you know you are.

Step inside this image, and as you do so *become* that really confident person. Remember, you have all the resources you need to be confident – you just need to BELIEVE IT!

Congratulations! You now know how to be a really confident student. I know I'm making it sound really easy but actually, it isn't that difficult to develop confidence, you just need to *believe* you are confident and *practice, practice, practice* being confident and practice, as they say makes perfect. If you practice being confident often enough then confidence, in time, will become your default way of being. Michael Jordan, the great basketball player said, "You have to expect things of yourself before you can do them."

James Woodworth, M.Ed, is a teacher, mentor, coach and NLP Practitioner with 23 years experience working in post-compulsory Education. He holds an honors degree in Fine Art, an M.A. and M.Phil in Visual Theories and a M.Ed in Educational Research from the Faculty of Education at the University of Cambridge in the United Kingdom.

Listen to this chapter at HowToLearn.com/amazing-grades-audio

How To Have an Attitude of a Winner

Did you ever wonder what makes a winner different from others? It is about making the right choices to create a positive outcome. Those choices will determine your future.

Whether you are top of the class or the bottom or somewhere in between, it doesn't matter. Your attitude determines your outcome period. It's your choice to either learn how to have the attitude of a winner or not.

Winner Formula

Take the opportunity to get on the right track - make your assessment and decide if the benefits outweigh the potential losses of not taking action:

1. Where will you be 10 years from now?

A true winner decides in advance to earn a certain type of income, have the job of their dreams, get higher education or not, and everything else they can think of. The point is to decide in advance.

2. Imagine an interview for employment, which requires certain academics.

How will you feel if you want the job but don't have the qualifications? Key ingredients include maintaining focus of your objectives while creating a plan and a regular pace to reach them. In order to make that a reality there are a number of contributing factors that can make or break you and all the while external influences can be your biggest enemy. So to begin with look inward and start communicating with yourself; know who you are and what you want. Ignore what others think or plan for you unless you want it too.

ATTITUDE KEYS = Work on improving your attitude

> *1. To achieve the best results try to balance your lifestyle.*
>
>> a. Take up 'physical exercise' fitness training.
>> b. Eat a healthy balanced diet (Never skip meals).
>> c. Aim for a stable weight based on your height and build.
>>
>>> ★   By being healthier your alertness and concentration will make enhancements while studying, thus contributing to improved performance.

> *2. Balance personal lifestyle with education.*
>
>> a. Make sure you have FREE time to stay in balance with your work time.
>> b. Focus on your objectives and do not fall prey to other people's problems.
>> c. Participate wholeheartedly in studies while at school.
>>
>>> ★   By concentrating on yourself, you will find it easier to keep up with the rest of the group, and excel.

> *3 . Work on anti-stress (self-awareness promotes a calmer, better you).*
>
>> a. Breathing and balancing exercises promote strength and inner calmness to achieve positive results. There are breathing exercises in this book and other brain balancing exercises too. See the chapter by Goldstein and the Dennisons.

Anti-Stress 1. Start by taking a few minutes to release the stress and glide into this transition at ease.

>   a. Sit or stand in a relaxed position.
>   b. Slowly inhale through your nose, counting to five in your head.
>   c. Let the air out from your mouth (don't hold it), counting to eight in your head as it
>   leaves your lungs. Repeat several times. That's it!

Anti-Stress 2. Take the next challenge.

Breathe in and hold your breath double the amount of counts that you exhale. So if you hold for 10 you will breathe out 5. This continues until you still feel comfortable but challenged. Feel your lungs open up and a sense of spiritual peace will flow through your body. By spending several minutes performing these exercises every day your lungs will become expanded and a sense of well being will fill your body.
The why behind the ATTITUDE keys is to provide a straightforward approach that will create the power from within to achieve greatness.

5 short statements to define the attitude of a winner:

★   Aim for perfection.
★   Time conscious effectiveness.
★   Analyze and think.
★   Passionate goal seeker.
★   Excellence producer.

Make a commitment today to add your ideas to the list and make a better tomorrow. Essentially a student needs to see the bigger picture in the choices that are available. Some students coach themselves into making changes and learn to ride the waves of emotion on the path to the attitude of a winner.

Another key to staying focused and objective is not to lose sight of why you are at school in the first place i.e. to learn. Small daily improvements will help you to get through obstacles that try to hold you back. Life has hardships that can be overcome. In fact it's a passage whereby everyone has the ability to cope and strengthen their character. It is how you handle the passages that matter and everyone has the capability to have the attitude of a winner.

The attitude of a winner will help you in your studies because it will allow you to think outside the box i.e. analyze things from different angles, which contributes to finding solutions. Try the exercises outlined above and you have everything to gain!

Carl Boniface is the founder of StudentsRatings.com. He lives in the U.K. No part of this chapter is intended to diagnose or prescribe medical advice. These are all well-known relaxation techniques.

Listen to this chapter at HowToLearn.com/amazing-grades-audio

Use Internal Awards to Achieve More!

Being the best person you can be may be met with various challenges but you have more than a hundred strategies in this book to help assure you of your success.

This success is not measured by superficial and materialistic barometers (money, toys, status, recognition, prestige, title, etc.) despite the fact many people think these are the best motivators. These motivators may provide some initial burst of joy but will not provide you with continuous meaningful motivation. You will not sustain any type of real personal achievement via the rewards, love and approval of anyone… other than yourself!

What is needed to drive and sustain success is not some external reward system but rather a strong intrinsic, *internal* reward system - one that you control.

Not only is this type of reward system more powerful, it is more lasting, and costs you nothing more than adapting your present ways of thinking. Let's be clear about one thing, the ultimate motivator is internal and is simply for the enjoyment and interest of an activity - like reading a book.

However it isn't always easy finding this type of motivation when achieving a diploma or degree. It is often said that if you have a career you love you will never have to "work" a day in your life. So here are some approaches to help achieve the same type of motivation at all academic challenges and perhaps many others in life.

Be present and engaged in your task.

In order to be sustained, this requires a healthy dose of energy, but not through energy drinks! Obviously doing a task you love will create this energy naturally; however doing a task that may be compulsory but not compelling, means finding ways to create interest even if it is artificial. Simple things like seating in class, participation, taking notes, or simply try to find some part of the lesson/topic that's interesting.

Making a constant conscious choice to be more engaged in the class/activity will help with your motivation when the subject matter does not do it alone. This may seem like an oversimplified approach but the results will prove it true - self motivation can be learned through repeated and conscious efforts to become and remain engaged in an activity.

Achievement begets achievement.

When we achieve an important goal we are left with a great sense of satisfaction that can tap into real internal motivation and become like an addictive drug. Striving to do your best on a challenging task can reward you with feelings of accomplishment and stronger self concept - making you feel like you can take on the world. Inevitably your drive to succeed on future tasks becomes stronger.

And if you have not achieved the level you had hoped, you must remain positive and look at what you can do – not what you can't. Achieving goals for your own internal desires of self-development becomes a self rewarding endeavor that has no limit and has no failures. By enjoying the fruits of your labor and taking pride in what you have achieved, it becomes a better motivator than any material possession that you could ever attain.

Become the journey.

Abraham Maslow was a famous American psychologist who believed everyone has strong desires deep in them to achieve their full potential thus achieving self actualization. Self actualization is simply a person's desire to be what they were meant to be. Fulfilling our potential by exploring our limits in the direction of interests and talents is one of the ultimate and most effective methods of becoming and remaining motivated. If you see each day as peeling back another layer of who you are and where you are going, each task becomes an exploration of the possibilities that lie before you. Like an artist carves a sculpture, you too are carving out the person you were meant to be. Embrace the surprises, rewards, challenges and yes - even the struggles.

You have direct control over your levels of motivation. Motivation is merely your internal desire and commitment to do things and is the basic and fundamental factor in achieving all of the goals you dream of. Being fully motivated is not a result of what happens to you, but a result of what happens in you. Tap into this and you are on your way to being better than you ever thought possible.

You are the embodiment of the information you choose to accept and act upon.
To change your circumstances you need to change your thinking and subsequent actions.
                                        - Adlin Sinclair

Donnie Holland, M.Ed. is a school principal in Nova Scotia, Canada and currently working on his Ed.D through the University of West Georgia.

Listen to this chapter at HowToLearn.com/amazing-grades-audio

How To Take Charge of Your Emotions

First of all I would like to acknowledge you for choosing to read this book. It shows that you are committed to improve your grades and life. I am so grateful to get this opportunity to add value to your life.

When you read the title of my chapter you may be asking "What do my emotions have to do with my grades and why is it so important?" Allow me to share with you why. As you go about your everyday life you may feel like your emotions are all over the place. It's natural to feel happy one day, sad the next, angry the next and fantastic the next. Heck, you can go through these emotions all in one day.

When I was younger, a mentor told me that our emotions are there for a reason. Just like the temperature meter in your car tells you whether your car is cool or overheating, your emotions help you determine whether your life is working for you or not. If you consistently have negative emotions it is a message that something is wrong and you must take action to change it before you "overheat".

When you feel happy your brain is in a better state for success, but of course you might not feel happy every day, so let's talk about how to get better grades even when you're not feeling happy. You may have heard success stories of athletes and others who came from very challenging environments to rise up and become great. They went through all kinds of emotions in their lives but the secret is that they used each emotion to their advantage to change their lives for the better. You can too.

Let me share with you how I overcame challenges of having very low self esteem and anger to excel in my studies and life. When I was in grade two my family moved and I went to a different school. The language I spoke was different than what most other students spoke so I was perceived as "different." My brother and I were bullied quite a bit. Over the years I developed very low self esteem, became angry as a teenager and did poorly in school. A turning point came for me when I went to camp.

A very kind teacher gave me unconditional love and respect. At that moment I made a commitment to change my life. I started to read self improvement books and attend seminars. I have learned many things over the years. In this chapter I am going to share with you three things and it is my utmost wish that will be a turning point in your life.

The first is about purpose. One of the reasons why I couldn't succeed in my grades was because I did not know what my purpose was or why I went to school. It is like a plane that takes off but does not have a destination. Please ask yourself "Why do I go to school"? Does the answer give you a positive emotion or negative one? If it is negative chances are you do not have a strong purpose why you go to school.

Over the years I did research on traits of top students. The one thing they all have in common is they all know their purpose and it is usually something bigger than themselves.

Example: The reason why I go to school is to learn and make a positive difference in the world.

That kind of purpose really helps you overcome the challenges and negative emotions that you may face in your daily life. So please find some quiet time to find your purpose.

The second thing I have learned is brain scientists say when we are angry, sad or frustrated our brain function gets very limited and we don't have access to the more thinking part of the brain.

That is one of the main reasons why I couldn't study initially. They say one of the fastest ways for us to switch from being angry to being able to access a more logical perspective and feelings, is doing a deep breathing exercise. Take a few minutes to slowly take a few deep breaths and notice how it feels. In the future when you are angry, sad or frustrated just keep on doing deep breathing and you automatically change your emotions.

Finally, one of the most powerful things I have learned about how to keep my emotions in a consistently positive state is to practice love and gratitude in my life.

In my class I do a powerful scientific experiment to show the power of love and how it affects our learning and life. It is called Muscle Testing and it is based on kinesiology which is the study of human movement.

I get students to volunteer. I ask them to lift up their arm and I tell them to resist when I try to push it down.

When I ask them to think of a negative experience or emotion their arms become weak and they can't resist.

When I ask them to think of someone they love and things they are grateful for their arms suddenly become strong and I cannot push it down.

What does that tell you? Yes! When you have negative emotions you become weak but when you practice love and gratitude in your life you become strong. Scientists have proven that love is one of the most powerful emotions you will ever have. It will change your life and all the negative emotions you are facing.

One of my daily practices is to forgive everyone before I go to sleep every night. Each morning I get up and say how grateful I am for everything I have and for people I care about. I would like to end this chapter by saying that it has been a privilege to be able to communicate with you. I wish you the best in your studies and life!

Zeal Zainuddin is the Principal Trainer and Life Coach of M&Z Empowerment Center in Malaysia and Singapore. He is a Certified Practitioner of Neuro-Linguistic Programming (NLP) and a Life Coach. Zeal started his own company with a mission to empower and benefit others with his personal experience and knowledge. Through his workshop Accelerated Learning in Action (ALIA) and Love & Respect life coaching he has helped many people to overcome their challenges in life and learn by applying the principles of Love & Respect and whole being learning (body, mind, heart and spirit). Mr. Zainuddin's mission is to provide the best quality education and learning in Malaysia, Singapore and around the world.

Listen to this chapter at HowToLearn.com/amazing-grades-audio

How Brain Healthy Foods
Relate to Higher Test Scores

Proficient learning and attaining optimal test scores are two skills necessary in achieving didactic proficiency. Your adroitness at attention, concentration and recall are the hallmarks of academic success. What other elements are obligatory factors in attaining these types of cognitive achievements? Brain healthy eating, as well as, brain and body exercise routines comprise a much larger role in brain performance than previously understood.

The food that we opt to consume to fuel our brain determines how adept these areas of cognition will function now and for the rest of our lives.

Research scientists know that nutrition and dietary habits have a momentous effect on learning and academic accomplishment. They also know that they have a critical effect on how our brains age. Not only is it important to know how certain foods effect our brain and thought processes, it is also equally important to know how the timing of food intake effects any type of performance either academic, athletic or leisure. The effects of academic examination stress on our food intake patterns also plays significant role. So not only is it important to have healthy nutritional behaviors on a daily basis; it is even more essential to know the effects food consumption has on cognition prior to and immediately following academic testing.

We have all heard the adage, "breakfast is the most important meal of the day". Research shows that kids who regularly eat breakfast score higher on standardized math tests compared to those who skip breakfast. Break-fast, is just that, after sleeping all night the brain (and the body) require refueling to function more optimally as we face our "activities of daily living".

Individuals who skip breakfast tend to have memory problems, much shorter attention spans and difficulty concentrating, all of which are at the core components of academic success.

The Human Brain is the most captivating organ in our body. It is the center of thought understanding and reason, requiring a variety of nutrients to function optimally. Proteins, carbohydrates both simple and complex as well as fats are all utilized by our brain in some special way.

Protein is one of the most important nutrients for healthy brain functioning. Proteins are the workhorses of the body, they make up the majority of cellular structure. Choline is a protein (amino acid) essential for neurotransmitters that play a pivotal role in memory retention. Consuming protein such as meat, eggs, chicken, tofu, almonds, navy beans, peanut butter also raises the levels of the amino acid tyrosine and this prompts the brain to manufacture other amino acids critical to memory and concentration. A moderate amount of daily protein is sufficient, timing the intake of the protein is critical to optimal brain functioning.

Complex Carbohydrates are essential for fuel, maintenance and repair of our brain and are composed of several kinds of sugars. The body takes longer to digest these sugars and release them as glucose in the blood streams, thus your blood sugar remains more stable. The more fiber in a complex carbohydrate the more prolonged the absorption. This allows for a constant source of "power up" glucose for the brain and body. The critical role of energy availability and optimal brain function is well established. The Mayo Clinic says that 45-65% of your daily calories should come from complex carbohydrates. Examples are whole wheat, brown rice, quinoa, black eyed peas, lentils and more.

Carbohydrate foods with high fiber content are essential in invigorating brain memory. These high fiber foods are the search engine for antioxidant health. The brain makes use of more oxygen that any other organ in your entire body. Good blood flow is essential to supply oxygen to these cognitive areas. Our brains are at high risk for damage as a result of the oxidation process. Balancing nutrient rich carbohydrates with foods high in protein will result in the best brain protection possible from a nutritional stand point.

Fats. Specialized brain cells that allow us to think and feel are created from fatty acids derived from fat. Monounsaturated and Polyunsaturated fats are "good fat" and they play a vital role in health brain functioning. The omega-3 fatty acid known as docosahexaenoic acid (DHA) is an important ingredient for optimal brain performance. Th at is why fish is known as a "brain food", it is a rich source of (DHA). The brain and its long spidery neurons are basically made of fat. Essential fatty acids are so important to the development and proper maintenance of the brain that "some scientists even postulate that it was the ingestion of omega-3 EFA's that allowed the brain to evolve to the next stage of human development." Check out the chapter called "Smart Fats" in this book for more information on omega 3 fats and why they are so important for optimal brain health.

The bottom line for you as a student is that choosing to eat more brain healthy foods puts your brain and body into the best shape to help you get higher grades and test scores.

Tell me what you eat, and I will tell you what you are.
- Jean Anthelme Brillat-Savarin

Stephen A. Konstenius, Ph.D., C.A.S.N.S. is a Certified Advanced Sports Nutritional Specialist and Director of 40Plusleap.com. He has extensive training in cognitive health, medical psychiatry & psychopharmacology from Harvard Medical School.

Listen to this chapter at HowToLearn.com/amazing-grades-audio

Self-Esteem: If It Get's Lost How Do I Find It Again?

Self-Esteem has become the new buzzword for students, parents and teachers. We all do our best in giving you the best chances to attain the highest self-esteem possible. With increased self-esteem there isn't anything you cannot accomplish. If you think you can achieve something you can.

High self-esteem even makes the nay-sayers irrelevant. If your self-esteem gets lost, you absolutely can find it again. When you speak to successful leaders, most often you will hear them recount stories of how others didn't believe in them but their own positive feelings about themselves pushed them to work harder and achieve more.

What gave them that ability? Healthy self-esteem.

Let's talk about how we go about gaining self-esteem and then keeping it in the face of difficulty, adversity and doubters. Self-esteem is the feeling we have about ourselves and how we carry ourselves in the world. If we feel good about ourselves then we feel more confident about taking on new challenges and succeeding in those challenges. So you may be asking yourself, how does one gain healthy self-esteem? It is developed in various ways beginning with your parents. If your parents provide you with the environment to try new things and support you as you struggle, healthy self-esteem is achieved. In that struggle come the great feelings. Once you have succeeded, the struggle seems worth it and your self-esteem increases because you were able to tackle it on your own.

If your parents jump in to rescue you and solve it for you, your sense of self-worth has the potential to go down. Yes, you might feel happy that you had the help, but in the end you know it wasn't all by your work and this nags at the self-esteem inside. The same is true for teachers, but they may have an easier time letting a child figure it out on their own. Parents, because of how much they love you want to help in any way they can often not realizing that in the long run, may not be so helpful. I am not suggesting that parents should never help their kids, but a little effort can go along way.

It is important to know that self-esteem may also not be a constant feeling. It may take some hits along the way as you encounter new struggles, new people, new environments, school assignments and exams. That may not sound very comforting, but here are some practical steps one can do to achieve and maintain healthy self-esteem.

Practical Ways To Higher Self-Esteem

★ Fake it until you feel it: Even if you feel your self-esteem has taken a hit and you have lost it a bit, fake it. Pretend to yourself that you are on top of the world. This may sound a bit nutty, but faking it until you feel it really works. For your next exam where you might be feeling a bit shaky, remind yourself what a great student you are and how you always ace these exams. Use your body language to propel self-esteem too. Sit tall and breathe deeply, holding your head high.

★ Practice some deep breathing: When your self-esteem becomes shaky, I want you to stop what you are doing and focus only on your breathing. Breathe in slowly and deeply and as you do you will find your body and mind become more relaxed. As you become more relaxed you can quiet the nerves and achieve what you want to achieve.

★ Practice relaxation and visualize your positive outcome: this can be one of the most successful and practical tools you can use to enhance your self-esteem and get back on track. When you close your eyes and imagine what you are trying to achieve and can see the outcome you desire, this is quite helpful in regaining and maintaining self-esteem. For example; imagine you have some difficult exams coming up and you want to get better grades than you did the last time. Close your eyes and picture yourself taking the exams and doing well. You see yourself as confident and capable and seeing the outcome of the wonderful grades you will achieve.

★ Surround yourself with others who enhance your self-esteem, rather than those who detract from it. If there are a group of kids that make you feel less confident and shaky about yourself because their behavior, morals and values are not in line with yours, then find like-minded people to share good times. Your peer group can be a wonderful support system assuming there are like minded individuals who are kind, supportive and do not participate in any type of bullying.

★ Reach out to your parents and teachers: when things feel a bit rough or your grades could use a lift gain some support to spur you on. If you need extra help then ask for it. You will be amazed at how a small amount of encouragement from your parents or teacher can go a long way in you regaining your self-esteem after you have lost it.

No one can make you feel inferior without your consent.
- Eleanor Roosevelt

Jennifer Kelman is a Certified Professional Coach, Licensed Master Social Worker, Entrepreneur and mother of twins. She is also the creator of the award-winning children's characters Mrs. Pinkelmeyer and Moopus McGlinden at MrsPinkelmeyer.com. She is also the founder of JenniferKelmanCoaching.com who credits her success to not counting the "no's." Kelman also founded Healing Connections, a non-profit organization to prevent eating disorders, lecturing to more than 10,000 students and parents.

Listen to this chapter at HowToLearn.com/amazing-grades-audio

Smart Food, Smart Brain = Better Grades

"Wake up Steve!" Ms. Nancy's voice boomed from across the room. That is the third time Steve had to be told to wake up during the class. He can't help it. He's really tired.

His sleeping in class is not because the lecture is boring. The subject is really interesting. Ms. Nancy is one of the most creative teachers around and Steve loves science. Yet he finds himself drowsy, sleepy and tired in class no matter how he tries to keep himself up. Not only that, every now and then, he is absent with a cold or the flu.

★   Have you ever felt tired and lethargic in school?
★   Do you find yourself getting sick easily?
★   Do you love fast foods and the sweet snacks?
★   Are you veggies your doom?
★   Do you skip your breakfast?

Would you actually like to be wake up fresh & stay awake in your classes? If you said yes to any of the above then this chapter is perfect for you! Imagine waking up fresh and alert, paying attention and getting terrific grades in the process. That would be great isn't it! Well here's one important secret you are about to learn about how to turn your brain and body into a smart machine!

The Biggest Secret is in Eating Smart!

Eating smart does not mean you have to eat vegetables all the time; it does not mean eating boring tasteless foods and it does not stop you from eating the foods you love.

Top 3 Eating SMART Tips for a Smarter Brain:

1. ZOOM ZOOM TURN IT ON!

Have you ever played a computer game on your phone and halfway through the battery goes dead because you forgot to charge your phone battery the night before? Well that's much like what happens to you when you feel tired from not charging yourself in the morning. Just like your car – you need to turn on the engine before it gets moving and you need to "turn on" your brain & charge it up before you go to class.

FUN FACTS: Do you know that studies have shown students who eat breakfast regularly score better in their tests? Breakfast gives your brain the charge it needs to you can think clearly and faster.

Here's a sample breakfast to help you get going.

Energy Breakfast
1 small cup fresh or frozen berries,; 1 small banana, ½ cup low fat yogurt, a handful of
almonds; 4/5 cup almond, rice or goat milk (check with your doctor to make sure you are
not allergic to any type of milk first); ice is optional.
Use your blender to mix enjoy the energy you feel.

2. HAPPY BRAIN = HAPPY BODY = BETTER GRADES

Imagine how you would feel if you best friend gave you something you love for your birthday. That would just make your day wouldn't it? Well that is how your brain would be too if you give it what it loves every day. Your brain will be so happy it will be tuned up and ready to absorb what you are learning in school just like a sponge!

So what makes your brain feel more efficient? Foods that are packed with omega-3's essential fatty acids. See the chapter by Dr. Marshall called Smart Fats for more information on what omega 3's are and what they do.

Some foods that are a great source of Omega-3 fats are salmon, tuna (make sure your tuna is mercury free though), walnuts, and seeds. There is a seed called Mila which is a Proprietary blend of Chia Seed and plant based source of omega 3. Flax seeds are also good.

Here is a Happy Brain Breakfast Full of Omega-3's

Organic oatmeal; add any fresh or dried fruits such as strawberries, peaches, blueberries, raisins, figs; handful of chopped walnuts sprinkle a teaspoon of MILA seeds, or flaxseeds. Eat and enjoy.

3. POWER SNACK

Do you get hungry in the middle of the day or while studying and find yourself snacking away on donuts, ice cream, chocolates, sweets, chips, yet you still end up hungry and feel more tired after the snack! This is what is called the ENERGY CRASH! Ever been on a roller coaster ride? Well that's how your blood sugar affects your body after you eat a lot of sweets. It's like a yo yo effect on your brain. What if you can snack on super snacks that can help you feel full, charges your brain and keeps your body energetic longer?

Here's some great examples:

★   A high grain with muesli bar; low fat yogurt; mixed unsalted nuts (almonds, cashews, or walnuts (make sure your doctor says you are not allergic to nuts first, banana muffins; fruit smoothies.

★   If you love bananas spread some almond butter on it and roll it in crushed nuts! Your brain and body will thank you for it.

★   It helps to keep a diary of what you eat so you can correlate food with how you feel. When you feel your best in brain and body, you can thank those foods.

Watch your thoughts, they become words,
Watch your words, they become actions,
Watch your actions they become habits,
Watch your habits they become your character,
Watch your character it becomes your destiny
- Lao Tzu

Suria Mohd, BSc, PGDE, is a certified nutritionist from Singapore and conducts a free course called "Secrets to Exam Success: 5 Reasons why Smart students Fail." Visit: Facebook.com/LearningDiscoveries to find out more. You can also find recipes at facebook.com/Mila.Miracle.Seeds Note: No part of this chapter is intended to diagnose or treat any illness. Be sure to check with your doctor first to make sure you have no food allergies.

Listen to this chapter at HowToLearn.com/amazing-grades-video

Laugh Your Way to Better Grades
Getting Better Grades May Be As Simple As Laughing...

As a student I had an on-going "love/hate" relationship with school. I loved the exposure to new information and ideas and was fortunate to have decent teachers, but dreaded trying to recall what I heard in lectures or what I had read after I studied. It was painful.

The harder I tried, the more painful my efforts became. I tried different diets and supplements for the brain (even went "raw" for several years). I tried exercise and a large number of other methods.

There were times when I felt like an "under-achiever," and yet because I was actually an "over-achiever," I was sabotaging most of my efforts to learn "smarter - not harder." Everything I tried had merit. It was the manner in which I pursued the acquisition of new concepts that kept me frozen. I was trying too hard. I would acquire a new "tool" and immediately "test" it to see how successful it would be. Each one seemed to take forever before I could experience noticeable results.

Through the years I noticed that many students were having similar challenges, at all grade levels. We were uncommonly stressed over learning. Endocrinologist Hans Selye defined eustress as stress that is healthy or gives one a feeling of fulfillment. As students, we were clearly not experiencing this "good" stress.

All were experiencing the stress that restricts the proper flow of blood and oxygen to the brain. So how do we get this "good" stress? Bernie DeKoven says that "Playfulness is one of the signs scientists look for when trying to determine the health of a herd of animals. The healthier the animals and the safer the herd, the more they play. The same is true of the human herds."

Does this playfulness help create the blood and oxygen our brains are screaming for? Yes! And when you add laughter to play, look what happens. Those "feel-good" endorphins, the "happy hormones," start to multiply. And are we calmer and more relaxed after laughing and playing? And does this help us focus in a more productive manner?

I first became aware of the benefits of laughter after reading Norman Cousin's book *Laughter, the Best Medicine*, in the 70's. Since then, much attention has been given to the power of laughter as it is embraced by many hospitals, psychiatrists and psychologists. The founder of the American School of Laughter Yoga, Sebastien Gendry, says that "Your brain at positive is 31% more productive than at negative, neutral or stressed.

This has a lot to do with the fact that dopamine (which floods into the system when you are positive) has two functions: not only does it make you happier, it turns on all the learning centers in your brain, allowing you to adapt to the world in a different way." Now that's what my brain wants to hear!

Dr. Madan Kataria and his wife created Laughter Yoga in India in 1995 which has resulted in laughter "clubs" all over the world. You're sure to find a "club" near you. They're free and they're fun. Sebastien Gendry says "Laughter is like gold: it can be molded into any shape imaginable, yet never lose its intrinsic value."

He says (based on many different research studies), "workers who laugh regularly, long and hard, focus better, think more creatively and problem solve better than co-workers who do not. People who laugh tend to be more efficient, more productive, and make fewer mistakes than their stressed-out co-workers. Because laughter reduces the damaging effects of stress on the immune system, people who laugh a lot are less vulnerable to illness and take fewer sick days from work."

I became fascinated with laughter (as a practice) when I saw the possibilities for improving my focus and recall in and out of the classroom. It was never enough to hear "lighten up" (which I heard often, along with "chill"). I needed to know how to lighten up and laughter has proven to be the quickest, most efficient way to study smarter, not harder and actually have fun. As Dr. Kataria says, "If laughter cannot solve your problems, it will definitely DISSOLVE your problems; so that you can think clearly about what to do with them."

Judy Watson is a clinical hypnotherapist, NLP practitioner, entrepreneur, Brain Gym instructor and co-founder of an organic apple ranch. She struggled with focus and discovered through laughter yoga that she could concentrate better. For more information see LaughterYoga.org.

Listen to this chapter at HowToLearn.com/amazing-grades-audio

The Big Brain Breakthrough That Makes Learning Naturally Easy

The more you understand about how your brain works the more you will realize how to influence your brain and have control over your learning and ability to get better grades.

The single most important factor scientists know about today is that the fact that the brain is not static. When you give the brain specific input it will change, grow and develop optimally. This is known as neuroplasticity.

The good news is that there are specific exercises that you can do that will improve your learning and memory simply because neuroplasticity makes this possible.

Brain development is naturally pushed forward by interaction of the brain with the environment through the sensory system, motor systems, and cognitive system under the control of the nervous system. That is, the brain develops in response to the movement of muscles, the visual system, the auditory system, touch, taste and smell.

Here are some specific exercises to enhance each of your systems and make learning easier:

tinyurl.com/nob2sy

★ Eye exercises such as looking right and left, up and down, follow targets and focus near and far strengthen your visual system and allow you to relax and focus as you read. As it turns out, you can relax your eyes and visual stress with specific exercises. (Google eye exercises to find out more.)

★ Hearing exercises such as being outside and concentrating on the sounds work very well to enhance your hearing. Keep your eyes closed and pinpoint where sounds are coming from and what they are, i.e. the swish of a birds winging through the air directly above you.

★ Muscle coordination and strength exercises such as the cross crawl and yoga postures will improve your core strength and coordination of the right and left sides of the body. When you engage both hemispheres of the brain, you are able to improve your ability to do everything academically.

★ Fine motor exercises improve your dexterity of the fingers, hands, toes and feet.

★ Touch exercises such as identifying what body part is being touched and massage are also helpful.

★ Smelling peppermint in the right nostril, and lavender in the left has lots of brain boosting benefits. Peppermint is used to heighten your senses and awaken your mind. It is one of the best oils to boost your creativity, energy and learning skills. Lavender, which is known as a linalyl ester stimulates the olfactory nerve, which in turn slows down your nervous system making you calmer, reduces anxiety, lifts your overall mood and helps you sleep better.

★ Breathing exercises such as five deep breaths, in through the nose and out through the mouth (with the exhale being twice as long as the inhale), help better oxygenate the brain and tone the nervous system. Distance running is one of the best brain exercises.

Using these exercises has been shown to increase brain development and enhance learning. The techniques being used to stimulate the brain represent an exciting new breakthrough in enhancing a brain's ability to learn.

The intuitive mind is a sacred gift and the rational mind is a faithful servant.
We have created a society that honors the servant and has forgotten the gift.
- Albert Einstein

 Albert Forwood, D.C., D.A.C.A.N, is board certified as a Diplomat of the American Chiropractic Academy of Neurology. He is the owner of the Brain Balance Center in Wayne, PA and has been helping people with learning and neurological problems for over 20 years. For more information visit BrainBalanceWayne.com.

Listen to this chapter at HowToLearn.com/amazing-grades-audio

Brain Matters That Make a Difference in Your Grades

Your brain is just 2% of your body weight but these brain facts will make all the difference in your learning.

Statistical Matters

Having a clear understanding of how your brain works will help you to get better grades. At the start let's make it clear that your brain is truly amazing for something so small and which is just 2% of your body weight. It does so much – it has a capacity bigger than the largest computer. It is very thirsty, sucking in 1.58 US pints (750ml) of blood every minute. It uses:

★   20% of your body's energy
★   66% of your body's intake of glucose
★   30% of calorie intake.

Your brain feels rather like a soft boiled egg and is made up of 75-85% water, 10% fat and 8% protein. Believe it or not its capacity is unlimited and it has 10-15 billion neurons (brain cells). Each neuron looks like a tree with over 5,000 branches. Gaps between neurons are called synapses and there are over 100 billion of these. There is no limit to the thinking power of your brain. To learn something new a signal has to jump across the gap to continue on its learning journey. To help this process it is essential:

★   To take in foods rich in Omega 3 fish oils (salmon, sardines and mackerel) as these make it easier for the signal to jump the gap. There are also Omega 3 supplements available.
★   To re-hydrate as the brain functions on electrical impulses and water is required as a conductor.

Fuel Matters

Blood which carries nutrients such as sugars and oxygen to the brain is 80-92% water so keeping rehydrated is essential. Drinking water and eating fruit and vegetables can improve your performance in assessments increasing your ability to learn by 30%. You need to reduce intake of drinks high in caffeine as these can have a diuretic effect and flush water out of your body. Also caffeine which gives you a quick lift has a downside as the effect is very short lived and you can end up with even lower blood sugar levels. Your brain needs the right food intake to work well. Some top tips:

★   Eat a good breakfast each day as it helps to avoid food lows later in the morning which will affect memory and performance. Try eating more protein at this meal.
★   Eat a good lunch. Avoid too much refined starch e.g. white bread.
★   Complex carbohydrates such as brown pasta and brown rice are good for maintaining blood sugar but eating too much before an exam can make you sleepy. Protein before exams is much better.

The brain needs sugar to work properly but:
★   Eating things high in sugar increases the amount of insulin produced however, this also increases levels of serotonin. Serotonin is known as the brain's natural sleeping substance, so it will make you feel sleepy too.
★   Too much fat also raises serotonin levels affecting memory and concentration. It will also prevent your brain taking up glucose. The brain needs a steady supply of glucose throughout the day as glucose is turned into electricity in the brain.
★   Glucose levels fluctuate throughout the day and work that is mentally demanding quickly reduces glucose levels in your body. So think carefully about what you eat.
★   Reduce levels of saturated fats which can clog blood vessels that take oxygen and nutrients to the brain and heart. Avoid processed snacks as these can also cause tiredness and slow down learning.

Oxygen Matters

Your brain needs lots of oxygen to help you learn:

★ Try aerobic exercise which helps your heart beat faster, increasing blood flow and oxygen in your blood stream. If your concentration lapses when revising try standing up – this puts 15% more oxygen in your brain or just go for a brisk walk.
★ Try deep breathing before and after study.
★ Playing sport or walking regularly will make your brain smarter and fitter.

Brain Exercise Matters

Physical movement and mental exercises are the best ways to spur the brain into action:
★ Doing exercises that link left and right sides of the brain, across the corpus callosum which is in the middle of your brain, means that you learn at 80% efficiency compared with 35% efficiency when you only use one side. One exercise that links both sides is double doodles where you write your name in the air with both left and right hands simultaneously and then cross your hands over each other.
★ Each person prefers a dominant side of the brain even though you are using both sides. If you are strongly right brain dominant you will like to learn using creativity, emotion and music. If you are strongly left brain dominant you will learn by using logic, order and reasoning.
★ Much successful learning occurs using the right side of the brain, visualizing facts and using fantasy to make stronger memory associations.

Timing Matters

It is best to remember that 80% of the stuff memorized is lost within the first 24 hours so it is best to go back to it and reinforce it within that period. Each time you reinforce the learning it will enter deeper into your long-term memory and recall of the information will be easier.

Relaxation Matters

★ Remain positive as positive feelings help your brain cells to connect more easily.
★ Cancel negative thoughts and comments and replace can't to with can do.
★ Stress can get in the way of learning and revising – over 80% of learning difficulties are related to stress. When stressed a primitive area of the brain known as the Reptilian brain is activated. Blood drains from the brain to arms and legs ready for a flight or fight response for survival. To overcome these feelings it is important to use techniques to relax which involves us anchoring ourselves into a more relaxed state by:
   ☆ Deep breathing – count to four as you breathe in through your nose, hold breath for three seconds and then exhale through your mouth. Repeat twenty times.
   ☆ Visualization – at the same time close your eyes and visualize a time when you were happy and relaxed or when you were in a location that was special to you. As you are doing this hold forefinger and thumb on each hand together. When you next feel stressed you can anchor yourself so that you are more relaxed by holding your thumb and forefinger together.

Sleep Matters

★ Sleep keeps your brain fresh and active. To ensure a good night's sleep you need to:
   ☆ Relax before you go to sleep – avoid playing games or watching too much television
   ☆ Get bedroom temperature right – not too hot
   ☆ Set up a regular routine with a similar bedtime each night
   ☆ Avoid taking in caffeine too near to bedtime
   ☆ Use relaxation techniques – such as deep breathing and visualization to help you get to sleep.

Dave Vizard (BEd, Cert Ed) is the Managing Director of Behaviour Solutions Limited and a consultant who works with schools and colleges in the UK promoting better behavior through successful learning. More information and free resources can be found at Behavioursolutions.com

Listen to this chapter at www.behaviourmatters.com/brainmattersaudio

Office Hours

- A Poem by Taylor Mali

A good teacher will often announce to his or her classes
that students who think they might need extra help
should feel free—*would be well advised*—to make
an appointment to meet with the teacher after school.

The word *behoove* may well be used.

In fact, good teachers always do this. And if they don't,
then they probably shouldn't be called good teachers.
There, I said it. Office hours: The time teachers set aside
to be around in case you need them;
the time they come to resent because
almost no one ever takes them up on this offer.

Office hours: an untapped goldmine of extra help
and motivation. Genius. All the difference in the galaxy.

But here's the black hole: The students who are actually
smart enough to take advantage of a teacher's office hours
are never the ones who need it most. Or if they are,
it's hard to tell because they quickly become something else.

Either way, be that. Be that student.

The one who appears in the door two days before a chapter test
and says: *I have five questions I'd like to ask you. Do you have a minute?*

The teacher is stunned.

Never in a million planets would the teacher have expected you.
The teacher was just going to get some coffee.
Because that's all the teacher ever does during office hours.
Drink coffee. Office hours = Coffee hours.
But you! Here, come in! Yes. Ask away. Th e teachers is all ears.

And wonder. And respect.

But now it's your turn. Now you have to have five questions to ask.
And they can't be idiot questions like: *What will the test be on?*
How should I study for it? Can you summarize everything.

I should have been paying attention to in class when you said it the first time?
This is the hardest part for you. Because you have to have completed
most of your homework to be able to ask a good question.
Bring in connections to old material. *This reminds me*
of what you taught us at the beginning of the year;
is that a valuable insight? Or just a curious observation
to make note of and move on?

The teacher is amazed. The teacher hadn't thought of that.
Inside, the teacher is pumping a fist like Tiger Woods.

I'm probably least familiar with the material at the end of the chapter.
Would it be wiser for me study that in the next few days?
Or maybe there won't be as much of that on the test?
Don't, of course, tell me anything you shouldn't.

The teacher actually hasn't written the test yet.
The teacher is deciding right now what exactly the test will be on.
The teacher says, *I don't want to tip my hand*
or give you an advantage that other students don't have, but . . .

The teacher is then likely to give you an advantage
other students will never have.

Right place. Right time. But you have to do the work.
Any idiot can ask an idiotic question.
But a good question, an informed question—
the word *trenchant* comes to mind—
is evidence of intellectual curiosity.

And that's all any teacher ever wants to see you have.
Call it a kind of spark, a cognitive fire to light up the dark.
Desire for learning akin to burning.
Physical proof that you actually are
some kind of amazing, shooting star.

tinyurl.com/7xh9cba

Taylor Mali curates the *Page Meets Stage* reading series at the Bowery Poetry Club in New York City. The author of two books of poetry, Mali was one of the original poets to appear on the HBO series *Def Poetry Jam*. His latest book, *What Teachers Make: In Praise of the Greatest Job in the World*, is based on a poem of his seen millions of times on YouTube. Visit Taylor at TaylorMali.com.

Listen to this chapter at HowToLearn.com/amazing-grades-audio

How Fitness Fortifies the Brain Fortress for Your Students

I finished high school with a solid "C+" average and graduated college cum laude. This could easily be the beginning to a novel about an experimental brain enhancement project, but in reality the difference between my "C" performance and "A" capabilities was physical fitness.

Plenty has been researched and written about the body/mind connection, but we have much to do in the way of implementing fitness in a meaningful way for high school students.

The Undernourished Roots

In 2009 a CDC survey found that only 18% of high school students were getting the recommended 1 hour of physical activity per day. This corresponds to the high rate of obesity and increased rate of Type II diabetes and cardiovascular disease that is diagnosed in increasingly younger individuals. But what has this got to do with academic performance?

Two decades of research and anecdotal evidence support the idea that physical fitness can have direct impact on cognitive functioning.

However, there was a time not to long ago when parents would refer to their children as "more of an athlete" or "more into computers" or fill in whatever you like. Somewhere in the last decade it became more common to encourage a more balanced scholar-athlete. While the concept is an improvement from the old single-label model, there is a particularly troubling problem: team sports.

Team sports (baseball, soccer, basketball, football) are so synonymous with the term "athletics" that unless a student participates in one of these (or several individual sports include track and field or wrestling), he/she is not considered an athlete. It is important to know that statistics show the vast majority of high school students do not participate in team sports. They are either cut from the team or have no interest in playing. If fitness is so important for physical and cognitive optimization, what is the answer?

The team sport model of athletics needs to go. So much more exists in the realm of physical activity than competitive sports. One of the fastest growing segments in the fitness industry is general fitness programming for teens. Different from sport-specific training, the best of these programs do what PE class is missing: introduce a variety of activities that enhance strength, speed, coordination, endurance, and power. These non-competitive programs also offer some crucial benefits by providing participants with a sense of accomplishment and enjoyment of physical activity.

Increasing physical ability will have generalization or carry-over to other areas of development. Forcing a student through a 30 minute game of soccer once or twice a week is not a surefire shortcut to good grades.

In order for fitness activities to be effective they must:
- ★ Be performed regularly (4-6x per week on average)
- ★ Be approached with a motivated, engaged approached
- ★ Include activities that provide initial success and eventual challenge
- ★ Provide opportunities for creativity and discovery

It's All Adaptive PE

I've spent a decade providing fitness programs for individuals with autism and related developmental disabilities as well as working with neurotypical or normally-developing adolescents and teens. Physical Education for special needs students is typically labeled "Adaptive PE." In reality, all PE and fitness

programs are adaptive. Any given gym class will have an extraordinary range of ability levels, and that does not just include physical skills. Adaptive, or behavioral skills (motivation, social abilities) and cognitive aptitude (what *type* of learner, with what speed of processing) are always a factor.

In a typical gym class of 15-25 students, perhaps six really want to do a 4-week unit of basketball drills. Five more students may participate out of compliance, and the rest will borrow from their drama class and play the convincing role of "Looking as though they are playing when the coach makes eye contact." Basketball, or any other competitive sport, is relatively closed-off to creativity. There are clearly defined and very rigid rules about how the game is played, how to win, and how to be successful or unsuccessful. For some teens, this situation works out well. For most, it just plain sucks!

I recommend that you do as I do and take a soft, 6 lb. medicine ball and put it one side of the room. I have a fifty foot nylon rope divided over itself to form two strands on the other side. Splitting the group in half, one "team" is going to find as many ways as possible to throw the ball in five minutes while the rope "team" is going to see how many variations of rope swings they can perform. After five minutes the groups switch to the other object (ball or rope). After another five minutes they switch again, only this time they have to jump to the other side of the gym on one foot. They are getting exponentially more physical activity than with a typical 30 minutes of soccer, and the activities are more general and less sport-specific. They also require more creativity and focus.

Creativity and focus are good, good things. They require an emotional "investment" in the activity. This is where the neurons of the brain pick up, in the figurative and literal senses. The more "open" activities invite participants to focus more and even expend more energy in pursuit of the goal, whether it be running across the room with a heavy sandbag overhead or figuring out a new way to jump over some low hurdles. Two of my friends and colleagues, Bill Meyer of Meyer Fitness in Norfolk, VA and Dr. Kwame Brown, creator of the FUNction Method are masters of these types of activities. Having fun while exercising also aids in fitness becoming a *lifestyle* rather than a keenly avoidable plague.

Outcomes the Goals

In the opening of this chapter I mentioned my improved academic performance over a decade. In the best case scenarios, appropriate fitness programs will: Increase general and specific physical health and abilities; increase cognitive functioning (particularly in frontal lobe abilities); decrease stress and anxiety; increase positive outlook and socialization; encourage exploration and play into adulthood.

To achieve these outcomes, educators, administrators, lawmakers, professionals, and parents must ensure that: Teens have access to PE and fitness programs that are movement and play-based rather than sport-specific; fitness is part of the classroom experience, have students stand up and move halfway through class; policies are passed to maintain and even extend recess, develop parks and outdoor play/fitness areas; group activities in noncompetitive settings do not marginalize the less talented students; healthy eating habits and choices are followed at home and available in schools.

Fitness is the gateway towards optimal physical, adaptive, and cognitive functioning. With the right programs and universal access, we can enhance the academic and lifelong success of students.

Eric Chessen, M.S. is the Founder of AutismFitness.com, creator of the PAC (Physical, Adaptive, Cognitive) Profile Assessment toolbox, and co-Founder of StrongerthanU.com. He is based in New York, presenting and consulting worldwide.

Listen to this chapter at: HowToLearn.com/amazing-grades-audio

Putting Happiness First -
Why Happiness and Gratitude Help You Produce Your Most Creative Work

I once heard an inspiring TED (a non-profit with ideas worth spreading) Talk entitled "The Happy Secret to Better Work" by Shawn Achor, CEO of Good Think Inc.

A big idea in his 12-minute presentation is that in our society people tend to believe that we should work hard in order to be happy. Achor suggests that this way of thinking could be backwards. He argues that happiness makes us more productive, creative, and successful. Consequently, happiness should come first.

My eighteen years as a classroom teacher tell me that Achor's words contain a great deal of truth. I know, for example, that when my students start their school day in a good mood, they are likely to work hard, get along well with their classmates, embrace challenges, and produce quality work.

tinyurl.com/772s6qw

On the other hand, when students enter the room angry about something that is happening with their friends or upset about something occurring at home, focusing on their school work can be a mighty struggle. It is an even larger struggle for kids who feel this way on most days.

Whenever I notice that someone in class appears to be off to a rough start on a given morning, I make it a point to speak privately with that person as soon as I can. As much as I want to jump in and focus on academic work, I understand that it is very difficult to relate to people on this level when they are preoccupied with other concerns.

I need to help them change their mindset first. Once students are in a more positive frame of mind, then we can talk academics. The question becomes, how do you achieve a more positive mindset when you're not feeling happy? At the end of his TED talk, Achor shares some ways that people can use to focus on the positive aspects of their lives and become happier.

One of his ideas resonated with me, and upon hearing it, I immediately decided to incorporate it into my teaching. Achor asserts that individuals who try this idea for 21 straight days can train themselves to think differently about their lives and actually re-wire their brains.

The idea is to think of three things in your life for which you are grateful. So, for three weeks (fifteen consecutive school days) my students and I did this. At the end of our daily, morning movement warm-up routine, I gave everyone about a minute of quiet "think" time.

Then several volunteers shared their ideas with the class. During this daily gratitude activity the primary challenge was to think of new things every day. By the end of our three-week endeavor, the hope is that students, over time, would realize just how many positive things they have in their lives, and as a result, the classroom environment would change.

That is exactly what happened. I have a few students who tend to pout or complain when things don't go their way, and that behavior largely disappeared. Of course, I can't know for sure whether out daily gratitude activity was responsible for causing that change, but it is reasonable to believe that it played an important part.

During this three-week period other positive signs emerged. The most powerful occurred anytime I met one-on-one with a student who seemed to be sad or lacking confidence. Though I met with the kids to discuss academic work, I didn't start talking with them about the task at hand right away. Instead, I first asked them to tell me their three ideas from that morning. Doing that seemed to bolster their spirits, and then we could address the school work. The overall mood and effort level in the classroom also improved.

Over the three weeks I was curious to see how student responses would evolve. Initially, I thought the kids might have difficulty generating new ideas after mentioning family, friends, school, food, shelter, and other familiar ideas, but that really didn't happen.

Instead, the kids shared a wide variety of responses, including: health, our country's freedom, classmates, freedom of religion, siblings, William Shakespeare, the environment, math, money, the opportunity to learn, peace, baseball teams, food, books, basketball, art, pets, the protection offered by police officers and firefighters, surgeons, trees, technology, the Sun, a warm bed, medicines, the library, grocery stores, tools, an efficient math system, and electronics.

Even though my students and I have concluded this initiative, I can now use it as a reference point for the remainder of the year. Our Putting Happiness First project is something we can revisit on a regular basis to help us build and maintain a sense of gratitude in our lives and a sense of perspective.

During those inevitable times when things don't go your way and the bad seems to outweigh the good, you can remember coming up with forty-five positive things for which you feel grateful. Maybe that can help you ride out those difficult times and maintain a positive attitude, even when it feels difficult to do so.

Give this idea a try. It may help you find that positive mindset that is so critical for performing at your highest level and producing your highest quality, most creative work.

Feeling grateful or appreciative of someone or something in your life actually attracts more of the things that you appreciate and value into your life.
-Christiane Northrup

Steve Reifman is the founder of stevereifman.com and a National Board Certified teacher, author, and speaker in Santa Monica, CA. He has written several books for educators and parents, including *Changing Kids' Lives One Quote at a Time* and *Eight Essentials for Empowered Teaching and Learning, K-8*. Steve is also the creator of the Chase Manning Mystery Series. Each book in the series features a single-day, real-time thriller that occurs on an elementary school campus. For weekly Teaching Tips, blog posts, and other valuable resources and strategies on teaching the whole child, visit stevereifman.com. Follow Steve on Twitter under the name: @stevereifman

Note: TED talk on Happiness by Shawn Achor Ted.com/talks/shawn_achor_the_happy_secret_to_better_work.html

Listen to this chapter at HowToLearn.com/amazing-grades-audio

How To Choose the Right College

Once you get the grades you want using the strategies found in this book, you may find you want to go to college. Your grades, extracurricular activities and test scores will all play a large part in determining which colleges will be available to you. There are still some things you can do to help identify your ideal college. Here are some pointers that are great to follow in narrowing your college choices and increasing your chances of getting offered admissions.

The first step is to determine the criteria of your ideal school. I would suggest creating a list with three columns marked need, want, and can live without. At this point you must sit down and consider what it is you are looking for in your school. In the need column begin writing down all the factors you feel are necessary for you to attend that school, for instance cost, location, and housing. In the second column, I would list factors that are not absolutely necessary, but would make the difference between two otherwise equal schools. In the third column mark down items that would be nice if available, but otherwise negligible, this may include things like extracurricular activities and services.

tinyurl.com/7k3ezrd

When you begin creating your list of criteria, you may want to consider some of the more subtle, yet important factors. By doing a little bit of research some interesting bits of information can be acquired.

When reviewing a college, I suggest looking at the graduation rate of students to see if the school is providing a solid education. Then, examine the student loan default rate to see how many students were able to meet their financial obligations after graduation. Finally, by comparing the default rate to the graduation rate, you can create a rough image of how many graduates find work after attending a given school. I recommend you stay away from schools with high default rates as this may represent a lack of quality instruction or a poor hiring climate for these graduates.

Next, I think it is important to consider what your goals may be. I am often asked questions regarding how to go about planning for the future; and I can tell you that the key is to identify what you want and make a plan to get there. I suggest you take some time and consider what it is you really want and if you are able to identify it, excellent. If not, do not be dismayed, most people do not know and sometimes it takes a while to find out what is you want to do.

The following is a breakdown of college types, their different functions and what they provide their students.

Career Colleges

Career colleges typically do not have transferable credits, and may or may not offer degrees. Usually a career college will provide you with a certificate or diploma that demonstrates proficiency in a particular field of study. Career colleges tend to offer instruction in high demand fields, and a school should provide some form of career placement services for graduates. An excellent indicator of a school's ability to assist in job placement is the number of internship locations offered by the school.

A higher number typically means more visibility and large alumni network that may assist in finding work. Another factor is the number of instructors working concurrently as professionals in the industry. Instructors who remain active professionally can also be a source for career mobility. Career colleges are typically more expensive than community colleges. Also, programs offered tend to be shorter due to a lack of general education courses and the ability to take accelerated courses.

Community Colleges

Community colleges offer a low cost alternative to a four year institution for the freshman and sophomore years, and can also provide technical or vocational training similar to a career college.

Community colleges tend to have agreements in place with public and private institutions within their state to simplify and expedite the transfer process. For example, the University of California System has an established cooperation with the Los Angeles Community College District students to transfer based on a minimum GPA and the completion of specified courses.

Students at community colleges are also able to easily find part time jobs due to their proximity to their home and minimized expenses from reduced tuition. A good community college should have a large number of programs, a relatively low student to teacher ratio, and should be conveniently located.

Four Year Institutions

Four year institutions can vary in size and scope. Private four year institutions tend to have higher costs and often times lower student enrollment resulting in a low student to teacher ratio. Conversely, a public four year institution usually has lower tuition costs due to public funding and a larger student body.

Many four year institutions provide housing for students through resident halls or nearby off campus locations. These colleges and universities tend to have more robust research programs, as well as a more active alumni community. Four year institutions tend to have more involved academic programs and offer more educational opportunities, such as internships or study abroad programs. When comparing four year institutions you must look at multiple factors, such as cost, location, and programs provided.

When choosing your school take in all the information you can and examine all the options. Take care to examine your list and compare it to what the schools you are looking at offer. Choosing the right college is an important decision and should not be taken lightly. For those that are uncertain about college degrees or career choices, I recommend entering a community college and trying out a variety of courses and programs to see what connects with you and then work toward making that your career. The "right school" is not the same for every person; take the time to discover what is best for you.

Koko Mouchmouchian, Pharm. D. founded and manages MatchCollege.com, a college and career search web portal. Through his educational career he has attended five different higher educational institutions of varying types. This experience inspired him to create a streamlined search utility for students seeking information on colleges and career pathways through MatchCollege.com.

Listen to this chapter at tinyurl.com/7k3ezrd

Community College Facts
to Help You Achieve Your Goals

Community colleges are an often overlooked but an essential component in the U.S. science, technology, engineering, and mathematics (STEM) education system.

About 1,200 community colleges in the United States enroll more than 8 million students annually, including 43 percent of U.S. undergraduates (Mullin and Phillippe, 2011; AACC 2011).

Community colleges provide not only general education but many of the essential technical skills on which economic development and innovation are based.

Almost half of the Americans who receive bachelor's degrees in science and engineering attended community college at some point during their education, and almost one-third of recipients of science or engineering master's degree did so (Tsapogas, 2004).

About 40 percent of the nation's teachers, including teachers of science and mathematics, completed some of their mathematics or science courses at community colleges (Shkodriani, 2004).

Community colleges provide professional development programs for teachers, offer alternate teacher certification programs for people who have a degree in another field, and in some states award baccalaureate degrees in teacher education and other disciplines.

Community colleges provide the most diverse student body in the history of the United States with access to higher education.

Community colleges serve people of color, women, older students, veterans, international students, first-generation college goers, and working parents. In particular, minorities who are underrepresented in STEM fields are disproportionately enrolled in community colleges. Fifty-two percent of Hispanic students, 44 percent of black students, 55 percent of Native American students, and 45 percent of Asian-Pacific Islander students attend community colleges (AACC, 2011).

Community colleges are more affordable as well as more accessible than four-year institutions. Average tuition and fees at a community college is about $3,000 per year, compared with an average of $8,200 per year for in-state four-year institutions, $21,000 per year for out-of state students at a state institution, and $29,000 per year at private institutions (College Board, 2011).

Indeed, it is this large difference between the cost of attending community colleges vs. even the least expensive four-year institutions, especially during these difficult economic times, that is serving as an impetus for many more students to begin their college careers at two-year institutions.

Community colleges also focus on teaching in an era when teaching in higher education is receiving particular scrutiny and calls for accountability. And community colleges are becoming an increasing focus of educational researchers as their contributions to education -- and to STEM education in particular -- are more widely recognized.

When you are choosing your career goal, community colleges may be one path to consider in the process.

Success comes in a lot of ways, but it doesn't come with money and it doesn't come with fame. It comes from having a meaning in your life, doing what you love and being passionate about what you do.

That's having a life of success. When you have the ability to do what you love, love what you do and have the ability to impact people. That's having a life of success.
That's what having a life of meaning is.

- Tim Tebow

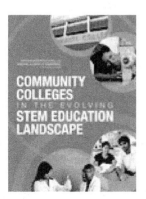

This chapter is Reprinted with permission from the National Academies Press, Copyright 2011, National Academy of Sciences. The book is called *Community Colleges in the Evolving STEM Education Landscape: Summary of a Summit* by Steve Olson and Jay B. Labov, Rapporteurs; Planning Committee on Evolving Relationships and Dynamics Between Two- and Four-Year Colleges and Universities; Board on Higher Education and Workforce, PGA; Board on Life Sciences, DELS; Board on Science Education, DBASSE; Engineering Education Program Office, NAE; Teacher Advisory Council, DBASSE; National Research Council; National Academy of Engineering (Quote added).

Listen to this chapter at HowToLearn.com/amazing-grades-audio

Visual Skills Needed in School
– Do You Have Any of These Symptoms?

This information was prepared to help teachers and consultants identify children's visual problems that could interfere with learning and classroom performance. Nearly all the visual problems that deter children from doing well in the classroom will NOT be uncovered by the Snellen eye chart, nor by most stereoscopic devices. The value of these school screening devices is to identify those children who cannot see clearly.

Vision Is More Than Clarity

It is the ability to visualize, understand and apply the information that comes through the eyes. Children with 20/20 sight may not have these abilities. Therefore, learning problems are often related to vision problems.

Teachers are the best screeners. They observe the child functioning in the classroom. The appearance of irritated eyes, squinting and frequent blinking are PHYSICAL signs of visual problems. A child's PERFORMANCE is affected by problems with eye movement, eye teaming, eye-hand coordination, and visual perception.

Eye Movement Problems

The information obtained by the child will be reduced if eye movements are slow or clumsy, if the eyes jump, "stutter" or lose their place on instructional materials.

Eye Teaming Problems

While our eyes are supposed to work as a team so that they perform as one, this teaming is not guaranteed by design. It must be acquired through use during the preschool years, and not all children adequately develop this skill. It can interfere with learning, especially in the areas of comprehension and spatial relations.

Eye-Hand Coordination Problems

Eye-hand coordination problems are noted as a lack of skill in drawing or writing. Paper work shows poor orientation on the page and an inability to stay within the lines when coloring. Often the child will continue to be dependent on his or her hand for inspection and exploration of toys or other objects.

Visual Form Perception Problems

Form perception problems usually are a result of difficulties in the discrimination of visible likenesses and differences. There is confusion with similarities, inattention to slight differences, reversals in reading and reversals of letter forms. This produces difficulties in spelling and writing.

Refractive Status Problems

Nearsightedness (myopia), farsightedness (hyperopia), astigmatism and focusing problems interfere with the child's comprehension processes and classroom participation. These problems can be developing even though the child may see 20/20 on a Snellen Chart. They need prompt attention by a behavioral optometrist who treats both vision and sight.

The Checklist

This checklist is designed to assist the teacher or consultant in communicating with clinicians and parents. It is particularly useful in identifying those children who did well academically in the very early grades and later developed problems.

Checklist Of Vision Problems

Student's Name
Date

APPEARANCE OF EYES

Reddened eyes or lids   ———
Eyes tear often   ———
Encrusted eyelids   ———
Frequent styes on lids   ———

COMPLAINTS WHEN USING EYES

Headaches   ———
Burning eyes   ———
Itching eyes   ———
Nausea after reading   ———
Print blurs   ———
Double vision   ———

TEACHER'S OBSERVATIONS WHEN STUDENT READS

Head movement   ———
Loses place often   ———
Needs finger to keep place   ———
Omits words frequently   ———
Re-reads lines   ———
Skips lines   ———
Short attention span   ———
Fails to recognize some words   ———
Confuses similar words   ———

WHEN STUDENT

Writes up- or downhill   ———
Repeats letters within words   ———
Omits letters, numbers or phrases   ———
Misaligns digits   ———
Covers one eye   ———
Tilts head   ———
Fails to recognize same word
when repeated in text   ———
Fails to visualize   ———
Makes mistakes when copying from
chalkboard   ———
Writing poorly spaced or crooked   ———
Unable to stay on ruled lines   ———
Poor placement of words on page   ———

OTHER PROBLEMS

Must feel things to understand   ———
Repeatedly confuses right and left   ———
Difficulty with similarities
and differences   ———
Avoids desk work   ———
Blinks, squints, rubs eyes   ———
Fatigues easily   ———

Consult a Behavioral Optometrist

If any of the problems listed on the Checklist of Vision Problems is marked, the child should be further evaluated by a behavioral optometrist.

OPTOMETRIC EXTENSION PROGRAM FOUNDATION Behavioral or developmental optometrists spend years in post-graduate, continuing education to master the complex visual programs prescribed to prevent or eliminate visual problems and enhance visual performance. Not all optometrists practice behavioral optometry, which includes developmental and functional optometry. Yearly vision evaluations are recommended to make sure the visual system develops properly. The Optometric Education Program Foundation is a non-profit international organization dedicated to the advancement of the discipline of optometry through the gathering and dissemination of information on vision and the visual process. You can find a behavioral or developmental optometrist at oepf.org

Listen to this chapter at HowToLearn.com/amazing-grades-audio

Outsmart Your Stress Before the Test

High school was a time for me when I became intimate, maybe too intimate, with being overwhelmed and feeling stressed socially and with the pressure of all the tests. Since that time, in the many years that I've been working as a Psychologist with teens, adults and stress, it appears that I'm not alone in that experience.

Recently, I wrote a popular book called *The Now Effect: How a Mindful Moment Can Change the Rest of Your Life* and now it's time to see how you can apply this to outsmart your stress before a test. In today's culture, students are constantly being told what to "DO" either to get better grades, how to manage their time or just how to fit in.

It seems like there's no time to "BE" and so it's no wonder why more and more kids suffer from heightened anxiety after feeling exhausted, unhealthy and burnt out. When it comes to stress around school, the fact is, stress itself isn't the problem.

The problem is how we relate to the stress

tinyurl.com/852kzlg

Let me briefly lay the foundation for how a stress reaction works. Back in the day when we used to experience life-threatening situations (e.g., getting chased by a tiger), our blood got redirected to our muscles as our bodies got geared up to either fight or flee from the situation. This stress response is critical to our survival. It can save our lives or enable a firefighter to carry a 300-pound man down twenty flights of stairs.

However, most of us don't face these types of threats anymore, but instead a stress reaction is often created in response to a thought, emotion or physical sensation we have.

If we're actively worried about not getting the perfect score on the next exam, this reaction will be activated.

The brain kicks into gear to try and "DO" something about this perceived problem. What it tends to do is think of all the "worst case scenarios," catastrophizing about the future.

If these systems don't slow down and normalize, our bodies continue to stay tense, our minds become unfocused, and it actually becomes more difficult to recall important information for the tests we're worried about.

In other words, we're creating a self-fulfilling prophecy. If the stress continues over a long period of time, forget about not doing well on the test, now we're talking about a variety of ailments including high blood pressure, muscle tension, anxiety, insomnia, gastro-digestive complaints, and a suppressed immune system which compromises the ability to fight disease. Okay, I promise not to scare you anymore.

The solution to this is engaging a simple practice that will help prime your mind toward the spaces of choice right before a test and even in other tough moments in the day. The effect of this short practice is strengthening the ability to readily refocus our attention on what is most important, turn the volume down on worrying, be less stressed and be more effective in the actual test itself.

See, Touch, Go

This three-minute video at tinyurl.com/852kzlg is the first video of many included in the book, but I want to share it with you to give you an experience of "see, touch, go." Give yourself a chance to practice it right now, then go ahead and bring it to the tests at school. If you don't have access to the video, the instructions are simply to breathe normally and naturally and notice where you are aware of the breath.

Is it at the tip of the nose, the belly or the chest? Then localize your attention that area, being curious about the sensation of the breath coming in and then again as the breath going out. Then whenever you mind wanders and you become aware of it, *see* where it wandered to, *touch* or note the thought, and then *gently* go back to the breath. Don't worry about what your mind says about whether this practice is worth doing or not, let your experience be your teacher, not your automatic judgments.

Come back to this practice throughout the day and bring it informally throughout the school day or whenever you notice your mind wandering from what's most important to pay attention to. You may even want to schedule a pop-up in your calendar asking yourself "Where is my attention now?" When it pops up, take a breath and then answer the question.

After you answer, redirect your attention to what is most important right now. You may do this dance over and over again. The purpose isn't to judge yourself if you're distracted, but just become aware of it and gently refocus your attention.

This mindful focus has been proven to grow the area of the brain involved with learning and memory (Hippocampus) and help us become less stressed and more effective at what we do. Try it out now!

In between stimulus and response there is a space, in that space lies our power to choose our response, in our response lies our growth and our freedom.
- Viktor Frankl

Elisha Goldstein, Ph.D. is a psychologist in West Los Angeles, California, the author of *The Now Effect: How A Mindful Moment Can Change the Rest of Your Life*, co-author of *A Mindfulness-Based Stress Reduction Workbook* and creator of multiple audio programs with practical applications integrating mindfulness and mental health at ElisahGoldstein.com/audio. He is also an international speaker and author of the popular Mindfulness and Psychotherapy Blog at http://blogs.psychcentral.com/mindfulness/ and writes for the Huffington Post. As a licensed Psychologist, he teaches mindfulness based programs in his own practice and through InsightLA and has also designed the 12 week Mindfulness at Work ™ program at tinyurl.com/7zhqr8j that is currently being conducted in many multinational corporations.

Listen to this chapter at http://elishagoldstein.com/amazing-grades/

Motivation Magic: 5 Steps to Move Off the Couch and Get It Done!

There are times when you just don't feel motivated to get up off the couch and do your work. Maybe the assignment staring at you is too difficult or just not interesting to you. You know that if you don't get yourself motivated to complete the assignment you will suffer the consequences. What can you do?

1. Make a connection between the assignment and what interests you!

Somehow, make a connection to this assignment. Is there a part of this assignment that you can relate to your life and what interests you? For example, can you apply the problem-solving methods needed to complete the assignment to a problem you are currently dealing with? Can you feel good about completing a writing assignment because you know that effective writing skills are needed in any career that you are considering? If you can connect the skills needed to complete this assignment to skills you need after graduation, you will increase your motivation to get up and get busy!

tinyurl.com/mu9rad

2. Use your fear!

This one uses your fear to help you stay motivated. Although it is not as powerful as moving towards a goal positively, it does work. If you realize all the negatives that happen when you don't get good grades, you're using your fear to motivate yourself.

3. Remember your goals!

We all have goals, and hopefully yours are written down and displayed in a prominent place. Being able to read and review your goals can be very motivating. One of my granddaughters stated that her goal is to have a successful life and for her that includes not having to struggle for money when she has a family. What is your goal? Will developing your knowledge and skills by way of this assignment lead you to your goals? Think of your goal and then get off the couch—you don't want to miss an opportunity to complete work that will help you achieve your goals!

© Erik Reis

4. Place value on this assignment!

The more value you place on an assignment, the more motivated you will be to complete it. If you feel that an assignment will be useful to you, you will place a higher value on completing it. Therefore, make each assignment useful to you, even if it's in some small way, so that your motivation increases to complete the work. Ask yourself how the assignment is valuable and useful to you. Will successful completion gain approval of your peers or parents? Will you earn an award or honors? Will you raise your GPA for college scholarships? Think of the value that this assignment provides to you to increase your motivation to complete it!

5. Take personal responsibility for your success!

A sign of maturity is accepting personal responsibility for your actions. Don't blame others if you experience a setback (the teacher didn't like me, the book wasn't good, the class was boring, etc.).

Watch two videos here that are shown in the scan tags in this chapter. Be sure to get the app to open them at http://gettag.mobi

★   "The Time of your Life" (run time 6:40 minutes)

★   John Beede (run time 6:06 minutes)

In conclusion, remember that you have the power to raise your expectations of yourself and thereby increase your motivation to do well. BELIEVE in yourself. Believe that you will be successful!

tinyurl.com/7toot6n

*Your belief determines your action
and your action determines your results,
but first you have to believe.*
- Mark Victor Hansen

Barbara Carder, M.S. is an adjunct professor at Franklin University in Ohio teaching principles of motivation and learning strategies. Franklin University was named the Best in Business for Online Education winner in the 2011 Columbus C.E.O. magazine reader survey. For information about attending Franklin University on campus or online, visit Franklin.edu.

Listen to this chapter at HowToLearn.com/amazing-grades-audio

How To Use Creative Visualization
to Get Better Grades

Creative Visualization is the scientifically based process of forming a detailed image in your mind of something that you want to achieve.

It helps you succeed in all areas of your life –school, home, work and even athletics. Most likely you've heard of basketball players using it as well as gold medal winning Olympic athletes to obtain the results they want.

The results of creative visualization are based on several factors. First you must determine what you want, your goal; then you get your brain into a relaxed state; and finally you create the pictures or images in your head. Ultimately, your actions are based on the images you create.

The process of forming a detailed image in your mind of something that you desire can be specific to a course, such as remembering information for a test, or more general, such as improving your grades faster.

Many studies have shown that "seeing" yourself achieve a goal in advance leads to success in that goal. In a well known study, prior to the 1980 Olympics, four groups of Russian athletes were studied. Each group was given different amounts of physical training and/or mental training. The mental training was a visualization in which they "saw" themselves competing in their sport and winning.

Group 1 received 100% physical training; Group 2 received 75% physical training with 25% mental training; Group 3 received 50% mental training with 50% physical training; Group 4 received 75% mental training with 25% physical training.

At the end of the study, group 4 had the best performance results, proving the effectiveness of their mental training, the creative visualization.

Creative Visualization is extremely helpful when you apply it to remembering something you have learned. It also has the added element of actually leading to success in any endeavor!

How To Begin Visualizing to Improve Your Grades

There are two parts to Creative Visualization. The first part is to relax and the second part is to create the image. So first of all, let's look at relaxing and what it really means. Lots of recent research on brain waves has shown that the ideal state for learning is when the brain is in a relaxed state, restful but still aware. These brain wave patterns are known as Alpha brain waves.

Without getting into all the science of it, there are basically four types of brain waves. The first is our regular waking state, this is where we are functioning normally, talking to our friends, doing daily tasks, this is the fastest brain wave called Beta State.

When we are relaxed, but still focused and aware, our brain waves slow down and we reach the Alpha State. This is the ideal place for learning new material, memorizing material, and for inspiring new ideas. There are two brain waves slower still, Theta State and Delta State and they relate to sleep and meditation. But for our purposes here, we will focus on reaching the Alpha State. The first part of Creative Visualization is to slow down to achieve the Alpha State.

How To Get Your Body and Brain to Relax

This can be done by focused breathing and draining your body of all tension and stress. To do this, get into a comfortable position, either laying down or sitting on a chair with your feet flat on the floor.

Close your eyes, because this takes away the immense amount of stimuli that your eyes take in every second. Then take three deep breaths, letting go of any tension as you exhale, and begin to relax. Starting at your feet, slowly go up your body, releasing tension from each part of your body, until your entire body feels heavy and relaxed.

Now see a set of stairs in front of you. Slowly go down ten stairs, counting down from ten to one, relaxing more and more with each step. By the time you reach the bottom of the stairs your body should feel heavy and relaxed. At the bottom of the stairs see a door, open the door and enter a room, allowing your mind to create whatever type of room it feels comfortable in, and trust that this room is perfect. Then in this room see a large comfortable chair, now go and sit in this chair. This will be your visualizing chair. In front of your chair see a screen. This will be your visualizing screen and you will use it to help you remember information and learn. In this space, on your chair and with your screen, you can begin visualizing whatever it is that you need to learn for your class or your exam.

How To Create Your Image

Here is where part two, creating the image, comes into effect. Let's say the topic you need to study is the French Revolution. Instead of trying to memorize random dates and names you cannot pronounce, instead create a mental image: Imagine hoards of French peasants storming the huge brick Bastille, see the tall turrets smoking, then paint the date 1789 across one of the turrets in bright red paint, maybe add a massive, gleaming guillotine in the middle of the square, and if you want to go further, perhaps include Marie Antoinette's head in the basket below with the date 1793 woven into the basket …. Get the picture?

If you can create a scene with color and drama, the history you think is boring becomes meaningful and much more memorable. Do this with scenes from Hamlet, the Periodic Table or with Algebraic formulae. Now comes the exciting part, an added bonus is that you can visualize yourself doing well on the exam or the assignment.

Think about any high level athlete from the high jumper to the platform diver to the field goal kicker: they always pause and visualize the result they are aiming for just before the attempt. This is creative visualization in action.

So, while you are in Alpha State visualizing – actually see yourself achieving an excellent grade in whatever subject you are focusing on. Make it as real as you possibly can. See yourself getting an A on your exam, FEEL how good it feels to do exceptionally well in your subject. The more real it feels, the more you are creating it. Enjoy it. Have fun with it. And remember the results are limitless.

Patricia Clark, M.A. is a graduate of UC Berkeley, Alaska Pacific University and founder of http://patticlark.wordpress.com. As a dual citizen of the U.S. and New Zealand, she has taught at the University of Wisconsin, Madison and created two non-profits in New Zealand: Figjam Workshops where she facilitates Creative Empowerment Workshops for women and Teen-Esteem Workshops where she facilitates Self-Empowerment Workshops for teen-agers. For over 30 years, Patti has used Creative Visualization in her workshops and classes supporting individuals on their journey toward an extraordinary life.

Listen to the chapter at http://patticlark.wordpress.com/

Balance Your Brain to Boost Your Grades

It can happen to any of us: we feel pressured, anxious, or spaced out in a way that affects our clarity and comprehension. For example, as you read you might be passively decoding words, and failing to catch the author's train of thought or to make associations from your own experience—needing to reread in order to grasp the main concept.

Or, in essay writing, you might be distracted and unable to internalize material to then reorganize it into your own words. When reading and writing during test taking that requires similar comprehension, you might lose access to your working memory. In stress and overwhelm, you can know the answer but not be able to express it.

Comprehension requires concentration, and your senses and movement provide the context— the landscape of familiar associations—for needed focus. You will do your best thinking, writing, and studying when you can bring your most relaxed sensory skills of seeing, listening, feeling, and kinesthesia to your immediate purpose.

By noticing your sensory involvement before and after taking a playful Brain Gym break, you'll begin to identify the specific kinds of movement that best help you to relax, self-calm, and organize your thoughts. You can quickly notice body language clues such as those listed below that inform you about what's happening with your sensory skills:

★ ease and coordination in sitting, standing, and moving about

★ playfulness and the curiosity to explore ideas in a clear- headed, responsive way

★ a focus on what you want to *do*, rather than what you're trying to avoid

★ the ability to appropriately engage and interact with people or objects in the room

★ comfortable shifting of attention from near-point to the distance and back, without visual stress or distraction

★ feeling no need for "adrenaline zappers" (rushing around, being late, or creating drama) to get yourself going

★ when reading or studying, relaxed sustaining of your focal attention

Use Brain Gym® Activities to Quickly Connect with New Learning

A few minutes doing Brain Gym activities can quickly release stress, ease visual tension, restore balance and equilibrium, and provide an expansive physical context for your ease of focal attention.

Explore using the following three movements to center your focus, let go of test anxiety, and improve your comprehension.

Use the three scan tags in this chapter and open to each movement described below. Be sure and get the app you need (http://gettag.mobi) to open the scan tags with your smart phone.

The Cross Crawl

Stand comfortably and reach across the midline of your body as you alternately move one arm and its opposite leg, then the other arm and leg, rhythmically touching each hand or elbow to the opposite knee.
You can also do this while sitting or lying down. Can you feel this contralateral movement originating from the core of your body? Repeat three or more times on each side.

You may notice . . . *ease when sitting or standing; improved left/right coordination; enhanced breathing and stamina; greater spatial awareness; enhanced listening or seeing; awareness of your whole body as a context for moving your eyes (e.g., moving both together across a page); improvements in spelling, writing, listening, reading, reading aloud, and reading comprehension.*

tinyurl.com/7yaavrg

The Footflex

Sit with one ankle resting on your knee. Place your fingertips below the elevated knee (at the top of your calf muscle) and just above your anklebone, holding these points firmly yet gently. Now slowly point and flex your foot three or more times.

Visualize as bands of clay the muscles and tendons that run between these two holding points. Search for tight spots at the beginning and end of these bands (but don't press directly behind the knee itself), and gently hold the muscle fibers apart until they seem to soften and "melt."

tinyurl.com/76ct7ho

Now continue lengthening the muscles in the same way on the front of the leg. Repeat the process on the other leg.

You may notice . . . improved creativity, attention span, writing ability, and listening and reading comprehension; more expressive spoken language skills; relaxed and lengthened calf muscles for easier standing and forward mobility.

Hook-ups

Part One: Standing, sitting, or lying down, cross your ankles. Next, extend your arms in front of you and cross one wrist over the other (palms together); then interlace your fingers and draw your clasped hands up toward your chest. Hold for a minute or so, breathing slowly with eyes open or closed. As you inhale, touch the tip of your tongue to the roof of your mouth at the hard palate (just behind the teeth), and relax your tongue on exhalation.

Part Two: When ready, uncross your arms and legs and put your fingertips together in front of your chest, continuing to breathe deeply. Hold the tip of your tongue on the roof of your mouth whenever you inhale.

You may notice . . . increased self-control and self-calming; better alignment and release of tension; ease of focus, organization, and concentration for improved recall, study skills, public speaking, and test or sports performance; release of fight-or-flight behavior.

tinyurl.com/78tj2bq

The Brain Gym program offers many further activities to support reading comprehension and test taking. And if you still have visual or auditory stress, remember the resource of Lazy 8s, the Thinking Cap, and other movements for relaxing those senses. These activities are profoundly simple, work well for all age groups, and can be done anywhere.

Successful learners are active learners, not just passive information processors. They move, interact, express themselves, and involve all of their senses. Your brain is *you*; it can't do anything without your participation—the choices you make to actively cultivate your senses and movement skills.

When you move with intention toward your goals and dreams, you're living your life to the fullest. And when you're active, moving, and expressing your intent, *that's* the brain that you're optimizing for your future.

Imprinted on the muscular memory structure of our bodies is not only the knowing of how to sit, stand, walk, and run, but where we are in space and how to move with grace and reason - even to create something beautiful and exquisite in the process. . . . Every number and letter have movement to it. It has a shape felt and imprinted on the musculature so it can be repeated and elaborated through the movement of writing.

    - Carla Hannaford, *Smart Moves: Why Learning is Not All in Your Head*

Paul E. Dennison, Ph.D., and his wife and colleague, Gail E. Dennison, are the co-creators of the Brain Gym ® processes and co-authors of the Edu-Kinesthetics book series on learning through movement, including *Brain Gym ® : Teacher's Edition* and *Vision Gym®: Playful Activities for Natural Seeing*. They are also the founders of Brain Gym ® International, see Braingym.org. Paul is an internationally known speaker in the field of movement-based learning, the originator of Dennison Laterality Repatterning, and the author of *Brain Gym ® and Me: Reclaiming the Pleasure of Learning*. Gail created the Visioncircles course for natural vision improvement. Learn more about the Dennisons' work at Edu-kinesthetics.com. The term Brain Gym ® is a trademark of Brain Gym ® International. See the book *Brain Gym ® : Teacher's Edition* for more information.

Listen to this chapter at HowToLearn.com/amazing-grades-audio

Goal Getting Goal Setting to Improve Your Grades Faster

Goals are the keys to great achievement. Goal-setting is extensively advocated by success coaches, top athletes, corporate high-flyers and motivational speakers because they understand the power of goals. If goal-setting is really as powerful as the experts say, what makes the difference between achieving your goals and not achieving them? The answer lies in the difference between goal-setting and *effective goal-setting*.

Goal-setting isn't about attaching ambitious 'A's to every subject and then hope your grades magically improve. Effective goals are like plans which must be followed through with <u>action</u> to be realized. You achieve results faster because goals give you direction, drive you forward and keep you on course until you get there. Whether you realize it or not, you set goals for things every day. They may be as simple as I'm going to meet my friends after class and we're driving to another city for the weekend. The difference between that goal is that it is short term and clear to you and one which is longer term and maybe not as clear is your attitude, how specific you decide to get, and whether you have a powerful "why" which is your reason to achieve a goal.

The basis of self-discipline is *attitude*. Attitude sets apart the excellent from the average. In order to achieve excellent grades, you must first think and act like an excellent student. If you observe excellent students, you'll find that achievement is directly linked to their attitude and their effort. Let me say this first: goal-setting is NOT a one-off thing. For goals to be effective, you need to continuously remind yourself of what they are until you know them by heart. Most people don't realize that goals are the first step to achieving desired outcomes. They either set ineffective goals or don't set goals at all and let whatever things happen along the way just happen. Your goals won't work unless you know what makes them *effective*. So what makes goals effective?

Here are the five keys:

★ **Effective goals are powered by belief**
Your belief is the most fundamental key to effective goals. If you doubt your ability to succeed from the get-go, your goal has no power. Believe undoubtedly that excellent grades are possible. More importantly you must believe you have what it takes to achieve them.

★ **Effective goals are specific and measurable**
Goals cannot be vague. 'I will get better scores on my exams' is not a goal. Specific details distinguish goals from wishes or wants. Clarity means seeing the completion of the goal in your mind. Measurable goals help you gauge how much effort you have to put in and whether you've achieved your target. If you write a goal that says, "I will receive an A in my cinema class at the end of the semester," it is far more specific.

★ **Effective goals are time-bounded**
Management guru and author Brian Tracy said, "There are no unrealistic goals, only unrealistic deadlines". Goals need deadlines because they push you to take action towards your goals. Setting deadlines activates your mind to look for solutions to help you meet them. Thus achieving something at the end of the semester compels you to do things each day to make this happen.

★ **Effective goals are challenging**
Goals must challenge and stretch you. Don't kid yourself by setting safe goals! If you set goals which you knew you'd probably achieve regardless of how hard you work, then you're underrating your own potential! People set weak goals because they're afraid of trying too hard or facing disappointment. But that's the problem: *weak goals lead to weak results!* Ask yourself - do you REALLY want to succeed? If you do, you have to raise the bar. If you've been getting 'C's or 'D's", go for 'A's this time. Even if you don't achieve your intended 'A', most likely you'll fall short slightly with a 'B'. That still beats getting a lower grade doesn't it? Do yourself a favor - aim a little higher.

★ **Effective goals have a strong 'WHY'**
Why do you want to achieve your goal? If you're serious about succeeding, you need good reasons

to do so! Will success get you into your dream college, get you a scholarship to graduate school, prove your critics wrong or make your parents proud? Whatever your reasons, remember them by heart. Your reasons will motivate you to get back up and keep going.

And now, here is the step-by-step method to effective goal-setting.

Step 1: What do you want?

Firstly you must know specifically what you want to achieve. An 'A' in math? A perfect GPA? What's great about academic goals is that the indicators of success are clear. You choose the standard.

Step 2: Write it down

Once you've decided, write your goals down or type them out. Then print them out and put them where you can see them. This is called goal-setting because you SET your goals down and make them concrete. The act of writing has more power than you think. Every study of great achievers shows that they wrote down their goals. Writing programs your goals into your subconscious mind which will automatically find solutions to achieve that goal. Unwritten goals are just wishes.

Step 3: Attach a deadline

If your goals are exam-based, your deadlines may be the respective exam dates. However, do be reasonable. You're not doing justice to yourself by hoping to turn your 'F' into a Distinction a day before exams without studying. Don't say I didn't warn you!

Step 4: Read it daily

For your goal to fully sink in, remind yourself of it. Place your goals somewhere you can see them daily. Your desktop, your journal - anywhere as long as you are constantly reminded of them. The best time to read your goals is just before bed and just when you awake when your mind is most ready to retain information. Th at way your mind primes you to move towards your goal and you can ask yourself whether what you do brings you closer to your goal each day.

Example of good goals

★   I achieve 5 'A's on my final exams by (put the date here)

Examples of ineffective goals

✗   I will achieve high grades for all my exams.
✗   I will pass chemistry with flying colors

Humans are naturally goal-oriented. We function with a built-in, goal-setting mechanism to get things done. When you say I want to go to the market today, you've just set a goal. And it means walking or driving there to achieve it. Once you've seen for yourself how much difference *effective* goals can make to your life, you will be eager to adopt effective goal-setting as a tool for success. You can use goals to achieve absolutely anything you want. The principles are the same: believe, write it down, commit and act until you've achieved them. I wish you well in your journey towards excellence, good luck!

Hyder Taufik is a success coach in Singapore. He also writes for young adults and is an entrepreneur.

Listen to this chapter at HowToLearn.com/amazing-grades-audio

Use Picture Mapping to Ace Your Exams

See if this sounds familiar. You start reading from the first page of the textbook to the last and just when you thought you've devoured all the information necessary for you to ace your exams, you realized you've forgotten most of what you've studied. This phenomenon is common. Don't worry, there's a phenomenal strategy in this chapter to help.

Most of the time, the most effective way of learning huge chunks of information is by first capturing the main theme of a particular chapter before you start memorizing the finer details. In psychology, this is called *top-down processing* – learning the main idea or concept of the chapter first, and then working your way down to the finer details of information such as definitions for technical terms. This approach to learning information is effective because once you understand what the main theme of the chapter is, you'll read the finer details in perspective. When you read in context, you'll begin to develop expectations of what you'll read, and confirm or reject these expectations as you proceed. This way, you'll be able to link it to the main concept, which enhances the ability for you to remember the information.

So what's the best way to learn the main theme of a chapter? Here are a few tips:

★   Read the learning objectives of the chapter first. It tells you the important information that you need to learn from reading that chapter.
★   Read the headlines and sub-headlines.
★   Read the first and last paragraph of each section.
★   Read the summary section at the end of each chapter.

And how do you compile and organize all these concepts so that you can remember it well? Use what I call *picture mapping* – a diagram filled with keywords (and pictures if you want) arranged around a central theme. An effective picture map consists of the following:

★   Colors – having colorful maps makes learning information easier
★   Keywords – make it succinct. Don't include the whole chunk of information inside. Otherwise, you'll defeat the purpose of picture map.
★   Pictures – a picture is worth a thousand words. Period.

An example of a *picture map* can be seen in the figure below (**Note:** it doesn't have pictures and is black and white because of the space constraint for the chapter. You are highly encouraged to include pictures in your own picture maps so you can memorize more effectively).

To explain the *picture map* below, let's take the "Prioritize" tab as an example. Let's pretend that there's a chapter on Time-management that you need to study, and "Prioritize" is a section under the chapter of Time-management. And this section explains how to make use of a to-do list. So, the "Prioritize" tab in the *picture map* links to the "To-do list" tab because in order to prioritize your tasks, you need to have a proper to-do list. You don't have to include any information on how to use a to-do list or any definitions under this section; you just have to include the main concept.

So friends, remember, whenever you read a chapter, make sure you know the main theme of the chapter first. And use *picture map* to help you learn the information more effectively. This way, you'll be able to remember the rest of the information in that chapter easier, which helps you to ace your exams!

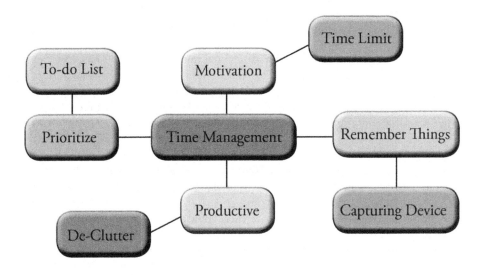

Note: Diagram created using the platform from bubbl.us

Xavier Tan, B.S. is the founder of GeninusOnPurpose.com and is getting his college degree in psychology in Singapore. Previously a failure in school, his turning point came when he discovered a proven system to getting better grades. Since that time he has become a distinguished student with honors in his classes at the university.

Listen to this chapter at HowToLearn.com/amazing-grades-audio

How Music Makes You Smarter

How many songs do you know? I'm sure that you could sing-a-long to at least a hundred. How about five hundred? Or even a thousand? Did you *study* those songs? Of course not! You learn them through an odd form of osmosis called *listening*.

The simple act of listening to a song for any number of repetitions permanently imbeds the song into your memory. Whether it's through a car radio, a song playing in a store or part of song heard in a movie, just a few seconds of any of them sparks a memory. I can remember many of the lyrics and most of the melodies to just about every song I heard through high school and college. But I'm not special, super human, and don't possess some miracle ability to memorize everything I see or hear.

We all have the same ability to store this musical data in our minds with little or no effort. But how do we harness this and use music to help us memorize? And the bigger question is how can we utilize the tool to increase our memory and give us the edge when studying for exams? We are going to explore this together with an added bonus. I challenge each of you to try these simple techniques and to revisit them in a year, two years, five years. I promise you that these memories will still be with you.

Have you heard of Don Campbell's book *The Mozart Effect*? It is a wonderful concept of how listening to concert music (sometimes the classical music of Wolfgang Amadeus Mozart) relaxes the brain and allows the synapses transmitting energy and memories to be faster, more streamlined.

This is in an effort to accomplish what all of our teachers know is the key to successful academics - retention. Memory *is not* mastery. Anyone can regurgitate facts. But if you have retention and are able to retain your memory over long periods of time it *becomes* knowledge. Knowledge is the key. So how can we increase our *knowledge* using music?

If you are among the few reading this that already have a deep love for classical music, wonderful! I suggest listening to Vivaldi's "Four Seasons" and the Bach cello suites as I find both are easily memorable, moving and great ways to attach memory to music. But for most of us, we just want to listen to Dance, Pop, Rock, Hip-Hop, etc. But can you use this music to increase your knowledge? Yes you can! Just follow these simple steps.

Step 1: Identify the mood

Think about yourself, what motivates you and what type of music gives you the most satisfaction. Are they pop sounding love songs? Perhaps some driving dance hall beats? Is it the groove and bass lines of hip-hop? Or is it electric guitar driven rock-n-roll? Whatever style it is, for this experiment, it's *your* style.

Step 2: Pick the right artists

Which artists should you select? Before you choose, consider these two specifications: what is the least distracting and what is the most catchy? You want to select a group that you find easy to listen to while being easy to remember. For example, if you choose Hip-Hop, you probably want to choose an artist that is less angry sounding than Eminem and more flow-based like Jay-Z.

Step 3: Make the playlist

Create a playlist of songs featuring those artists and include a couple favorites that fit your mood and criteria by other artists to break up the sound. The list should be at least two hours long. Don't spend too much time determining the order of the playlist. Five minutes is more than enough time to create it.

Example:

For my memory retention mood, I choose rock. The patterns are catchy and the back beat is good and heavy. I created a playlist featuring Metallica and Muse with a couple songs by Stevie Ray Vaughn and Eric Clapton. It runs about three hours in total and for me it was best to randomize my playlist rather than to create the order myself.

Now you have the tool but how do you make it work for you? Let's try it as if we were studying for a math exam. Start your playlist and begin studying. You will immediately feel the 'mood' that you have planned on creating based on your above selections. Your body will start releasing adrenaline, or in the event you selected slower and softer music, your heart rate will slow, making you more relaxed. Whatever the case may be, that 'mood' is making you an open vessel for knowledge based on your own preferences and learning style.

As you study, allow yourself to get into the music, but don't start singing along with it. Instead, focus on the text and numbers you need to memorize. What you are doing is tapping into the memories you *already* have created with the music. Since you know and are familiar with the songs, your mind is simply adding facts to them. Here are two methods that can increase your retention:

Linear

Simply listen to the playlist while you study. The trick is to be aware of both the facts you are trying to add to your memory while still listening to the music. The combination of both will increase your retention rates and those memories will become knowledge.

Association

Focus on what you need to remember and continuously repeat one song of the playlist until you are satisfied that you remember it. This is the more traditional method of studying through repetition, but by adding the aural component you are making a powerful association.

For example, let's say you are studying for a complicated math exam and you needed to memorize a specific set of equations to solve a certain problem. Let's use my example and say that I associated Muse's "Uprising" with some complicated equation. When I come across the problem on the test and have difficulty recalling the memory where that equation lives, I will playback "Uprising" in my head for a few moments and the equation somehow pops back into my head.

I suggest giving both a try and stick with the one that gives you the best results. There is one drawback though. Ten years from now when you hear that song on the radio, those academic memories will pop up and you may find yourself reciting that equation.

Gregory Pavliv, M.A. is Director of Training at Little Kids Rock at LittleKidsRock.org where he designs and implements trainings and strategies to help teachers mold the creative problem solvers we so desperately need today. A graduate of Berklee College of Music in Boston, he also earned his Master's Degree in Curriculum Design and Instruction. Gregory spent five years as a public school music teacher and was part of the NEA National Representative Assembly where he authored a bill to protect music and the arts in our public schools. Gregory is still an advocate for the importance of the arts on a national level.

Listen to this chapter at HowToLearn.com/amazing-grades-audio

How To Use Mental Photography to Improve Test Scores

You are under pressure to perform – everyone is watching you. Your confidence is shot. The stress can be unbearable – you feel so alone. Your mind goes blank and a sense of dread overwhelms you. No, you're not on the maiden voyage of the RMS Titanic. You are sitting down to take another "TEST".

This scenario is repeated millions of times each day. What would you be willing to do to turn it all around? What if YOU could be the "confident" one that did not need to spend your life studying just to get mediocre grades?

What if something called Mental Photography could change everything? What if it was the one thing that could bring it all into focus for you? Many of the people that are excelling past you are probably already using it. But they are not telling their secret.

Let's Roll Back Time.

Before you entered school, you were a genius! Your parents knew it. And if you are a parent yourself, you see it in your own young children. Read kids a story, then after two or three weeks you read it to them again, and they will point out any mistakes you made. They only heard it once, and they do not even know how to read yet. Yes, you were born genius too.

Your parents saw in you every opportunity to become what they were not. You were an information sponge, just taking it all in; every experience, fully, in every sensory detail. You were born with an eidetic memory. Since the word "eidetic" is a little hard to pronounce, we refer to it today as the Photographic Memory. And yes, we were all born with it.

Most people believe we lose our photographic memory. We don't! We have misplaced our remote control - our accessibility to it. We gave it up as just an infantile way of learning. So, how do we regain access to our Photographic Memory now?

Visionary Discovers Mental Photography

tinyurl.com/735e58c

In 1975, the "Father of Mental Photography", Richard Welch, Ph.D., my Mentor, invented Mental Photography from speed reading. Richard found that under specific conditions, and through reconditioning the mind, the faster you speed through the reading material, the more you get out of it by sending the information directly to the long term memory. The long term memory is your storehouse of information you have "learned" and keep.

The information gained with Mental Photography bypasses the short term memory altogether. Therefore, you gain the information because the information is not encumbered by most learning challenges.

What is Mental Photography?

In essence, Mental Photography is your natural ability to tap into your photographic memory (eidetic memory), and make it work for you. It is a natural learning process that everyone possesses that allows you to rapidly take in books, and any other type of information, at levels way beyond speed reading. As a brain exercise, Mental Photography capitalizes on neuroplasticity to grow and strengthen your brain. Your benefits last a lifetime.

How to Develop your Mental Photography, and Use It for Test-Taking

You can take steps to develop Mental Photography and to use it to succeed with test taking.

Relax – The most important thing for doing well on tests is also the most important thing when developing your Mental Photography. Like meditation teaches you to relax to gain access to your whole mind, likewise Mental Photography needs access in the same manner. So, relax, like you would when you are daydreaming.

Turn pages rapidly – Staying relaxed, turn pages in your book so fast you cannot read them. You are using a different part of the brain.

Do not read – Do not attempt to read or remember anything while you are Mentally Photographing. You won't feel like anything is happening because the brain functions differently during mental photography than when you read. Your subconscious is processing the information to your long term memory, where you keep it permanently in high detail.

Reading vs. Mental Photography: Reading is like looking at the surface of the ocean, while Mental Photography is getting the volume of the ocean without seeing the surface. The volume is much greater than just the surface.

Using Mental Photography to Boost Study Efforts – A habit of using Mental Photography every day along with your current study routine will boost your test results in the areas you are weak in. With consistent use, your study time will go down and your scores will go up in any subject.

Superior Information from Mental Photography makes Testing Easy – One thing you must accept about test taking is that it is designed to see how well you perform under stress and expectation, as well as whether you retained what you know. When you understand the "Rules of Engagement", you eliminate stress. It allows you to relax and pull out information as you need it to answer questions correctly.

Your Support System

Doing the steps above will only address the application. You must do them continuously over time to recondition your mind for gaining and retrieving information using Mental Photography. Having a strong support system in place makes your transition easier and our complete training offers that support. You are not the same as everyone else. Your support should be personalized, to address the things that affect you and your success. Your success is based on your results as well as all the other aspects of your life. You should be given every opportunity to be successful. Your study time will shrink amazingly and you will exude confidence once you have Mental Photography working for you. You may be doing things that are considered outlandish or impossible by others.

Test-taking Does Not End In School

Your school-life experiences will follow you throughout your life. Testing does not end with school and you will be tested often as you go through life. Choosing to gain the ability to access your photographic memory with Mental Photography throughout your life can be one very helpful way to achieve your goals.

Shannon Panzo, Ph.D., is a Mental Photography and Brain Management expert, creator of ZOX Pro Training and the advanced eBrain Executive Seminar. You may find out more at http://ZOXpro.com. He also has another site at http://MINDtoMIND.com.

Listen to this chapter at tinyurl.com/burghkl

Memory Skills Made Easy

Memory is as simple as knowing the strategies to improve it so you can always rely on it. As the research goes, you must use your memory and practice the strategies or you will lose it.

Just as knowledge is software to the brain's hardware, you can improve your hardware by committing time to the following best memory systems I've spent years researching. (Some are free and some are paid.)

1. Dual N-Back game has initial studies which indicate that it develops such key aspects of intelligence as short-term memory, concentration span, differentiation and creativity. You may find this at http://brainworkshop.sourceforge.net

2. Neuro Programmer 3 is audio-visual software that includes memory and intelligence-improving sessions. With the correct techniques you will soon be able to remember things naturally, while having much more fun doing so, and possibly even equal or better the achievements of the great mnemonists!

3. How To Develop A Brilliant Memory Week By Week book by Dominic O'Brien is one which pretty much covers everything and sets a pace you can comfortably maintain with your studies.

His Dominic System is, for me, by far the most user-friendly for memorizing the strings of digits we use in math, scientific formula, computing etc., in part because it uses a standard set of people (rather than objects) and associated action for each pair of digits from 0-99.

Further persons and actions for use in your Dominic System may also be found in the Files section of the Yahoo Group: World Wide Brain Club, whose members also share tips on memory improvement and so on. Dominic also introduces in this book a key memory technique, the journey (also generally known as the memory palace or Roman room) system.

Looking around the room you are in you may notice the following string of objects: aquarium, blinds, ceiling, door, envelope

Applying a number to each of these in turn:
1   aquarium
2   blinds
3   ceiling
4   door
5   envelope

This will give you a mental journey of numerically-consecutive objects, to which you may attach keywords (or, as in the Dominic System, mnemonically coded) pieces of information such as:
★   instructions
★   lines of dialogue, speeches or textbook passages
★   mathematical or scientific workings-out or formula etc.

One way to memorize π to nine decimal places (3.14159265) using the journey system, for instance, you would break it down into manageable chunks (as with a credit card or, say, an international phone number) such as:
3
14
15
92
65

Then attach (using your imagination) in turn each of these digits to a consecutive object in a mental journey. Thus in the journey we have just created:

3   in the aquarium (perhaps a fish's mouth)
14   behind the blinds, glowing in the sunlight
15   painted on the ceiling
92   standing by the door
5   printed (or perhaps a hook - resembles a 5 - through) on the envelope

4. I tend to use Tony Buzan's mind mapping process (thinkbuzan.com/iMindMap) and *The Mind Map Book* by Tony Buzan) as an efficient method in which you use a visual memory of what you have drawn. Each item around the center relates to the whole, so this is especially great for recalling information in a textbook.

5. The one great book using mnemonics for most subject areas I have found is Every Good Boy Deserves Fudge The Book of Mnemonic Devices by Rod L. Evans, Ph.D.

6. You may also wish to try one of many books or courses on speed reading and the self-explanatory How To Read A Book by Mortimer Adler and Charles Lincoln Van Doren is a model on efficient study and note-taking.

7. If you are an auditory learner, dictate key or most difficult parts of your study into your computer's sound recorder for private listening when you are walking around and studying at your desk, etc.

8. Another great course I live is Harry Kahne's *The Multiple Mentality Course* for cross-exercising underused parts of the brain. Several of the exercises can be practiced in one's head during the more mindless parts of the day: This is at http://www.rexresearch.com/kahne/kahne.htm

9. Lumosity is one of the best programs online. While there is a small cost associated with it, it gives your whole brain a full workout to enhance not only memory, attention and creativity. You can find this course at lumosity.com.

Best Way to Review Your Material To Increase Recall

Research shows that we recall what we learned first (primacy) and what we learned last (recency) more easily that what we learned in the middle of a lesson. Thus, reviewing in the following way increases your memory: After a one-hour period of study you should review your material:

Approximately after:	Approximate review period (in minutes)
30 minutes (following a 10-minute break)	10
1 day	2-4
1 week	2
1 month	2
6 months	2
1 year	2

James Smith, BA (Hons) is the author of *Memory Palace Definitive* and member of British MENSA. He is currently writing a guide, with Phil Chambers of Learning Technologies, Ltd., to memorizing mathematical and scientific formula for publication in late 2012. Memory improvement is also discussed at the following Yahoo Groups: Memory Sports and Art of Memory and on the Facebook Community page for Memory Palace Definitive.

Listen to this chapter at HowToLearn.com/amazing-grades-audio

How To Get Better ACT, SAT, GRE... Test Scores

Standardized tests, including the ACT, SAT, GRE and many others, are one of the most important factors in determining your chances of getting into a school. A bachelor's degree can increase lifetime earnings by more than $2 million, further amplifying the importance of getting into a good school.

Given the high stakes, it is highly recommended that you devote enough time preparing for the required standardized test and approach the process with diligence and discipline. To make it easier for you, I have broken down the complete process into three steps:

★ **Phase I: Research**

Before you pick a book and start taking practice exams, take a step back and put together a plan. Start with doing research on your goals and setting up the right expectations. Jumping into the preparation phase without doing research will lead to waste of time and energy.

Goals: Ask yourself a simple question- what's the end goal? Which school or university do you want to get to? Once you answer this, work backwards from the goal. Figure out the admission criteria, requirements, historic scores, and grade expectations for the desired universities.

The Test: Once you have figured out your goals, you need to "get to know" the test. Understanding the test will certainly set you up for success. A majority of students waste precious time practicing and preparing without having a clear understanding of what the test stands for. This research should include questions like how does the test scoring work? Are there penalty points for skipping questions? What are the different areas and skill-sets it is trying to test you on? Are some areas more important than others? Do you have to write an essay?

Talk to Friends, Advisors, Classmates: If you are thinking of going to college or taking another test beyond college, look around and find friends who are thinking the same or have already gone to college. Many of them have most likely already taken the test. Pick up the phone and talk to them. It helps to talk to someone who has gone through the process and can tell you the mistakes they made. Learn from their mistakes and experience before you invest your time.

Diagnostics: The fourth step is to know where you are before you start preparing. Most of the standardized tests test you on general analytical, math and verbal skills. The topics covered in these tests have already been covered, in some shape or form, in your classes. However, you need to objectively assess where you stand. I highly recommend that you take a diagnostic test to understand how much of a gap you need to fill to be able to achieve a score that will land you in the college you want to go to. By knowing your goals, strengths, weaknesses and requirements, half of the battle is already won.

★ **Phase II: Preparation**

If there is one thing that will guarantee you a good score, it's PRACTICE! Preparing with a systematic approach is the other half of the battle. Be sure to read the learning styles section in this book and use the style that works best for you.

Mobile Solution to Study: If you are not one of the students who can easily focus for extended periods of time, find a mobile solution, which provides you access to material and practice at your fingertips. You can

tinyurl.com/z4536lu

also connect with friends this way. If you have a difficult time memorizing certain aspects of the test like vocabulary and their definitions, make sure you use their digital flashcards and techniques you learned in this book to make the process more efficient.

In any of these study styles, tracking and identifying confidence levels is very important. If you don't understand a concept, mark it as low confidence, if you feel good about a concept, mark it as high. Mark everything else as medium. Every week go back and review everything you have marked as low/medium and the goal should be to bump it up a level.

Take-Aways: There is one more thing that can help you improve your score: making a journal of key takeaways while practicing. I call them cheat-sheets. Essentially, once you start practicing questions, you will notice that you are making similar mistakes on certain question types. As soon as you realize this, take a note of the key takeaway. Do this over as many different question types/areas and you will end up with 30-50 key take-aways in the form of a cheat sheet. This is gold. You just condensed days of re-practicing into hours. Well done.

Resources: In case you still don't understand certain concepts, there are plenty of amazing free and paid online resources like Khan Academy to help you out further. Also, BenchPrep courses are from top publishers which are augmented with relevant open educational resources including Khan Academy videos, all in one place, which can save you a lot of time searching.

★   **Phase III: Execution**

By this time you have been at it for month; you have cut down your social life, reduced the number of shows you are watching and missed couple of NBA playoff games. Hold steady, the big day is coming. It is very important to be relaxed on the day of the exam. Here is a checklist of things you should make sure you do:

Sleep: Don't break your sleeping schedule. If you have to wake up at 8 am in the morning to take a test, make sure you are waking up at 8 at least 2-3 days continuously before the exam day. Breakfast: Eat a healthy breakfast, including protein on the day of the test to make sure you have enough physical and mental stamina to go through the test completely.

Breathing: Take a deep breath. During the exam, every now and then (let's say every 30 mins), just take a deep breath, clear your mind and close your eyes for 10 seconds. Don't worry about losing 10 seconds. It is not a lot of time to lose but it will help you re-practice again.

Time: Don't spend too much time on any one question. Don't get emotional about answering every question. Make an educated guess and move on to the next question if the test doesn't do negative scoring. Good luck!

 Ujjwal Gupta, Ph.D. is the Founder and CTO of BenchPrep.com, the world's first and only cross-device exam prep and assessment platform. The company was voted "most innovative and best-in-class test prep and assessment platform" at the Education Innovation Summit and won the 2010 New Venture Challenge at Chicago Booth. He, along with BenchPrep, has been featured in Wall Street Journal, NY Times, TechCrunch, Publishers Weekly and Fast Company as a leading education innovator. BenchPrep is bringing best-in-class education to the masses. Mr. Gupta has won multiple awards and published 15+ papers in various international journals including Langmuir, ACS Nano, Chemical Physics Letters, etc.

Listen to this chapter at HowToLearn.com/amazing-grades-audio

8 Ways to Beat Exam Anxiety
Before and During Your Exams

Got the jitters before your exams? During your exams? Here are 8 practical tips to nix them.

★   **Review the subjects you dislike the most in the morning before the exam**

Sometimes it is just easier to stomach the things you don't like in the morning rather than after a long day. Successful people in all walks of life attribute their success to one simple technique: if you have a set of jobs to do, you do the most difficult thing - the thing you don't like - first. This means when you first get up, immediately after breakfast, your mind is the freshest.

★   **Read and take notes using picture maps**

If you have a textbook you think is boring, reading it alone will not cement the information in your brain. You have to do something with the information. Take notes, use pictures and make connections of the information you read with something you enjoy. Use all the memory techniques in this book and you will find you actually recall the information when you need it most.

★   **Manage your time properly in the exam**

This is the most vital of all techniques. Make sure you spend the most time on the questions that give you the most points. Often these are the last ones, and there is a very solid argument for looking at the whole exam first if you can, just to plan your time better and see which questions carry the most weight. Do these first.

★   **Answer the question asked**

While this seems very obvious, you would be surprised to know how many times it does not happen. Teachers always talk about their concerns to other teachers when students don't actually answer the questions they are asked. Make sure you answer the question in front of you, not some other question you've made up, because that question is asking you for things you know. Do this by underlining three key words per question and checking with yourself that you know – exactly what is being asked.

★   **Plan your answer**

Think about a wedding. If it wasn't planned properly, then the bride and the groom would turn up at different churches, the priest would have taken the day off, and nothing positive would have happened. The same thing applies to any essay work you have to write in an exam. Fail to plan and you plan to fail. Brainstorm your ideas, mark each idea with the paragraph number they go in, and only then should you go about writing the essay. Make sure your plan is on the exam paper, where the examiner can see it. There is a great chapter in this book on how to write essays and I recommend you spend a bit of time reading it.

★   **Check your paper**

If an exam is one-and-a-half hours long, you have exactly one-and-a-half hours to squeeze every point you can out of it. If you find yourself towards the end of an exam, lounging in your chair trying to catch your friend's attention in the next row, wake up! You are sabotaging your own chances. There is only one point difference between a pass and a fail. Checking your paper at the end could be the thing that gives you that one, crucial mark.

★   **Use positive self-talk**

People who tell themselves they can't do things invariably find that they are right. People who tell themselves they can are right too. During your study time and during the exam itself, keep telling yourself, "I can do this." You'll find you can.

★   **Take your time and do your best**

When the examiner says, "You may turn your papers over now," everyone else in the room will try and do so at the pace an Olympic sprinter leaves the blocks. Don't do this. It puts you in a stressful state, and saves you exactly 0.41 seconds, (which is a useless amount of time to save). When the examiner says to turn your paper over, don't. Take a breath, count to ten, then do it. You are the one in control of your destiny.

Stay calm and focused. If, at the end of the day, you are able to honestly say to yourself that you have done your best, you have a right to be happy with yourself no matter what the grade. No one has any right to ask any more of you.

Anxiety does not empty tomorrow of its sorrows, but only empties today of its strength.
- Charles Spurgeon

 Phil Beadle is both an internationally recognized expert on teaching and learning and an inner city English teacher specializing in working with students in challenging circumstances. He has won national awards in the United Kingdom for both teaching and broadcasting and an international award for his journalism. His books on teaching and learning have been translated into five different languages. His *How to Teach* book was awarded 10/10 by the Times Educational Supplement. More recent publications include *Dancing about Architecture* and *Bad Education*, a compilation of the columns he wrote for the Guardian. His TV programs, 'Lessons from the Best' are used in universities across the west coast of America. For more information, visit his website at PhilBeadle.com or follow him on Twitter at twitter.com/@philbeadle

Listen to this chapter at HowToLearn.com/amazing-grades-audio

How To Get Good Grades in College

College students spend untold hours worrying about what they will major in at college, when the choice of major is less important than getting good grades in college. The skills that you will need to carry you through a life filled with many jobs and multiple careers can be found in most traditional majors and the required core courses that most colleges demand.

An employer or graduate school is going to look at the GPA to see how smart you are. If you are passionate about the ideas in your philosophy courses and get good grades in them then the 3.5 there is going to serve you better than the 2.7 gotten in majoring in accounting which you hate but think is more useful. It is not useful if you are not good at it and can't get good grades in it. Parents, with all loving intent, will try to guide you to a practical major, but be sure that it is one that also aligns with your strengths as that will make a difference in the grades you are able to get.

Usually professors will spell out in the syllabus how they calculate a grade—particular percentages, for instance, for quizzes, papers, class participation, and final exams so you can figure out how to get a good grade. If the elements are not spelled out, ask for a breakdown. This way you can track how you are doing, so you can calculate the kind of grades you may get based on what you have done in each of the elements being graded. Good grades reflect how hard you work and that you know the material.

tbit.ly/1HgbSD9

Also track how well you are doing as the year goes along. If you see a pattern of low grades in a particular arena, like the sciences, then you need to see what is going on. Is it the way you are studying or is it that it is not your strength then? If so, shift direction to focus on and major in the areas that grab you and where the strongest grades come most easily. Make that move early in your academic career so that your final GPA reflects you at your best.

Look at your course catalog to see how the GPA is calculated and keep a record. If an F has crept in find out how to make things better rather than dropping out totally. This is what advisers are for.

It does not serve you well to demand good grades because you want or need them. If you have not done the work, done well on tasks assigned, or engaged in class activities, you cannot expect a professor to change a C grade to a B because, say, your scholarship is at risk.

Study tips for getting good grades:

★   If you love the subject, the material just comes easily to you, or there is not a lot of work required. Think about the ones that are difficult. You typically approach the easy ones with a willingness to tackle them first. Instead figure out how much time you need to do the work of your hardest class and then tackle it when you are freshest and most alert and able to focus. Do tough work first to get a good grade in it. Hold out the work you enjoy for last—make it dessert.

★   If you're not a good writer plan to spend time with your professor and in the writing center, and have someone look over your drafts. You must have a longer planning horizon for writing papers.

★   Find a viable study space for how you study best. Some students need total silence, so the library or their dorm room may work. If your room is too distracting—the TV and the bed tempt you— then find somewhere else. Your space should allow you to have your notes, laptop, and texts handy.

★ Learn how to read. Making it to college does not mean you know how to read there, where it will be more about comprehension and interpretation. Read with access to a glossary or dictionary. You must understand what you're reading to get good grades. Turning pages when you don't get it does not make sense. Ask an upperclassman, a TA, or your professor, if necessary. I have seen far too many students sit silently, not understanding a word of what is going on, and then blow the test, midterm, or paper.

★ When reading you're looking for key concepts, and evidence to support them. Look at the table of contents, the index of a book, or the introduction to see where the author wants to lead you. Then read the middle, looking for examples of what the author wants you to understand. Once you know what you're looking for, you can read faster. Make notes if you disagree with the author's premises and why. Use whatever tools work for you to highlight key points.

★ It helps you get good grades when you read in a difficult field if you ask yourself (or others) why it is important and relevant. The key point about studying is to find the most important ideas in whatever you're working on Ask your professor what the most important concepts are that you're expected to master.

★ Devise your own tools to help you retain material. Make flash cards and carry them around. Make notes in the margins of your class notes. If you keep notes on your laptop, print them out so you can review them offline. Record the key concepts you're learning as you go, and how they hang together. Develop a short summary of that week's material. If you're a visual learner, make diagrams or pictures to remember material. If you can't summarize, then you have not learned or understood the material.

★ The students who get good grades are not going it alone. If math or science is hard for you, again, seek out the professor, the TA, or a tutor. Your school may have resources which provide online tutoring. Some subjects, often quantitative, lend themselves to the use of study groups.

Good grades are about working smart and hard. You can do it if you try and make it your own process that plays to your own strengths.

Marcia Y. Cantarella, Ph.D., is the author of *I CAN Finish College: The Overcome Any Obstacle and Get Your Degree Guide*, which is available on Amazon or at icanfinishcollege.com. Dr. Cantarella is the president of Cantarella Consulting, has been a dean at Princeton University, Associate Dean at Hunter College and part of the Dean's staff at New York University's College of Arts and Science. As Vice-President of Student Affairs at Metropolitan College of NY she was responsible for web development and rebranding of the College as well as admissions and student services.

Listen to this chapter at HowToLearn.com/amazing-grades-audio

Cracking the College Code:
5 Study Secrets Excellent Students Use

Excellent students share common traits and strategies. If you want to get amazing grades and have the best chance to get into the college or other training program of your choice, do what they do.

1. PREPARE

Prepare your <u>space</u> by creating a "home office" for study. Most kids don't give any thought to where they study. To get ahead of the pack, spend time creating an area where you love to spend time that supports your style. Do you like more structured desk space, or a comfortable supportive chair with a rolling adjustable computer stand that comes to you? Create good lighting (look for full spectrum), possibly a floor stand with a goose-neck light and a place for all the materials you need in easy reach. Hang affirmation and content posters, and play baroque music or the Mozart Effect while you're studying and upbeat music for breaks to add to the ambiance.

bit.ly/1WcwbvD

Prepare yourself by remembering your <u>ABCs</u> – Attitude, Beliefs, Curiosity. Your **attitude** has a tremendous effect on your success and has everything to do with your energy and results. Have you ever tried something new and were convinced you wouldn't be able to do it right? What was the result? You need to have an upbeat attitude and positive **beliefs**. Henry Ford once said 'whether you believe you can or whether you believe you can't, either way you're right.' When you believe in something it shifts your thinking and makes it real in your mind. Along with your upbeat attitude and positive beliefs, add a touch of **curiosity**. Ask yourself, I wonder what this means? I wonder what's coming next. Your attitude, beliefs and curiosity can be the deciding factor between boredom and fun, between failure and success, between staying in one place and moving forward. And remember, the way you hold them is a choice – only you can choose.

2. FOCUS

Focus by being clear on your <u>outcome</u> – what you want to achieve and in how much time. **Chunk** your content into small sections and take short **breaks** between them.

Focus by getting into <u>state</u>: *Pull up and Picture, Breathe and Release, Look and Listen.* Sit or stand tall by imagining a string attached to the top of your head that pulls you up. Picture what you want to achieve. Take a breath deep from your belly, and release your jaw and shoulders. Now look and listen and focus your attention on one thing – what you are learning.

3. MAXIMIZE

Maximize your <u>style</u> by using strategies for all learning modalities – visual, auditory, tactual/kinesthetic. All learners benefit from visual notes and posters. Map out your content in color while you are reading, studying or listening to your teacher. Make posters and hang them for review. Talk to yourself – yes out loud. Move around and emphasize main points by making up motions that remind you of the points. We like to say – See it! Say it! Draw it! Do it!

Maximize your <u>memory</u> by creating imaginary pictures or mental images in your head of the content, much like a movie. Connect the new content you are learning to something you already know to make it meaningful.

Maximize your <u>motivation</u> by finding the WIIFM (what's in it for me). Why would I want to learn what the teacher is teaching? How might I use this information to benefit me? Is it to pass the exam and get a good grade? Is it that if I pay good attention I'll get through my homework faster? Will I find the content interesting and something I will use later? When you come up with ways this lesson will benefit you, your ability to focus and learn the information increases, it's more fun and time goes faster.

Maximize your <u>thinking</u> by analyzing the content. Ask yourself such things as: Is this fact or opinion? What do I think about this? Is there evidence to support the author's conclusions? What problem needs to be solved? Is the author making assumptions I don't agree with? What values are projected that differ from those of my family? What is the cause and effect (could the outcome really result from the event)? Become an active participant in your learning.

4. REVIEW

Review your learning by making a plan. Know the important points and sub-points and review using 10-24-7. Do a quick review of small chunks every 10 minutes, overview the important points and sub-points in 24 hours, and again in 7 days. Make a chart as a reminder. Find fun ways to review and incorporate visual, auditory, tactual and kinesthetic strategies.

Review with a theta scan. Your brain moves information from short-term to long-term memory during sleep. Just before you turn off your light, scan your notes and think about what you learned during the day.

5. GIVE YOUR BEST EFFORT

Give your best effort to the task at hand. You can't guarantee an "A" grade, but you can guarantee you will give your best effort in learning the material. Be sure to keep charts to track your progress and ask yourself, "What happened, what was the result? What did I learn? What will I do differently next time?" When you give your best effort, track progress, and learn from your results you learn, grow and succeed. You become an excellent successful student!

Remember to celebrate your learning!

Bobbi DePorter, author of 18 books, is co-founder and president of Quantum Learning Network, an organization that produces SuperCamp, a learning and life skills summer enrichment program held on prestigious university campuses across the U.S. and 14 countries with over 64,000 graduates. She is also the co-founder of Quantum Learning Education, which develops positive school cultures focused on the quality of learning with programs for administrators, teachers and students that have transformed thousands of schools and millions of students. For free test taking tips visit SuperCamp.com and QuantumLearning.com.

Listen to this chapter at HowToLearn.com/amazing-grades-audio

Your High Tech Brain and Technology:
How to Use Technology to Enhance Your Brain

It is fairly common for every student to be connected to some type of technology. Let's face it, most of you reading this are in some way plugged in.

Whether, Facebook, video chat, text, or your smart phone, you have a need to be in constant communication with your peers. I am not going to tell you to cut the connections; I am going to tell you to use them to your advantage. You can use your need to be connected to your friends to learn faster, learn better, retain more, and develop methods of collaboration that will serve you for a lifetime. Oh yes, all of this will raise your grades. Higher grades should always be the result of better learning.

I'm sure you have heard the old saying, "two heads are better than one" and this is true in many aspects of life, including learning. It is through social discourse, talking with friends, that learning can truly be solidified in the brain. Stick with me here for a bit of neuroscience.

Learning is a mental thing but it is a chemical, physical thing too. When you learn something it is recorded in the brain as new connections between neurons, this is why it takes a while to learn something new. When you do not have any neural connections linking concepts, you have to experience it enough to develop the connections. These connections are called pathways. Most of us tend to memorize new material because the act of rote memorization is a quick way to build neural connections. BIG problem… Memorization only creates one pathway to knowledge.

© Nikolai Sorokin

The best way to make sure you can use that information in many ways is to create several pathways to the knowledge, not just one. I know it sounds a bit confusing but it is really quite easy to do. You have to connect new knowledge to things you have experienced and things you know already, and, most importantly, you must involve your emotions. These can all be done by using what you already love, connecting with friends through technology, and putting in place a few new guidelines to ensure you accomplish your goals of learning.

The best thing is that not only will your grades go up but your desire to learn or your motivation will increase too. Oh, you need to know that this is not a "night before the test fix", this is an everyday, set aside at least twenty minutes of designated connection time. Most of you already spend more than twenty minutes connected with your friends. This is just asking you to designate of that some time to specific discussion.

So how do you accomplish this? It is easy. First of all, you will need to develop a list of friends that are either in your class, are studying the same thing, or enjoy the topic being studied. Second, you will need to inform the others of the guidelines of discussion. Just what are these guidelines? In the discussion you will need to discuss the following questions in relationship to the topic. Now, before I give you the questions, I need to explain why they are all important. Each question represents a facet of understanding. **Each facet creates a unique pathway.** In other words, you can create at least six ways of accessing your new knowledge if you take this seriously and reflectively discuss the material using the questions.

6 Questions To Create New Pathways In Your Brain

1. What is the information? Explain, tell or recount the information.
2. What personal connection can I make to this information? Ask – 'what does this remind me of?'
3. How can I use this information?
4. Why is this information important?
5. How would someone else look at this information? How would a mathematician, scientist, doctor, lawyer, etc. look at this information? The more perspectives you can come up with, the better you will be.
6. What do I understand, not understand, and want to know more about?

A really neat advantage of using this format for thinking is it is reflective in nature; therefore you will be strengthening the area of your brain that deals with making good personal decisions, self-control, and assessing cause and effect of situations and personal choices.

Finally, the part you like is here. You can create a blog, designate a time for a conference call or use whatever technology you love to communicate with your peers. As long as you use these questions as guidelines and stick to topic, you will make neural connections; you will learn, and your grades will increase. This is an authentic long-term way of thinking that will result in enhanced understanding, more knowledge, and the ability to remember better.

I'm a great believer that any tool that enhances communication has profound effects in terms of how people can learn from each other, and how they can achieve the kind of freedoms that they're interested in.
- Bill Gates

 Deborah Crowder, Ph.D. is an Assistant Professor and member of Graduate Faculty at Texas A&M University Central Texas. She is a member of American Educational Research Association, International Reading Association, Professors of Reading Teacher Educators, National Speakers Association and the Global Speakers Federation.

Listen to this chapter at HowToLearn.com/amazing-grades-audio

Tablets: The Backpack of Tomorrow to Raise Your Grades

If you're a student these days, you've more than likely heard someone make the comment, "He has some sort of addiction to that device; he's fixated on it for endless hours; he never leaves home without that technology thing."

I used to try to defend technology to everyone who made those comments about me; however, I quickly came to terms with the fact that the world would soon catch up to speed. I don't think what some realize is that these 'technology things' actually take the place of many 'things' we previously used. So, naturally, it would seem as though we are always fixated on our mobile devices.

For example, in high school, I used to carry around a loaded backpack with several books, numerous well-organized notebooks, a few highlighters, different colored pens, literature books for reading, my day planner, and my homework binder. People use to say, "Her head is always in the books." Interesting how that comment was perceived as positive when compared to today's comments regarding being addicted to technology. Don't they realize students are multi-tasking while on their mobile devices?

What used to put a heavy strain on my back has been replaced by a single, ultra-thin, social device: the tablet. By a superficial glance, it may appear that today's students are plugged in so much that they are oblivious to what's happening around them. I'd argue quite the opposite. In a matter of moments, today's students can connect with peers across the globe, share content with thousands of people with the click of one button, and collaborate in real-time with anyone, anywhere.

Students today are using tablets to modernize, streamline, and enhance the same study habits we all practiced in our youth. Studying, researching, and note taking remain core competencies in which all students must excel.

The tablet is simply a tool to support students. It is similar to the Encyclopedias and highlighters we used. What the tablet now adds is the ability to create, publish, and share student-created content in a visually stimulating and interactive format.

Note-Taking and Research:

Applications such as SoundNote (soundnote.com) allow the student to record their classroom discussion, or lecture, while taking their own notes. Students can go to any section of their notes and, with one click, have the audio jump to that exact portion of the discussion or lecture. Evernote (Evernote.com) is an application that focuses on streamlining student creativity and ideas. With this app, students can record notes, jot down important details, snap photographs to save, and have all of this content synced to one account for access anywhere, even on one's computer.

Staying organized with Awesome Note (bridworks.com/anote/en/main/index.php) allows students to enter homework or assignment tasks, personal items, maps, calendar and event items, and more all with colorful tabs that categorize each topic.

Studying:

Having access to your flashcards at all times without having to carry around stacks of index cards bound together is made simple by StudyBlue (studyblue.com). This application separates your cards into ones you've mastered and ones you need to continue studying.

Students can create their own specific cards or search the archive of shared content to extend their learning. Then, students can take the notes they've been studying and sort their research with iCard Sort (tinyurl.com/28jvnvt) to truly gauge their understanding of each concept.

One of my favorite applications is GoodReader (tinyurl.com/y2v9h3g). GoodReader allows you to read PDF documents and have the ability to annotate your personal notes on top of the text. Students can highlight, underline, add arrows, text boxes, call out features, and free hand drawings to mark-up their text.

Creating:

Developing and sharing content is an engaging and critical aspect of studying and learning. I know when my students work through the process of creating a product, they've synthesized their learning at a much higher level. Pages (http://www.apple.com/iwork/pages/) is a rich application that allows students to have access to word processing on their tablet by importing text and images in a beautiful layout that can be published.

Animoto (animoto.com) is a digital storytelling application that enables students to share their work through video, images, text titles, and music. This app creates emotionally charged , creative products. KeyNote (keynote.com) is an app that is similar to PowerPoint in which allows students to showcase their learning to a public forum. Students can also use SonicPics (sonicpics.com) to create a slideshow comprised of images with student annotation through voice over.

With great tools such as these available, it's easy to see why successful students don't leave home without their tablet.

If we teach today as we taught yesterday, we rob our children of tomorrow.
- John Dewey

 Erin Klein, M.A. is a teacher, Michigan Reading Association's co-Technology chair for the state and a member of the National Writing Project. Klein has also been recognized as a SMART Exemplary Educator by SMART Technologies. She has been a guest blogger for several sites including Edutopia, Really Good Stuff, and Edudemic. Her own blog, Kleinspiration.com has received several awards for education and technology. You can connect with her on her blog or on Twitter here: @KleinErin

Listen to this chapter at HowToLearn.com/amazing-grades-audio

How Can You Tell When You "Know" Something?

As you go through school, you may find yourself wondering whether you really know something. I have outlined some steps below so that you can tell if you know, for sure.

★ **Inventory of Facts and Principles**

The first step in "knowing" is to find out exactly what has to be learned in any given field, such as geology, math, etc. What is the lay of the land, so to speak? What are the parts that make up the field of study? What principles and facts need to be learned? Make a list.

★ **Absorb the Knowledge**

Using the learning strategies in this book, learn the principles behind what you are learning, and the facts that support the theories in the field you are studying. Each field has methods to learn these. Learn how to think according to the field of knowledge you are learning. Find out what these are.

★ **Application of Facts and Principles to real life**

Apply what you have learned in order to discover what works and what does not work in real life. Make the adjustments necessary so that what you learn will work in the real world.

See how others have dealt with the problems you encountered. What steps must you take in order to find the solution to a problem in your field?

★ **Modification of Facts and Principles with Respect to Real-Life Applications**

Know what works well enough so that you can use it in the real world. Consult experts. Do not take experts at face value and test their information against other experts. Apply your knowledge of the field to real life problems and situations.

Find what weaknesses there are in your knowledge. Is there something new you have to learn? Modify your knowledge accordingly.

Always be eager and enthusiastic to add to your knowledge. You will need to re-modify your knowledge as you gain more experience. Learning is a lifelong never ending process.

★ **Teach what you "know" so others can learn it also**

When you feel comfortable that what you have learned works well, and you can easily apply your knowledge to real world problems and in every situation you encounter, then you know your field well enough to pass this knowledge on to others.

You can then teach what you know.

At this point you can say you "know" your subject, even though you realize that you must continue to learn and modify as long as you live, ever learning more in order to know more. It never ends.

The more careful you have been in learning your material, the more you will have to share with those who need to learn it. Don't teach superficially. Research the material you teach so that you teach the solid truth about the field being taught.

Wisdom is the principal thing; therefore, get wisdom; and with all thy getting, get understanding. Exalt her,and she shall promote thee, she shall bring thee to honor when thou dost embrace her. She shall promote thee, she shall bring thee to honor when thou dost embrace her.
-Proverbs 4:7,8

I hear and I forget. I see and I remember. I do and I understand.
-Confucius

Ralph Sirvent, Jr., M.A. was a Senior Adjunct Professor of English at Atlantic Cape Community College. He attended and graduated from Binghamton University.

Listen to this chapter at HowToLearn.com/amazing-grades-audio

3 Ways To Make an A: How One Student Went From Failing to 4.0!

I struggled in school. From kindergarten through 12th grade, I struggled to earn mediocre grades. I would study for hours…then fail a test. Over time, I had no motivation to study. "Why should I bother?" I wondered.

As I entered college, I knew something would have to change. Based on my track-record, I would never survive. So, I found two books on the subject of "preparing for college." Most of the information in these books was awkward and frustrating. A few strategies, however, were attractive. They were simple. I could easily remember them. So, I tried them.

They worked! I earned a 3.9 GPA my first semester of college. Before long, I earned a 4.0 and graduated from college with the highest honors. After 13 years of chronic struggle in school, this was a miracle!

What Made the Difference?

It turns out, the strategies I learned were "study skills;" skills that allowed me how to learn more efficiently. After a lifetime of struggles, a few simple concepts completely transformed my experience in school. My confidence soared! I discovered I can do anything I set my mind to.

Do Study Skills Really Make *THAT* Much Difference?

Study skills changed my life. It turns out, I'm not alone. In 2009, Ohio State University published results from a long-term study on the effectiveness of study skills. They found that: Students who had struggled in high school, were <u>45% more likely to graduate</u> from college if they took a study skills class as a freshman. Students who had been considered "average" in high school, were <u>600% more likely to graduate from college</u> after taking a study skills class!

Employers Are DESPERATE for Study Skills!

In the workplace, these skills are known as "soft skills." And, employers are desperate for them! In a 2008 survey, hundreds of employers in "emerging sectors" (fields that are expected to grow in the next 30 years) listed the skills they needed most. Of the top 57 skills, only four related to technology. The remaining 95% were skills such as: * Reading comprehension (which ranked at the top of the list for every individual sector) * Critical thinking * Active learning * Written expression * Time management * Organization * Active Listening * Attention to detail * Learning Strategies * Independence…these are "study skills" and they represent 95% of the top skills in the workplace!

We Are Preparing Students for Jobs That Do Not Yet Exist!

Is it any wonder that employers need students to learn these study skills? Information is changing at an unprecedented pace! The top 10 in-demand jobs ten years from now…do not exist today. Employers need to hire people who can keep up with changes. They need students who can access information, organize it, recall it for later use, think critically, and manage time appropriately. National and state education standards place all of the emphasis on *content*. Content is easy to test, but students need to learn how to learn that content so they are prepared to learn *any* content.

Study Skills Are for Everyone!

Study skills level the playing field for everyone. Straight-A students appreciate learning short-cuts to make their study time more efficient. Struggling students appreciate the clarity and confidence they develop once they unlock the mystery. Even students with learning disabilities and ADHD benefit from study skills.

In fact, it wasn't until just a few months ago (nearly 20 years after I began teaching study skills) that I learned I have ADHD and a couple of learning disabilities. This explains why I struggled through school. But it also demonstrates how powerful study skills can be in overcoming major challenges.

What Are These "Magic" Skills?

I could write a whole book on the tips and strategies that helped me go from failing to a four-point (and, actually, I have). But I'll share a few of my favorites now:

Visual Networking for Textbook Reading

You have heard that a picture is worth a thousand words; the brain is hard-wired to absorb images instantaneously. Words, on the other hand, require several additional layers of processing before the brain can generate meaning. Take advantage of the brain's natural strengths by "reading the pictures" in the text. Reading the pictures is a three-step process:
1. Look at each picture, chart, graph, and visual.
2. Read the caption.
3. Ask yourself, "Why do I think this picture is here?" Answer this question to the best of your ability; make an educated guess if you are not sure.

The third step is the most important in this process. It forces your brain to make connections; connecting visuals with the content in the text. These connections will greatly improve reading speed and comprehension!

Take Ten

"Take Ten" is a daily, ten-minute routine that improves the two most important keys to improving grades: organization and learning. It works by using the first ten minutes of daily homework to organize papers and review notes: Two minutes to clean out the book bag and organize papers in folders or a binder. Eight minutes to review all notes and handouts that were distributed throughout the day. This daily review transfers new information from short-term to long-term memory and dramatically reduces study time for tests. It also helps the brain process homework more efficiently, which means homework can be done faster.

Power Down

The concept of "powering down" has become one of the most eye-opening for the students in our classes! I always tell students, "If you don't learn how to control electronics now, they will always have control over you." Students tell us that this sound bite sticks with them. This is the first time they have ever noticed that electronics do, in fact, run their lives.

As you might guess, the idea behind "powering down" is simply to turn off electronic distractions long enough to finish. Students think they can multi-task. In reality, their attention ping-pongs back-and-forth: Homework. Texting. Homework. TV. Homework. Music. Texting. Homework. The brain is only capable of multi-tasking for routine activities such as walking while talking. It is not capable of multitasking with learning. All of these electronic distractions simply reduce efficiency and make homework take 2-4 times longer.

In conclusion, national K-12 curriculum does not teach students *how* to learn, but there are simple brain-based strategies for learning more efficiently. There is no reason why any student should be denied the ability to meet his or her best potential with these strategies. If I can go from failing to a 4.0, anyone else can, too. It's time you had the strategies to make that happen!

Susan Kruger, M.Ed. is the author of the international best-selling study skills book, *SOAR Study Skills* and is the founder of StudySkills.com. She has combined her struggles as a student with her professional expertise to create a student friendly and effective system for earning better grades in less time. Download her FREE guide, *Six Steps to Conquer the Chaos: How to Organize and Motivate Students for Success* at www.StudySkills.com.

Listen to this chapter at: StudySkills.com/amazinggrades

3 Strategies Guaranteed to Reduce Your Study Time

Is it possible to study less and make better grades at the same time? Actually, yes! Although it may sound impossible, if you learn to study strategically, you can actually decrease the amount of time you spend studying while simultaneously improving your GPA. It's all about making the most of each moment of your study sessions by using efficient and effective study strategies.

Strategy 1. Prioritize

If you feel you have too much to do and that you can't possibly do it all, the only solution is to prioritize. Identifying the goals that are most important and pressing and then making a practical plan to achieve these goals can help you maximize the time you do have and help boost your success in short order.

★   **Define your goals.**

Before you can begin prioritizing the tasks you need to accomplish, you first need to identify your goals. Although it's good to set long-term goals because they help you keep your eye on the end goal, the most important kind of goal when it comes to time management is a short-term goal. Short-term goals are more manageable and can prevent you from becoming overwhelmed. For instance, even though you may not have all the answers when it comes to achieving the long-term goal of increasing your overall academic success, you likely know exactly what type of help to ask for in order to increase your grade in math class.

★   **Make a plan.**

Once you've defined your goals, it's time to create a plan for achieving each of them. This plan should include all of the ways you intend to accomplish your goal. For instance, if you want to make better grades in math, your plan could include strategies such as creating an open dialogue with your teacher, completing all homework assignments on time, and studying daily to be better prepared for quizzes and tests.

tinyurl.com/8xwspe3

★   **Create a daily task list.**

After you have a plan to achieve your goals, the next step is to create a daily task list. This will help you break up tasks into smaller, more doable steps that you can complete each day. Your daily task list may include items such as completing an assignment, studying for thirty minutes, or asking your teacher for extra help with a particular skill.

Strategy 2. Manage Your Time Effectively

We are all given the same twenty-four hours in a day, yet it's a fact that some people get more done in any given day than others. While many people seem to struggle to beat the clock, others navigate their day easily, checking tasks off of their "to-do" lists with ease. How do they do it? They aren't blessed with an inherent or unattainable gift; they've simply learned the skills to manage their time more effectively than others. Consider implementing some of the time management skills below to become more productive in less time and enjoy academic success without the need for cramming:

★   **Take small steps.**

It's often natural to push the idea about an upcoming test to the back of your mind, but the truth is this will make you more anxious later. Once you are informed of a major assignment or project, make a conscious effort to devote a little time each day to working on it. Using this approach, you'll begin to slowly cut away at the overall work that needs to be done, and as a result, you'll begin to feel more at ease and in control.

★   **Eliminate distractions.**

How often do you allow yourself to become distracted during your study sessions? You may not realize it but these "mini-breaks", when you allow your attention to wander elsewhere, are probably taking up a huge chunk of your time, causing you to become less productive and efficient while studying. Of course, like anything else, the first step in eliminating distractions is defining the problem.

Make a list of time-wasters that eat away at your productivity and then take action to get rid of the temptation. For example, do you constantly find yourself looking up at the television when you know you should be studying?

If so, keep the TV off during study hours, or better yet, study in a room where there is no television. Are you bombarded with phone calls, text messages, or emails while you're trying to get your assignments completed? Turn your phone off and close out your email to prevent losing focus on your schoolwork. While this may seem like a sacrifice, the reality is that you'll actually have more time to do the things you like to do. By eliminating distractions from your study time you'll be able to get more done in a shorter amount of time.

Strategy 3. Combat Stress

Some forms of stress in moderate doses can be good for us while other forms of stress, or too much stress, can render us ineffective. Here are a couple of tips for combating the negative effects stress can have on your academic performance.

★   **Eliminate unnecessary stress.**

Students have to deal with many sources of stress whether from social functions, academic responsibilities, or extracurricular activities. Sometimes it may appear as if there is more to do than time to do it. Therefore, it's best to get rid of the sources of stress in your life that are negative or unnecessary. Evaluate what you are doing and eliminate extra things that you simply don't need so you can become stress-free.

★   **Learn how to manage stress.**

Everyone deals with stress, and there's no magic wand that will remove it from your life completely. That's why it's necessary to learn how to manage stress and keep it from controlling and limiting you. Try using things that are already medically proven to help like regular exercise, meditation, breathing exercises, adequate sleep and nutritious foods to manage your stress. If you're still feeling frazzled, talk to your parents, teachers, or another trusted adult about how you're feeling. Chances are, they'll have some good advice.

By prioritizing your goals, managing your time effectively, and dealing with stress in a positive way, you will study more effectively in less time and achieve better grades. The more you practice these strategies, the more natural they will become, and the more success you will enjoy in school and out of school.

Study and life skills expert Rick Kamal is an authority on effective learning for students in middle school through college. He works with other experts at top universities to produce resources that prepare students to thrive in the global economy. Learn more at Edu-Nova.com

Listen to this chapter at Edu-Nova.com/studytime.html

Learn More, Study Less

Here's a quick question. What matters more in determining how much information you remember before a test?

1. Motivation to learn
2. What you think about while learning
3. How much time you spend studying

It turns out the answer is #2. In a ground-breaking study, researchers tested learners' ability to remember information under a variety of conditions. Motivation is important to get you to start studying, but it turns out it doesn't affect how well you remember information. Time, of course, matters too, but it doesn't help if your learning strategy is broken.

The most important factor tested in the study was what cognitive psychologists call "depth of processing". When students thought about the information at a deeper level, they remembered twice as much information without spending more time.

How you learn, not just how much time you spend, matters a lot. Most students don't realize this, however. Whenever they struggle, their answer is to just study more. Unfortunately this blind strategy often leads to exactly the inefficient studying techniques that result in worse grades.

Smart students don't study the way normal students do. They deliberately read and listen at a deeper level of processing. While most students try to frantically memorize information to pass tests, smart students learn faster by making connections between ideas.

Make Connections, Don't Memorize

Many students subscribe to what I'll call the "robot brain" theory of memory. This is the idea that the goal of learning information is to have a perfect copy of the information in your head. These are students who rewrite definitions verbatim and use flashcards to remember equations.

I call this the "robot brain" theory because it would make sense if you were a robot. Computers have no difficulty remembering information perfectly once it is stored in memory. Human beings, on the other hand, often require several exposures to make an idea stick, which is time consuming and difficult.

Smart students don't do this. Instead they realize that learning comes from understanding things deeply and creating connections between ideas so you don't need to memorize.

Learn by connections, not memorization. Now how do you do that?

Metaphors and Mental Pictures

One simple way to do this is to create metaphors, examples, analogies or mental pictures whenever you learn something important. You can do this by asking yourself questions like:

What does this remind me of?
What would be an example of this?
What would this look like?

Let's say you're studying calculus and need to learn the definition of a derivative. You could be like most students, and endlessly repeat the information. Or you could create a metaphor—the derivative measures rate of change, just like the speedometer on a car.

What if you're studying psychology and learn about opponent processing theory for color vision? You could connect that to an example—opponent processing is the reason you never see any colors which are reddish-green.

Maybe you're learning chemistry and want to remember that an acid and a base reacting create water and salts. You could visualize this by viewing the acidic hydronium ions like a ball of fire and the basic hydroxide ions as a chunk of ice—they cancel each other out to leave only water.

Examples like this show how most smart students actually learn. They process the material at a deep level so that it sticks in memory without repetition. However it can be a little daunting to start learning by connections for the first time, so how do you actually come up with all these metaphors and mental pictures?

How to Find Good Connections

The first step is simply to look for them. Many students get so caught up in memorizing that they forget to be curious about the material. Asking yourself questions about how things would look if you visualized them or what they remind you of seem like silly studying tactics but they are extremely effective.

Another source of ideas can come from your teachers and textbooks directly. Teachers often spend years coming up with the best analogies and examples to convey the meaning behind an idea. See if you can extend their explanations just a little further—so if you're given only one example, try to find a related one on your own. If that fails, sources like Wikipedia and YouTube can provide alternative explanations which can clue you into possible metaphors.

Studying in this way takes practice, so don't be concerned if it takes you awhile to develop the habit! Once you develop the right attitude about learning, you can learn faster with less studying too.

Scott Young is the author of *Learn More, Study Less*. You can get a free rapid-learning ebook from his website: http://www.scotthyoung.com/blog/newsletter/

Listen to the chapter at: http://www.scotthyoung.com/AG/learnmorestudyless.mp3

Conquer Algebra Quickly by Making Concepts Concrete

Are algebraic equations and word problems a challenge for you? Solving algebraic linear equations is an essential skill for success in algebra and other math and science classes.

Algebraic equations can be intimidating, especially the first time you encounter one. After all, what are letters and numbers doing together? Here is an approach that will help you to understand the meaning of an algebraic equation such as 4x + 3 = 3x + 9.

First let's transform this abstract equation into something concrete. We will say that x is the name of a game piece, a pawn. Now we place four of these pawns on the left side of a drawing of a balance scale to represent the 4x part of the problem.

The problem says to add a 3, and so we place a cube with the number 3 on the same side as the four pawns. That's half of the equation. On the right side of the balance scale we place three pawns and a cube with the number 9.

Now the concrete representation for the abstract equation looks like this:

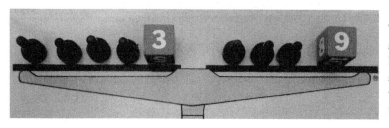

The equal sign in the equation says that both sides of the balance scale are equal to one another. The goal is to find the value, or weight, of the pawn that will make the sides balance.

Trial and error shows that not all values for the pawn will work. For example, if we give the pawn a value of 2, the left side of the balance will have a value of 11 and the right side a value of 15.

We need to discover a value of the pawn that will make both sides the same. You could just keep trying different values for the pawn and eventually find the answer that way.

However, using an algebraic strategy will give you the answer directly. If a scale is in balance, then removing the same weight (or value) from each side will maintain the balance.

So we can take three pawns from each side in our problem and the scale will still be in balance. Now we have a pawn and a 3-cube on the left side and a 9-cube on the right side.

If one pawn plus 3 equals 9, then the pawn must have a value of 6. The pawn represents x in our equation; therefore, you can write the answer as x = 6. Wait! We're not quite finished.

tinyurl.com/7tsyeq5

We need to verify our answer by conducting a check. Here's how to do it. Go back to the original setup shown above and substitute the value of 6 for the pawn. When we do this step, we see that both sides have the same value: 27. The sides are in balance when x equals 6.

Another way to make a concrete representation of the above problem is to draw the pawn-and-cube setup. You can use arrows to show that you are removing the same number of pawns from each side of the balance scale.

Representing and Solving Word Problems

Being able to represent a word problem in the form of an equation is another powerful tool for success in algebra and the sciences.

This process can be simplified by first representing the problem as a concrete or pictorial equation. Here's an example problem: "Twice a number, increased by 1, doubled, will give the same result as twice the original number, increased by 10. Find the number."

We can approach this problem using pawns and number cubes, just as we did before. Each pawn stands for our unknown "number" and so two pawns and a 1-cube represent "twice a number, increased by 1." That quantity is "doubled" and so we add another two pawns and a 1-cube. That's the left side.

For the right side we need "twice the original number, increased by 10," which gives us two pawns and a 10-cube. On the drawing of the balance scale, our problem looks like this:

Now we remove two pawns from each side and cube values equal to 2 on each side. That leaves two pawns on the

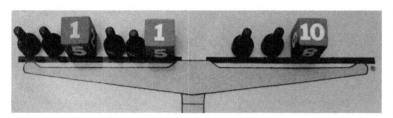

left and a cube value of 8 on the right. If two pawns equal 8, then one pawn must have a value of 4. So the answer to the problem is, "The number is 4."

You can check this answer by noticing on the left that twice the number 4, increased by 1, is 9. When that is doubled we get 18. On the right side, twice 4 is 8, increased by 10, also is 18. This shows that a number value of 4 satisfies the conditions of the problem.

From the above concrete representation, we can write the abstract equation using x for the number that is represented by the pawn. The items on a scale are additive, and so the equation would be 2x + 1 + 2x + 1 = 2x + 10 or 2(2x + 1) = 2x + 10. Being able to solve algebraic linear equations will empower you to succeed in algebra. Using a concrete or visual representation of an equation or a word problem will give you greater insight into the meaning of the problem and its solution.

Dr. Henry Borenson is the inventor of Hands-On Equations, founder of Borenson.com and president of Borenson and Associates, Inc. You can get the Hands-On Equations app at the itunes store here: http://goo.gl/mti8t

Listen to this chapter at http://goo.gl/RddIf

5 Strategies To Master Precalculus

Precalculus is the bridge that connects geometry and algebra to calculus. Everything you learned in mathematics from arithmetic through algebra has prepared you for precalculus which focuses on functions, their properties, and their graphs. Here are five strategies for mastering precalculus and helping you to learn it faster.

1. Learn the concept of functions

Concepts are the ideas behind a subject or topic. Precalculus is designed to teach the concept of functions in preparation for calculus. In calculus you will perform operations (finding derivatives and integrals) on these functions. Without understanding the functions, it will be difficult to perform these operations.

Functions are rules with a specific relationship between two sets of numbers. One set of numbers is composed of independent variables (a symbol, often a letter, which signifies a value). The other set is composed of dependent variables. For each independent variable, there is up to one dependent variable assigned to it. For example, for each person (independent variable) in the United States, there is up to one social security number (dependent variable) assigned to that person. No individual is assigned more than one social security number.

Functions can be described as formulas (e.g., y = mx + b), as a verbal description of a relationship (e.g., for each student, there is a unique student identifi cation number), or as a graph (e.g., the graph of a line). In precalculus, you need to know how to describe each function in either format and you need to make the connection between all three representations of functions in order to fully grasp the concept of functions.

2. Understand graphs of functions

Graphs provide visual representations of functions. In precalculus, the Cartesian coordinate system (x-axis and y-axis) is used to graph functions using coordinates x and y or (x,y). When written as a formula f(x) represents the "y" coordinate. Given any formula of a function, you can sketch or draw its graph: select values for x, substitute the values in f(x) to get values of y, plot the corresponding coordinates (x,y), then connect the points to complete the graph of the function. For example, when you graph the linear equation y = mx + b, a common function used in algebra, the result is the graph of a line.

Graphs provide information about functions such as the x-intercepts (where the graph crosses the x-axis), the y-intercepts (where the graph crosses the y-axis), the domain (input values), the range (output values), and the shape of the graph. Understanding the graphs of functions will provide a visual representation of the graph that will help you understand why each function has certain properties.

3. Lose the calculator, grasp the concept

When completing math problems you may have the tendency to hold your calculator in one hand while writing with your other hand. However, in precalculus it is important to lose your calculator and grasp the concepts being taught.

Although calculators are useful tools for graphing functions, they are a hindrance to learning why functions operate the way they do. Get in the habit of calculating values of functions and graphing those values by hand. This will help you understand the formula, the limitations (why x or y cannot equal certain values), and the properties of each function you study.

It is imperative that you understand the precalculus concepts being taught, not just the outcome of working through problems. Calculators give you outputs, but not an understanding of the concepts behind those outputs. If you understand the concept of the material you learn, you will master precalculus.

4. Read your textbook

Your textbook is there to help you understand precalculus concepts. The text offers explanations of the solutions to the problems displayed throughout the textbook. These explanations help form a better understanding of the concepts applied to the problems.

The biggest challenge most of my students face is reading their precalculus textbook. My students who earn higher grades take the time to read their textbook before completing their assignments. You must do more than work through the examples and homework problems. Reading the textbook will provide a deeper level of understanding than working through problems alone.

If you struggle with the writing style of the author of your assigned textbook, go to your local library and find a textbook that has a writing style you like. Keep in mind that your teacher or professor develops their lessons based upon material they read in textbooks.

5. Learn and use mathematics terminology

One of the biggest complaints many of my students have is that they do not understand the questions on a test or quiz. Their problem is not their ability to comprehend what is asked, but their knowledge and understanding of the vocabulary used in the problem. Once I explain what the question asks they are able to answer the question. Unfortunately, this often happens after a test or quiz has been graded.

You will be more successful in precalculus if you understand the vocabulary used by your precalculus teacher. As you progress through higher level mathematics courses, your professors will use math terminology more frequently than in earlier school years. Professors often write about mathematics topics and discuss their ideas with their peers. Making the transition to every day math terminology can be tricky, so professors rarely "water down" the vocabulary. Make the effort to know and understand the terminology used in precalculus. This will cut down the confusion when listening to your teacher, completing homework assignments, and taking tests.

These five strategies will make your learning experience more fulfilling and enriching. When learning precalculus, make meaningful connections between the formula, written representation, and graph of each function you encounter. Read your textbook and learn the terminology used in precalculus. This will increase your understanding of the concepts taught and ensure your success in mastering precalculus.

Nneka Kirkland, M.Ed., is a professor of College Algebra and Precalculus at Temple University in Philadelphia. She is a co-founder of Citywide Math and Science Institute, a math and science tutoring company in Philadelphia, committed to advancing STEM education. For more information visit her website at CityWideMathScience.com.

Listen to this chapter at HowToLearn.com/amazing-grades-audio

Developing Your Higher Math Intuition

Our initial exposure to an idea shapes our intuition. And our intuition impacts how much we enjoy a subject. What do I mean? Suppose we want to define a "cat":

★ **Caveman definition:** A furry animal with claws, teeth, a tail, 4 legs, that purrs when happy and hisses when angry...

★ **Evolutionary definition:** Mammalian descendants of a certain species *(F. catus)*, sharing certain characteristics...

★ **Modern definition:** You call those *definitions*? Cats are animals sharing the following DNA: ACATACATACATACAT...

tinyurl.com/7xd7tnv

The modern definition is precise, sure. But is it the *best*? Is it what you'd teach a child learning the word? Does it give better insight into the "catness" of the animal? Not really. The modern definition is useful, but *after* getting an understanding of what a cat is. It shouldn't be our starting point.

Unfortunately, math understanding seems to follow the DNA pattern. We're taught the modern, rigorous definition and not the insights that led up to it. We're left with arcane formulas (DNA) but little understanding of what the idea is.

Let's approach ideas from a different angle. I imagine a circle: the center is the idea you're studying, and along the outside are the facts describing it. We start in one corner, with one fact or insight, and work our way around to develop our understanding. *Cats have common physical traits* leads to *Cats have a common ancestor* leads to *A species can be identified by certain portions of DNA*. Aha! I can see how the modern definition evolved from the caveman one. But not all starting points are equal. The right perspective makes math click — and the mathematical "cavemen" who first found an idea often had an enlightening viewpoint. Let's learn how to build our intuition.

What is a Circle?

Time for a math example: How do you define a circle?
There are seemingly countless definitions. Here's a few:

★ The most symmetric 2-d shape possible
★ The shape that gets the most area for the least perimeter (the isoperimeter property)
★ All points in a plane the same distance from a given point (drawn with a compass, or a pencil on a string)
★ The points (x,y) in the equation $x^2 + y^2 = r^2$ (analytic version of the geometric definition above)
★ The points in the equation $r \cdot \sin(t)$, $r \cdot \cos(t)$ for all t (really analytic version)
★ The shape whose tangent line is always perpendicular to the position vector (physical interpretation)

The list goes on, but here's the key: the facts all describe the same idea! It's like saying 1, one, uno, eins, "the solution to $2x + 3 = 5$" or "the number of noses on your face" — just different names for the idea of unity.

But these initial descriptions are important — they shape our intuition. Because we see circles in the real world before the classroom, we understand their "roundness". No matter what fancy equation we see ($x^2 + y^2 = r^2$), we know deep inside that a circle is round. If we graphed that equation and it appeared square, or lopsided, we'd know there was a mistake.

As children, we learn the caveman definition of a circle (a really round thing), which gives us a comfortable intuition. We can see that every point on our "round thing" is the same distance from the center. $x^2 + y^2 = r^2$ is the analytic way of expressing that fact (using the Pythagorean theorem for distance). We started in one corner, with our intuition, and worked our way around to the formal definition.

Other ideas aren't so lucky. Do we instinctively see the *growth of e*, or is it an abstract definition? Do we realize the *rotation of i*, or is it an artificial, useless idea?

A Strategy For Developing Insight

I still have to remind myself about the deeper meaning of *e* and *i* — which seems as absurd as "remembering" that a circle is round or what a cat looks like! It should be the natural insight we start with. Missing the big picture drives me crazy: math is about ideas — formulas are just a way to express them. Once the central concept is clear, the equations snap into place.

Defining a Circle

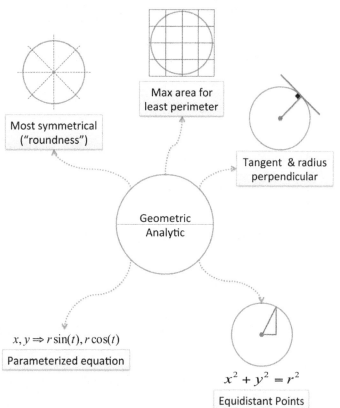

Here's a strategy that has helped me:

- ★ **Step 1: Find the central theme of a math concept.** This can be difficult, but try starting with its history. Where was the idea first used? What was the discoverer doing? This use may be different from our modern interpretation and application.

- ★ **Step 2: Explain a property/fact using the theme.** Use the theme to make an analogy to the formal definition. If you're lucky, you can translate the math equation ($x^2 + y^2 = r^2$) into a plain-English statement ("All points the same distance from the center").

- ★ **Step 3: Explore related properties using the same theme.** Once you have an analogy or interpretation that works, see if it applies to other properties. Sometimes it will, sometimes it won't (and you'll need a new insight), but you'd be surprised what you can discover. Let's try it out.

A Real Example: Understanding *e*

Understanding the number e (2.71828…) has been a major battle. *e* appears everywhere in science, and has numerous definitions, yet rarely clicks in a natural way. Let's build some insight around this idea. The following section has several equations, which are simply ways to describe ideas. Even if the equation is gibberish, there's a plain-English concept behind it. Here's a few common definitions of *e*:

The first step is to find a theme. Looking at e's history, it seems it has something to do with growth or interest rates. e was discovered when performing business calculations (not abstract mathematical conjectures) so "interest" (growth) is a possible theme.

Let's look at the first definition, in the upper left. The key jump, for me, was to realize how much this looked like the formula for compound interest. In fact, it is the interest formula when you compound 100% interest for 1 unit of time, compounding as fast as possible.

★ **Definition 1:** Define e as 100% compound growth at the smallest increment possible.

Let's look at the second definition: an infinite series of terms, getting smaller and smaller. What could this be?
$$e = 1/0! + 1/1! + 1/2! + 1/3! + \ldots$$

After noodling this over using the theme of "interest" we see this definition shows the components of compound interest. Now, insights don't come instantly — this insight might strike after brainstorming "What could $1 + 1 + 1/2 + 1/6 + \ldots$" represent when talking about growth?

The faces of e

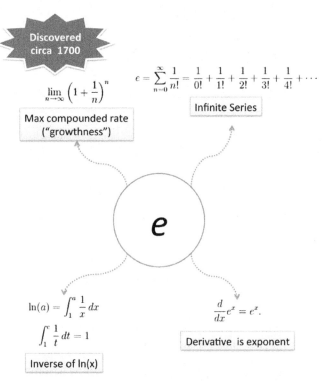

Discovered circa 1700

$$\lim_{n \to \infty} \left(1 + \frac{1}{n}\right)^n$$

Max compounded rate ("growthness")

$$e = \sum_{n=0}^{\infty} \frac{1}{n!} = \frac{1}{0!} + \frac{1}{1!} + \frac{1}{2!} + \frac{1}{3!} + \frac{1}{4!} + \cdots$$

Infinite Series

$$e$$

$$\ln(a) = \int_1^a \frac{1}{x}\, dx$$

$$\int_1^e \frac{1}{t}\, dt = 1$$

Inverse of ln(x)

$$\frac{d}{dx} e^x = e^x.$$

Derivative is exponent

Well, the first term ($1 = 1/0!$, remembering that $0!$ is 1) is your principal, the original amount. The next term ($1 = 1/1!$) is the "direct" interest you earned — 100% of 1. The next term ($0.5 = 1/2!$) is the amount of money your interest made ("2nd level interest"). The following term ($.1666 = 1/3!$) is your "3rd-level interest" — how much money your interest's interest earned!

Money earns money, which earns money, which earns money, and so on — the sequence separates out these contributions (see each level of interest as growing independently). There's much more to say, but that's the "growth-focused" understanding of that idea.

★ **Definition 2:** Define e by the contributions each piece of interest makes Neato.

Now to the third, shortest definition. What does it mean? Instead of thinking "derivative" (which turns your brain into equation-crunching mode), think about what it means. *The feeling* of the equation. Make it your friend.
$$d/dx\ \text{Blah} = \text{Blah}$$

It's the calculus way of saying "Your rate of growth is equal to your current amount". Well, growing at your current amount would be a 100% interest rate, right? And by always growing it means you are always calculating interest – it's another way of describing continuously compound interest!

★ **Definition 3:** Define e as always growing by 100% of your current value Nice — e is the number where you're always growing by exactly your current amount (100%), not 1% or 200%.

Time for the last definition — it's a tricky one. Here's my interpretation: Instead of describing how much you grew, why not say how long it took? If you're at 1 and growing at 100%, it takes 1 unit of time to get from 1 to 2. But once you're at 2, and growing 100%, it means you're growing at 2 units per unit time! So it only takes 1/2 unit of time to go from 2 to 3. Going from 3 to 4 only takes 1/3 unit of time, and so on. The time needed to grow from 1 to A is the time from 1 to 2, 2 to 3, 3 to 4... and so on, until you get to A.

The first definition defines the natural log (ln) as shorthand for this "time to grow" computation. ln(a) is simply the time to grow from 1 to a. We then say that e is the number that takes exactly 1 unit of time to grow to. Said another way, e is the amount of growth after waiting exactly 1 unit of time!

★ **_Definition 4:_** Define the time needed to grow continuously from 1 to as ln(a). *e* is the amount of growth you have after 1 unit of time.

Whablamo! These are four different ways to describe the mysterious *e*. Once we have the core idea ("*e* is about 100% continuous growth"), the crazy equations snap into place — it's possible to translate calculus into English. Math is about ideas!

What's the Moral?

In math class, we often start with the last, most complex idea. It's no wonder we're confused: we're showing students DNA and expecting them to see a cat. I've learned a few lessons from this approach, and it underlies how I understand and explain math:

★ **Search for insights and apply them.** That first intuitive insight can help everything else snap into place. Start with a definition that makes sense and "walk around the circle" to find others.

★ **Be resourceful.** Banging your head against an idea is no fun. If it doesn't click, come at it from different angles. There's another book, another article, another person who explains it in a way that makes sense to you.

★ **It's ok to be visual.** We think of math as rigid and analytic — but visual interpretations are ok! Do what develops your understanding. Imaginary numbers were puzzling until their geometric interpretation came to light, decades after their initial discovery. Looking at equations all day didn't help mathematicians "get" what they were about.

Math becomes difficult and discouraging when we focus on definitions over understanding. Remember that the modern definition is the most advanced step of thought, not necessarily the starting point. Don't be afraid to approach a concept from a funny angle — figure out the plain- English sentence behind the equation. Happy math.

Kalid Azad graduated from Princeton University and has been writing professionally for over a decade, from chapters in the best-selling *How to Program* textbooks (from Deitel, Inc.) to technical whitepapers for Microsoft, Corp. In 2006 he founded BetterExplained.com, which has grown into a popular, highly-acclaimed mathematics resource with hundreds of thousands of monthly readers. Kalid has tutored math since high school (99% percentile for SAT/ GRE/GMAT) and is enamored with finding intuitive insights for complex topics.

Listen to this chapter at http://betterexplained.com/amazing-grades/audio

Biology Bits and Tips:
How to Get to the Head of the Class!

So, biology just 'isn't your thing', or 'science is just too confusing…' here are some tips I've shared with students over the years. I hope they will help you to learn and remember information and make it more manageable and memorable.

TIP 1. Study prefix and suffix meanings. Knowing the Latin name or meaning can simplify scientific vocabulary by helping you deduce the meaning. In Greek, Bios means "life" while logos, means "the study of." Thus Biology literally means "the study of life." Photosynthesis, the way plants make food can be figured out in this way. Photo means 'light', Synthesis means 'putting together' = putting together with light. In short, many terms used in biology are composed from Greek or Latin root words and once you learn those root meanings, it is much easier to understand the subject.

TIP 2. Identify key vocabulary. Make notecards/flashcards to study. Some websites allow you to print your own cards. On one side, write the word, on the other a description, definition, or a picture that represents the word. Use the 'definition' side and try to remember the word, or use the word side and say the description or definition. Flip the deck over and repeat. Make mental images of the pictures and the meanings of the words.

TIP 3. Draw it, sign it, sing it. Sketch designs to help you remember information. Draw the carbon or nitrogen cycle using pictures and arrows then label. Make cartoons with dialogue. Create silly rhymes or jingles to help remember difficult words. Use the tune of a nursery rhyme or popular jingle and put words to it. I use the tune of 'Row, Row, Row Your Boat' to remember that mitosis results in body cells that are diploid and meiosis leads to sex cells that are haploid. (You might try songs and poems out loud and alone in a room with the door closed – after all it is easier to remember and hear it in your head later when taking the exam!).

> *'In Mitosis cells divide, chromosomes are diploid,*
> *meiosis makes the gametes form; their number is haploid.'*

For the 6 kingdoms of life I use 'He's Got the Whole World in His Hands',

> *'I've got the whole world in my hands, I've got the whole world in my hands,*
> *I've got the plants and the protists, in my hands,*
> *I've got Archaea and Bacteria in my hands,*
> *I've got the Fungi and the Animals in my hands,*
> *I've got the whole world in my hands.'*

This song is accompanied by hand motions and a diagram in my notes with fingers representing each kingdom. Archaea and Eubacteria, the simplest kingdoms share the pointer finger, the thumb is for plants (green thumb!), the middle finger is animals (think about shooting the 'bird')….you get the idea. Rhymes are strong and predictable and the meter is solid and consistent. Rhyme and meter, together with body movement can serve as a powerful memory trigger.

TIP 4. Use mnemonics like acrostics and acronyms. These don't substitute for understanding, but are great tools to remember lists, dates, formulas, or other facts. Remembering key information 'the scaffold' enables you to remember and understand more complex material with which you can 'build the house'. Mnemonics make information in long-term memory easier to recall and organize new material by comparing it to information that is similar and already known.

ACROSTICS use the first letter of each word you are trying to remember, to make a sentence. The sillier the sentence, the easier it is to recall. Some common well known examples are: **D**o **K**ids **P**laying **C**atch **O**n

Freeways **G**et **S**quashed – or **D**on't **K**ings **P**lay **C**hess **O**n **F**unny **G**irls **S**tomachs (Levels of Classification -Domain, Kingdom, Phylum, Class, Order, Family, Genus, Species).

Kangaroos **H**op **D**own **M**ountains **D**rinking **C**hocolate **M**ilk (The order of prefixes in the metric system, for every power of ten from 3 to -3; **K**ilometer, **H**ectometer, **D**ecameter, **M**eter, **D**ecimeter, **C**entimeter, **M**illimeter) There over 30 phyla of animals in the animal kingdom. In my class we learn the most familiar seven invertebrate and the vertebrate phylum with this sentence:

People **C**an **P**lay **A**nd **A**lways **M**ake **E**xcellent **C**hoices (Porifera, Cnidaria, Platyhelmenthese, Annelida, Arthropods, Molluska, Echinodermata, Chordata).

ACRONYMS use the 1st letter from each word in a group of words to form a brand new word. They are used every day. SCUBA (Self Contained Underwater Breathing Apparatus) and LASER (Light Amplification by Stimulated Emission of Radiation) are acronyms; as are NBA (National Basketball Associations) and NASCAR (National Association for Stock Car Auto Racing). Suppose you have to memorize the names of the four stages in Cell Division (Mitosis); 1) Interphase, 2) Prophase, 3) Metaphase, 4) Anaphase, 5) Telophase.

Take the first letter of each: **IPMAT**. In this case they resemble a familiar word and are easier to remember.

Students can remember nature's recyclers as the **FBI** (Fungus, Bacteria, and Insect Larvae). These organisms all recycle nutrients in ecosystems to be re-used by other living things. Darwin used **GPA**; Geology (the fossil record), Population studies, and Artificial selection (breeding) to come up with his theory of evolution based on natural selection.

A disadvantage using acronyms is that all words don't work similarly well and/or lend themselves to this technique. Acrostics and acronyms can be simple to remember and helpful when remembering items in a specific order, but acrostics take more thought to create and require remembering a whole new sentence rather than just a word. Do realize that these types of mnemonics don't aid comprehension. They help with memorization.

TIP 5. Get a live or a virtual Study Buddy. Studying with someone makes you more accountable and allows another 'point of view' when it comes to course material. No time to meet a study buddy in person? Make out your own test of 5, 10, or 20 questions. Trade the 'home made' tests with each other, answer and trade back. Grade your friend's test. How well did they do? How well did you do? Hopefully these specific ways to recall information will get you an A in your next biology course. And know too that any of these bits and tips easily transfer to other subjects.

There once was a student who said:
Biology – it's hard and it's bad!
He used all these tips,
and a couple of bits,
And he got an A and was glad!

Cindi Smith-Walters, Ph.D. is a full professor of Biology at Middle Tennessee State University, and co-directs the MTSU Center for Environmental Education. Nationally recognized for excellence in teaching and learning she is a frequent presenter at conferences, has held various offices in state and national organizations and received numerous awards for teaching, public service, and public outreach.

Listen to this chapter at HowToLearn.com/amazing-grades-audio

How To Get Better Grades in Science Courses

In this chapter, we'll be covering two areas in relation to science: study skills strategies and answering exam questions. These areas are important to help you improve, but most people stick to familiar ways of studying and tackling exam questions for obvious reasons. Your previous techniques may not be as efficient in getting you the best grades so you need to modify them to improve.

Study Skills Strategies

Whatever course you're studying you need to be clear about:

★   what you need to learn (a question for your teacher/ tutor),

★   when your exams are

★   when you need to start a study routine.

The more organized and prepared you are, the less scary the exams will be. Every study technique has its purpose. You need study techniques that are fit for your purpose.

1. Vocabulary Cards

The main reason for using vocabulary cards is to learn keywords and definitions. You can write your own on index cards or use a website such quizlet.com in the USA or http://getrevising.co.uk/revision-cards in the UK to make your own. This is just a starting point; you can expand this to include questions and answers to help you break down your revision topics into chunks.

Try a bit of physics by matching these together:

mass	Newtons
length	Joules
weight	kilograms
frequency	Watts
energy	metres
power	Hertz

2. Mind Maps ™

Mind Maps™ have been around for a while and are attributed to author Tony Buzan. If you like things neat and tidy, the mind map can be off -putting. If this describes you, you might want to use mind mapping software. You only need to search 'mind map software' in a search engine and choose one. If you don't mind things getting messy, then do it by hand - make it colorful and detailed.

Start with the topic you want to review and put it in the center of your paper. Build your knowledge around it with pictures and words. Ideas will branch out as well as loop back and link to other words and pictures. You can make your own; all you need is your notes.

ANSWERING EXAM QUESTIONS

What I want you to get out of this is:

★   To identify different types of questions using the command words
★   To understand questions by breaking them down.

You've made your mind maps, vocabulary cards and you're ready for the next step... exam questions!

Command Words

Command words are the words used to let you know what kind of question you are being asked. Many high marks have been lost because the question has been misunderstood. Here are a few command words you need to be familiar with (check with your teacher if there are any more you should be aware of).

★ Identify, State, Give, Write down – a short answer to point out reason or words. This does not require a description or explanation.
★ Describe – give information about a process, diagram, or other event. In the case of graphs 'say what you see'.
★ Explain – to provide the how or why something
★ Compare – describe the similarities and differences between the objects. You must mention both not just one.
★ Contrast – Not the same as compare.
★ Evaluate – give evidence for and against then come to a conclusion.
★ Calculate – use the numbers in the question to work out the answer. Remember to show your working and use units.
★ Suggest – use your knowledge and understanding in an unfamiliar context.
★ Use the information to... – you must look at the diagram, graph, table provided to inform your answer.

Use one of your revision (study) strategies to become familiar with these key terms.

The Questions

When attempting questions, take your time and start by dissecting the question into its constituent parts. Be prepared to write on the exam paper when practicing. Let's take a typical exam question:

★ Circle the command word
★ Circle the number of marks
★ Underline the keywords
★ Draw arrows from keywords to the key information, e.g. if the question is asking about the graph/ table/ data, draw an arrow to the actual graph/ table/ data to remind you to use that information.
★ Check your understanding of words you are unfamiliar with when practicing.

Physics Question

Use this technique to break down the questions to improve your understanding and avoid missing crucial instructions. Only then try to answer the question. *How would you have answered these questions?* This is a starting point to you improving your opportunities to do better in science exams. Keep practicing and revising, and you will be as ready as you can be for your exams.

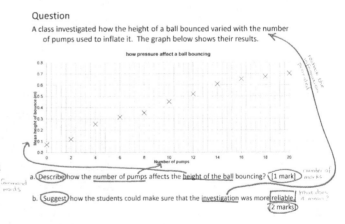

Question

A class investigated how the height of a ball bounced varied with the number of pumps used to inflate it. The graph below shows their results.

a. Describe how the number of pumps affects the height of the ball bouncing? [1 mark]

b. Suggest how the students could make sure that the investigation was more reliable. [2 marks]

Lorraine Smith, BSc Physiological Science, is a science teacher in Buckinghamshire, UK obtaining her doctoral degree in education. She teaches biology, chemistry and physics to secondary school students.

Listen to her chapter at HowToLearn.com/amazing-grades-audio

Got Chemistry? How to Master It Faster!

There is no escaping molecules and atoms. They are everywhere literally and when you understand their properties you begin the process of unlocking the secrets of the universe!

That statement is for motivation but let's face it. Chemistry is exciting but intimidating for some at the same time so let's conquer the beast and pull up our sleeves. By following these five strategies you have the know-how to do well in the course.

First strategy, you must have strong math skills in Algebra because in chemistry you will be asked repeatedly to find the value of some unknown. See the Borenson chapter in this book to insure you have strong algebra skills. Most problems in chemistry can be solved by dimensional analysis which is a problem solving skill that is similar to algebra, but uses physical dimensions. Dimensional analysis is introduced in the beginning of the course and must be mastered before you begin another chapter.

Dimensional analysis and determining the significant figures from problems will never go away in chemistry, so if you want to succeed practice, practice and practice some more! If you haven't had any Algebra for a while, the Borenson chapter in this book makes algebra a snap.

The second strategy to understanding chemistry is that you must imagine a beautiful building and in order for this building to exist there must be a strong foundation; the foundation in chemistry is the periodic table.

By understanding the patterns of the periodic table and studying the properties of the major elements you will start to build that strong foundation. The periodic table must become your best friend and to master the subject you must sleep, eat and dream with your periodic table, because you will refer to this table for the rest of your chemistry life. As we start to build on this basic chemistry foundation with topics such as stoichiometry, limiting reactant, ideal gas laws etc. You will have to refer to the periodic table and if you spent time learning the patterns you will do well in the course. See chapters on memory in this book.

The third strategy is making flash cards. On each flash card write the purpose (which can be found at the end of your chapter under key concepts,) then the equation and the conceptual plan to solve the problem.

© Robert Marmion

Go through these flash cards everyday because chemistry is a selfish subject and requires time. That is why it's best to make flash cards to give you a quick reminder of why? If you have been reading this chapter you will see I used the word understand several times because this is what chemistry is all about. I still sometimes refer to my old textbook for equations, but understanding a subject relieves the stress so that you can just relax and read and make flash cards for reinforcement. There are lots of chapters in *Amazing Grades* to reinforce your ability to understand any subject because they build the foundation.

The fourth strategy is to bring this mantra into the laboratory. All chemistry courses are laboratory intensive and if you start asking yourself, 'why are we doing this lab', you will be able to correlate the lab with the chapter and that is the most exciting part.

The fifth strategy is to keep your cool. Relaxation is key to your success. If you take the time necessary to understand the beginning chapters you will succeed and chemistry will open doors in any field of science. By taking the time to build that strong foundation that beautiful building will never collapse.

Again, you can't connect the dots looking forward; you can only connect them looking backwards. So you have to trust that the dots will somehow connect in your future. You have to trust in something - your gut, destiny, life, karma, whatever. This approach has never let me down, and it has made all the difference in my life.

- Steve Jobs

Chalon Downs, M.S. is an adjunct faculty in the biology department at Delaware County Community College and co-founder of Citywide Math and Science Institute in Philadelphia, PA.

Listen to this chapter at HowToLearn.com/amazing-grades-audio

Creative Critical Thinking

In this chapter I am going to show you a few techniques which will allow you to become a better critical thinker.

Critical thinking will give you the skills to understand and evaluate the arguments and beliefs of others as well as to develop and defend your own arguments and beliefs. This is a skill that can be applied in almost every situation. Critical thinking is also valuable for the personal enrichment it brings to your life.

Many of my students begin this type of course by defining critical, to mean judgmental, and take initial fault finding approaches to various issues. This idea must be put out of your mind completely and you must approach each new issue with an open mind.

Critical thinking is a valuable skill that can be learned and developed. In order for this to be effective you must make a cognizant effort to avoid egocentrism, sociocentrism, wishful thinking, and any other impediments that will inhibit you from being open-minded. These barriers must be broken down to begin this process.

Keep in mind you must be willing to welcome opposing points of view and welcome criticisms of beliefs and assumptions. This can seem difficult in the beginning and will take some practice, but once you make a conscious effort to think critically ideas will flow. I am going to provide you with a three-step technique which will make the critical thinking process less daunting.

© Konstantin Li

Step 1

Begin with a clear definition of critical thinking. Critical thinking is defined as disciplined thinking that is clear, rational, open-minded and informed by evidence. Clarity ensures that when you are discussing a topic there are no vague or ambiguous terms.

Relevance keeps you on topic so as not to stray off on a tangent. The most important fact to remember is to be open-minded as this will allow you to feel empathy towards others and think beyond yourself. Research informs your audience that your premises are factual and therefore trustworthy. Once you are able to achieve this the next two steps are relatively simple.

Step 2

Think creatively and outside of the box so you can be as creative as possible. To apply this definition you must put aside preconceived notions and be open to a variety of ideas which in many cases will be outside of your comfort zone. This is where you want to brainstorm as many ideas relating to the topic as possible. Your thoughts may be outrageous however you want them all to be factual. Do not hold back here this is where you can be imaginative and allow all of your ideas to flow freely.

Step 3

Analyze all of your previous ideas in order to make a clear, concise, and logical decision. You will be able to make conclusions two ways based on the premises you come up with. One way is by inductive reasoning which is where you apply the most probable conclusion based on the information provided. The second is by deductive reasoning. Deductive reasoning is based on what is actually stated and drawing a conclusion from that. This is where you are able to list all of the premises you were able to come up with and make conclusions based on what you have researched. Keep in mind that you want to avoid incorrect conclusion, so make sure you verify each of the premises you come up with and stay consistent. Following these simple steps will help you become a better critical thinker. The more often you apply them makes the process easier.

Knowing a great deal is not the same as being smart;
intelligence is not information alone but also judgment,
the manner in which information is collected and used.
- Carl Sagan

Lisa M. Hornick B.A., CPhT is an instructor at Lincoln Technical Institute and has worked in the pharmaceutical industry for over 10 years. She has been teaching proprietary education for 3 years. Hornick graduated from Rutgers University and is contributor to the NHA EXCPT study guide.

Listen to this chapter at HowToLearn.com/amazing-grades-audio

Don't Know Much About History?
How to Master it Faster

For many students history often ranks quite high on the list of 'most boring subjects.' There are many reasons for this which I won't go into now, but it is this pre-conception which can be counter-productive and become a self-fulfilling prophecy. So, in order to succeed in your history class you must first have the **right attitude**. It also helps to have an inspiring teacher. Unfortunately you can't always be so lucky so what can <u>you</u> do?

First of all, it is good to start off by understanding that history is far more than the study of dates, places, past events and dead old men. Mostly, history is about relationships: people's relationships with each other, their families, with institutions and governments within and outside their society. Now, instead of focusing only on dates and obscure facts, let's focus on the <u>stories</u> of people. Yes, you still have to know the names and dates stuff , but we can address that later.

The key to enjoying and consequently doing well in history is to make it come alive, make it something you can relate to.

Primary sources in history can be more interesting than text book interpretations. Reading the diaries or log entries of immigrants crossing the Atlantic in search of a new home in America gives insights into the historical context of the period. What were they fleeing? What were the working and living conditions they left behind? What did they encounter in their new home? Or how about first hand accounts of the people who knew General George Custer? We can see the arrogance and delusions of one of America's most celebrated. Reading newspaper stories and interviews written at the time of the event gives us a look at what people thought at the time rather than how historians have interpreted and repackaged the events according to their own personal biases. Because, remember history is only partially about facts (dates, names, places). History is very much about <u>interpretation</u> of the facts. So, since we all enjoy a good movie, why not look at history from the point-of-view of Hollywood? Actually, watching **historical movies** is a great way to make history more real, accessible and definitely, more interesting.

For example, the word *Holocaust* and 6 million Jews killed during WWII certainly leaves an impression, but watching Schindler's List, Life is Beautiful or The Pianist gives a dimension to that event which words fall short of. Give new meaning to *Colonization* by viewing The Mission, The New World or Dances with Wolves. *The Industrial Revolution* becomes clearer after watching Hard Times, Modern Times or Moulin Rouge. Understanding the *Civil Rights Movement* is deepened through watching To Kill a Mockingbird, Malcolm X and The Help. Then there are the biographical movies which bring to life the stories of history's big names. Think Gandhi, JFK, Marie Antoinette, Braveheart, Lawrence of Arabia, Elizabeth, to name a few. Although generally feature films will have more appeal than **documentaries**, there is a lot of value in watching a good documentary. TV can be useful here. The History Channel or similar is all about making history visual and meaningful.

For those students who enjoy reading but resist the drudgery of some textbooks, **historical novels** are great for enhancing your study of history (many end up becoming movies). What these novels do that textbooks fail at, is focus on the <u>people</u> who <u>are</u> history. The complex stories of personal relationships—families, friends, rivals, lovers and enemies—are what make history. Some non-fiction books also do this with one standout needing mentioning.

Howard Zinn's *A People's History of the United States* is a stunning attempt to tell history through the eyes of the people who made, participated, experienced, and were victims of, history. Not the generals, kings, heroes or villains but rather, the common everyday observers: The mothers, factory workers, slaves, Indians, farm workers, unemployed. The ones whose perspectives are absent from most textbooks but whose story gives depth, relevance and real-life to history.

So, you can find **primary sources** to read, watch some great **films** and **documentaries** and even enjoy a fascinating **historical novel**. You can do all these things to fuel your interest and add to your knowledge of history.

Mastering History Exams

In addition to the above, you are still going to have to do the basics which will determine your grade. In other words: tests, exams, essays, research papers. This book is chock full of the learning strategies you need to do very well on your exams and get better grades.

Everyone has their favorite technique. Most history evaluations are either objective-type (true/false, multiple choice, mapping, timelines) or essay-type. Unfortunately, many teachers still require students to remember dates, places and people's names in order to pass tests. Memorization is an unavoidable requirement for success in history. Therefore, it is back to basics: reading, re-reading, note-taking, highlighting key ideas, graphic organizers, summarizing, flash cards, studying with friends and family, mnemonic devices and lots of repetition. For essay writing, knowing the facts is certainly essential but equally important is understanding the <u>context</u> of your subject/theme. In an essay you can show the 'extra' depth you have gained through the other media like film, novels and primary sources.

The other common type of work you will be graded on in history is the report or research paper. My one tip for you is to make sure that you are absolutely clear on what and how you will be graded. A good teacher will provide the criteria and samples of exemplary work in advance for you. But not all teachers do; so it is up to you to get this important information. Ask your teacher and be as specific as possible so that you can prepare appropriately and ensure the best results. Review the chapter in this book on how to write an essay.

If you want better grades in history, you're just going to have to have a little more fun. Go ahead, read the intimate details of someone else's diary; or lose yourself in the personal stories found in a good historical novel; turn the TV on and catch a well produced documentary; or get out the popcorn and sit down to a good action packed movie. Enjoying history will result in succeeding in history.

The complex stories of personal relationships—
families, friends, rivals, lovers and enemies—
are what make history.

- Jeff Memler

 Jeff Memler, M.A., graduated from the School for International Training and his B.A. in Education is from the University of Arizona. He has taught at high school and university in the U.S.; and at primary, secondary and tertiary levels in New Zealand. Jeff has taught Social Studies, Geography, English and ESL, done teacher training and developed curricula internationally for over 25 years. He currently lives in New Zealand.

Listen to this chapter at HowToLearn.com/amazing-grades-audio

7 Simple Steps to Accelerate Your Language Learning

If you're trying to learn a foreign language, you have one thing in common with others trying to do the same thing: you want to accelerate your learning so you can begin communicating NOW!

It's a typical reaction shared by anyone beginning a new skill: guitar players, dancers, singers, you name it. You want to find a way to get to the finish line tomorrow. Well, unfortunately, language learning (like the guitar, etc.) is something that takes time and persistence. You need to learn the basics like the rules of grammar, how to conjugate and all the rest. As time goes on, you build up a base of knowledge and start to progress. There is no real shortcut to fluency. Nevertheless, there are some tricks to speeding up the process so that the finish line arrives earlier than expected.

As a language learner you have your tools: books with activities and explanations, DVDs, MP3s, online exercises, etc. These remain a vital part of the learning process.

However, by adding a few simple tips that you can incorporate into your daily routine, you can progress even faster than you imagine.

Here are some tips to accelerate your learning that you can use beginning today:

★ **Memorize a Song In The Target Language**

This is something that we all do in English. We hear a song so many times that it gets stuck in our head. Well, we want to achieve the same effect but in the target language. There is no better way to improve your speaking and pronunciation than to repeat a song over and over again. It will seem impossible at first. You'll find your mouth can't keep up with the words. That's not a problem, trust me. Your brain and mouth muscles will catch up. Just stay with it and you'll see how easy it really is.

What you want to do is find a song that you like (look on YouTube), download it and find the lyrics there or on Google. Then, for the first couple of days, just listen to the song. Don't worry about the lyrics. Once you get the song in your head, you'll want to look at the lyrics and sing along. The secret is to find a song that you like because when you do, it isn't focused repetition...it's fun.

★ **Find A Speaking Buddy**

One of the best ways to kick start your language learning is to have someone to practice with on a constant basis. This way, you can work out the mistakes you're making and progress even faster. There are two ways to go about this. The first way is to look for a community center nearby that teaches English to newly arrived immigrants that speak the target language. Once you find a center, go there and speak with the English teacher. Explain to them that you're interested in meeting with a native speaker so that both of you can practice your language skills. Once you find someone, you can set up a meeting and speak English (to help them) for 15 minutes and then speak the language you want to learn for 15 minutes. This way, both parties are satisfied.

A second way to find a speaking buddy is to go to Google and type in Language Learning Communities. You'll find a list of web pages that are sites where people find partners to practice their speaking skills. Once you find a partner (who speaks the language you're learning and wants to learn English), you connect via Skype and you're on your way.

★   **Find your target language radio stations.**

Depending on where you live, you can find a radio station in the target language. That may be possible in your car or you may have to go to the internet. Either way you have quick and easy access to native speakers. The only decision you have to make is what type of program you like to listen to. I would recommend a talk show because it involves different voices and authentic speech.

★   **TV/Movies in the target language**

Whether it's online or on your TV, you can find shows, movies, documentaries, anything your heart desires in the target language. Depending on what you're watching, you can use the subtitles or change the audio to the target language. Just make sure you find a program/series/movie that you like and look forward to seeing.

★   **Practice tongue twisters**

Next to singing a song, there is no better way to learn how to pronounce correctly. There will be sounds in the target language that your mouth muscles are not accustomed to saying. (i.e. the RR in Spanish). By repeating tongue twisters with a focus on one particular sound, you are developing the muscles necessary to pronounce correctly. Once your brain understands the movements involved in the sound, it becomes automatic. You'll begin pronouncing that sound correctly each time. Then, as soon as you master one sound, you move to the next.

★   **Set up your cell or smart phone in the target language**

A cell phone is something you look at again and again during the day. For this reason, it is the perfect place to have the target language. All you have to do is change the language settings on your phone and each time you reach for it you'll get a mini vocabulary lesson.

★   **Read out loud**

Once you have reached a certain level of understanding in the target language, it's time to get the flow of the language in order. By that I mean, getting used to speaking like a native speaker. You can do this by getting a newspaper in the target language, a book from the library or using the reading sections in the textbook. The idea is to read the same paragraph(s) out loud various times until it begins to flow. That is to say, until it begins to sound like a native speaker. The key to this activity is to do it with no one around so that you can really imitate a native speaker. Don't hold back. Take this time to pretend you're already fluent and you'll be amazed how good you sound.

If you follow the tips mentioned above, you'll be adding practice time to your day. However, since the practice time involves things you like (ex. watching movies, listening to music, etc.) it won't feel like more studying. It'll actually be fun. Good luck!

Jim Sarris is the author of *Comic Mnemonics for Spanish Verbs* and *Memory Skills Made Easy*. He is a Spanish teacher with over 20 years experience.

Listen to this chapter at HowToLearn.com/amazing-grades-audio

From Loathing to Loving Literature:
Questions to Ask So You Can Master Any Book

Are you one of those people who prefer to watch a movie rather than read a book? Do you have trouble answering the teacher's questions in Literature class? Don't have a clue about what is going on? Think that books don't have any relevance to your life? If so, then I would like to help! Here are a few things to think about.

Art is an expression of thought and emotion drawn from experience. Cinema is art in pictures, but Literature is art in words. Authors tell about human experience, each through his own media (whether by poem or play or story), using words to paint pictures in your mind. Reading about experiences of others allows you to share in those experiences, broaden your own knowledge, help you to avoid errors and imitate successes.

Your mind can be a mode of transportation through the dimension of others' experience. Without leaving your room, you can travel to anywhere in the world, anywhere in history.

★ Have you ever wondered what it was like to live during the Great Plague? Read Nobel prizewinner Sigrid Unset's *Kristin Lavrensdatter* or Alessando Mazoni's *The Betrothed (I Promessi Sposi)*.

tinyurl.com/88g36ef

★ Do you like action or mystery? Try G. K. Chesterton's *Father Brown Mysteries*, Baroness Emmuska Orczy's *The Scarlet Pimpernel*, or Robert Hugh Benson's *By What Authority*.

★ Have you wondered what the results might be if you murdered someone? Read Edgar Allen Poe's *The Tell-Tale Heart*, Fyodor Dostoyevsky's *Crime and Punishment*, or Shakespeare's *Macbeth*.

★ Are you interested in romance and human relationships? A few books of lighter fare are Jane Austen's *Pride and Prejudice*, Mary Roberts Rinehart's *The Amazing Interlude*, L. M. Montgomery's *Blue Castle*, Gene Stratton-Porter's *Girl of the Limberlost*, and Regina Doman's *Fairy Tales Retold* series.

Of course, once I start naming books that I enjoy, there is no way to stop me! I want you to love books as much as I do; not only do they help you to be a better person, but reading makes you smarter, too! The more reading you do (of good books), the better you will do in school and on tests. Did you know that the SAT is primarily a reading test? Better readers get higher scores.

How do you become a better reader? Well, before you open a book or read an excerpt in a Literature anthology, ask yourself these questions (and, no, you won't know the answers yet):

★ Who is the book/story/poem, etc. about? (The answer to this question will provide a list of CHARACTERS.)
★ What problem(s) does each main character face? (This gives you PLOT.)
★ Do the characters solve their problems or do the problems overcome them? (The first, in a classical sense, is a COMEDY; the second, a TRAGEDY.)

As you read, look for answers to those three questions (WHO is the story about, WHAT is the problem, HOW is it dealt with) – you might even jot down some notes about what you think the answers should be. These questions should allow you to check your comprehension; they will also form a baseline on which the details of the story (and your perceptions) can grow and build.

After you've read the selection and know WHO, WHAT, and HOW, then these questions can be asked:

- ★ What might I do if I were in the same situation? (Have I ever been in a situation like this? When would I be in a similar situation?)
- ★ Did the characters make any mistakes that I would like to avoid? How would I avoid them?
- ★ Was there anything about the characters that I would like to imitate?
  With what character do I feel the most sympathy? Why?

Here only some of the benefits that can come from reading. Can you add to this list?

- ★ Reading – with comprehension – makes you smarter, makes your brain work better (this is scientifically proven – just do an Internet search for "reading makes you smarter")!
- ★ Reading increases your vocabulary, which helps you to have more interesting conversations, to be a better writer, and to get better test scores – all of which will help you to get a better job and live a happier life.
- ★ Reading broadens your horizons, allowing you to experience many things outside your own world.
- ★ Reading is a means to connect with great minds from more than three millennia.
- ★ Reading is enjoyable, entertaining, relaxing, motivating.

And last, but not least, relate this story to others you've read. "What other stories have I read that dealt with the same problem? How did those characters behave compared to the ones I just read about?" By asking yourself these questions and looking for answers, your understanding of what you read and the parallels to your experience (to "real life" – to your life) will flourish. And just maybe, that loathing that you might feel for reading literature will change into a real love (or at least an appreciation) for this very beautiful art form – this expression of experience.

Sister Maria Philomena is vice principal, teacher and curriculum supervisor at Immaculate Heart of Mary School in Richmond, New Hampshire at http://ihm.catholicism.org. In 2011, the National Society of High School Scholars (NSHSS) selected Sister as a Claes Nobel Educator of Distinction. You can download free books at http://www.gutenberg.org

Listen to this chapter at: HowToLearn.com/amazing-grades-audio

How To Make Reading Easier
in High School and College

There are two kinds of high school and college reading – pleasure and for the purpose of gaining knowledge and getting better grades.

What if you were to find a written text that, from its title, promised such a mystery unveiled? Would you continue reading? Wouldn't you feel, at least, a little curious about what could make this story not just *very* interesting, but more likely, the last word on the subject?

What would happen if it *actually were* "THE ULTIMATE STORY EVER!"? Would you read on until your curiosity was satisfied? It seems to me that, if your answer was "Yes", you could consider yourself to be a really lucky person to have found such a rarity!

But, let's face it: such a situation might also be a bit… odd. I mean, who can honestly say they have ever found all the following characteristics in a text together?

1. Texts with such an attractive and promising title that they automatically hook you into the reading and breeze all the way through its lovely, logical contents non-stop. Love at first sight.

2. Words, sentences and vocabulary are so familiar to you that their reading makes you feel as if you were actually talking to yourself, or to your best friend. Or to both.

3. Lots and lots of images (for the visual learners, of course). Pure delight.

4. Texts with ideas so common, so easy to digest that, just as in number 2, they could even save you the trouble of challenging your preconceptions and your as-you-know-it previous understanding of the world.

And last, but not least:

5. Imagine these texts are academic. Homework, essays, reports; you get the picture. If you got a positive answer on the first four in a row, you were most likely thinking of a reading you did for pleasure. I am almost certain that once you reached number five, numbers 1 to 4 stopped making sense altogether.

Academic reading can be more challenging than those we do for pleasure in many ways: they tend to be more complicated by nature, both in language and contents; they're not the type of texts you would usually not be able to put down like fiction reading; if illustrations decorate their pages they might end up being just as complex as the text itself. And, more importantly: they are compulsory. This can be a creepy word for students. "I *have* to do it, but I just don't get it!"

But please don't get me wrong: The examples above are in no way patronizing. They are ironic, yet clear examples of what I've witnessed in my 15-year teaching career: students who honestly struggle with reading academic texts. If you are one of those, don't stop reading here. Keep going until the end of this chapter and, with any luck, you will be able to get some useful advice from it. Ready?

1. Give the text a chance. Have you ever been in a situation where you've found yourself talking to someone you've never met before? Or when your friends arrange a meeting between you and a stranger because they thought that person might do you good? This is a somewhat *compulsory* situation. It might be a little awkward at first, but once you start talking to each other, once you've given yourself the chance to get to know that person better, who knows what might come next? The same happens with texts: if you do not even give them a chance, who knows what you might be losing?

2. Take your time to read it. Even advanced readers take their time to go through the texts. Remember that reading well does not imply reading fast, although it can. I recommend that you take the text reading more slowly. Take your time to go through the title, subheadings and illustrations.

This will familiarize you with the contents and will make the first approach run more smoothly. Check with your instructor how much time you have. It is most likely that there will be an outcome to the reading task, such as an essay or a class debate. In this case, if you try to read everything the night before the final outcome you won't be able to digest the information properly and you will end up writing a poor essay or coming up with weak arguments for the debate. And, the worst thing of all, you will soon forget all about it, which will have rendered your effort useless. High schools and colleges demand from students a higher degree of knowledge and critical thinking. I'm sure you're perfectly capable of achieving this, you just need to organize your schedule.

3. Engage in a *conversation* with the text. Some texts are harder to approach than others. Let's suppose you have to work on a very challenging reading. "How can I see the words, but not understand what it says?". First of all, it's not always about you. Some authors write for a very small, specialized audience and they assume everybody from that group will understand what they say.

If this is the case, ask your teachers for some basic terms or ideas they would like you to be aware of as you read. Then, ask questions of the text. Start with the basic ones: *what/who/when/where*, then move on to *how* and *why*, and finally go for the *how far/to what extent* sort. Having a specific goal in your reading (which is to answer these questions) will make it more significant as you will be playing "Sherlock Holmes" following the leads. Taking notes in a notebook or on your computer is always useful. This will help you with the *conversation* and the revision process later.

4. Get as much help as you can. Do not be afraid to ask. We teachers appreciate the hard work students put into their tasks and, therefore, we are willing to help. For humanities and social sciences readings, you might imagine what it would be like if you were one of the characters from the reading and, by personalizing it in this way, you will be less likely to forget. If drawing the stories or concepts helps you remember and learn better, then go for it! There are many techniques available on the web. Remember that, whichever technique you use, it won't work unless you are really constant, and all four tips I've described here work with all of them.

Summing up:

- ★ Read with a purpose and ask questions to answer before you read
- ★ Establish a time frame for reading
- ★ Question the text and have conversations with the material
- ★ Ask for help

Cristina Camacho is a college professor at Churchill College in Mexico City. She graduated from Universidad Nacional Autónoma de México (UNAM) and is the author of *La fiesta de Nuestra Señora de Guadalupe*.

Listen to this chapter at HowToLearn.com/amazing-grades-audio

How To Integrate Technology Into Your Learning for Better Grades

Overwhelmingly, research shows us people learn larger amounts of information faster when technology is integrated into instruction.

You are able to do more and complete more if you use the resources available properly. This is true whether you study for an upcoming exam but also for your research, when you create projects, and present your ideas. In today's digital age, it is more important to be able to adapt to new technologies than necessarily understand the details of a specific program.

We live in a technology infused world, where information is at your fingertips. Having technology on your side may be the difference between a passing and failing grade, or landing the post-college job. Recruiters are increasingly using social media to find new prospects. Through this chapter, we will discuss real, practical ways to use technology to improve your grades. We will also learn methods for each learning style to utilize technology. Do not worry if you do not have the latest, greatest device or even internet access. You will quickly learn ways to navigate through these barriers.

Interpersonal Learner

You enjoy learning in a group. You are a social person and work well in cooperative environments. Use these skills and technology to help increase your knowledge and earn better grades. Create social groups about your topic of study. Set-up video chats with classmates for discussions and study sessions.

tinyurl.com/6n65jkn

Intrapersonal Learner

Learning content is easier when you are on your own. Making personal connections to learning is extremely important for full understanding. Try keeping an electronic journal for each area of study. You will begin to see patterns in what you are learning and its relationship to your life. Blogging may also be a good outlet for your learning process. Whether you decide to publish your writing or keep it confidential, your knowledge will improve.

Visual Learner

Seeing is believing for the visual learner. You will make lasting connections if you can associate your studies with visual cues. This can be accomplished through searching for images correlating to your area of study. You may also find it helpful to watch web video tutorials. Note taking in a lecture style classroom will be difficult for this type of learner. There are several programs available to combat this issue. Free applications will take audio files and convert them into notes. When you have a written form, make sure to add a picture to each section, further solidifying the information.

Auditory Learner

Listening skills are high on your list of attributes. Technology is easily adapted to assist your learning style. Podcasts, songs, and lectures are available about almost anything. Search and download resources to amplify your understanding. You may even find it beneficial to create your own songs.

Kinesthetic Learner

tinyurl.com/7zoyl7o

Hands-on activities help you learn. Finding simulation type activities will be most beneficial to your studies. Try on-line learning labs and modules. Games may also help you to learn. If you are unable to find an activity to fit your learning need, it will help to study while you move. Listen to a podcast or your lecture notes while going for a run or working in the yard. Stimulating your senses and concentrating on your motions will improve your education.

Logical Learner

You benefit from understanding the reasons behind your learning. Researching deeper into an area of study can help you tremendously. Brain teasers and strategy games will help you gain knowledge. Taking the information you learn in class and converting it into a flow chart, spreadsheet, or data table will assist your brain in creating logical associations with your studies.

Verbal Learner

You thrive in learning environments where you can talk things through. Attempt recording yourself discussing a topic. Listen back to the recording and make sure what you are saying is the same as what you are learning. Mnemonic devices and songs can also support your learning.

Across the world, educators of all levels of instruction are encouraged to integrate technology into their learning environments. If your teachers are learning these techniques, chances are you will benefit from learning them. If you do not have access to the internet or a computer, check with your school or public library. Your librarian is a valuable resource. When you try one of the methods above, be sure to inform your professor about these activities. It may not only help you understand the material, you could earn extra credit.

Kendra Chambless, B.A. is teacher of the year at Vineville Academy of the Arts in Macon, GA. She specializes in integrating technology into the classroom. Kendra is a certified special education and gifted teacher. Currently, she is working on her Master's in Adult Education.

Listen to this chapter at HowToLearn.com/amazing-grades-audio

How To Use Google to Help You Get Better Grades

Have you ever typed a search term into Google and noticed that you get hundreds of millions of search results? Google tells us that less than twenty percent of people look at the second page of search results, but what if the answer you are looking for is on page 30! How can you be sure that you are finding the most relevant and appropriate information?

If you are anything like most students (and teachers) your Google Search strategy will go a little something like this...

You randomly type in some loosely related search term – quickly scan over the first 5 or 6 search results – nothing grabs your attention so you delete your search term and repeat the process, but alas there is still nothing that seems to jump off the page at you so you again delete that search term and randomly type in another hoping that this time the Google gods will favor you and give you what you are search for. Sound familiar?

If you want to get better grades then you need to know how to find the right information that is relevant to your subject and age level. **Here is how you do it.**

1. Type in your search term. When you are choosing your term, try and write your question as a statement not a question. Google will give you results based on the words you type (these are called keywords). If Google can find a question the same as yours then they will deliver that question to you but not necessarily the answer. So instead of typing *"What is the habitat of polar bear like?"* It would better to type *"The habitat of a polar bear is like".*

2. Decide how you want Google to recognize the words you have typed in. If you type more than one word into the search bar then Google can give you a result based on any or all of the words you have typed in. For example, if I wanted to search for the term native animals, Google would give me results for the following three search terms; native, or animals, or native animals. So in this example I could receive results for native plants, native Indians and so on because they also have the word native in them. To help narrow down your search results you always put a " " around your search term. So in the above example, if I wanted to search for native animals and filter out any result that just had just animal or native I would type my search like this "native animals". As soon as I do this I only receive results that specifically have the keywords native and animals joined. When you do this you can literally see your search results drop by tens of millions.

3. Use the related search tool. After you have typed your search term, if you don't see the result you want then it is time to further filter out your results. On the Google webpage you will find a link on the left hand side of the page that says **more tools** (see the graph).

Once you click on this link you will see a range of new options available to you. In the example below I have clicked on related searches. When I have done this you will notice that there are a number of suggestions offered by Google just under the search term.

Rather than just typing in another random search term, it is far better to ask Google to suggest some search terms that are similar to the topic you are searching for.

The related searches suggested by Google are the most frequent search queries typed into Google. By using the related search tool you get the benefit of seeing ideas from of people and therefore have a better chance of returning a result that is more relevant to your needs.

4. Use the reading level tool. This is one of my favorite tools. When you click on this link, Google will filter all the results into three reading levels; basic, intermediate and advanced. By using this tool you can instantly filter out results that will be either too basic or advanced, once again narrowing your search results dramatically.

For the college students who might need to look at journal articles, the best place for you to conduct your search is www.scholar.google.com

Here you will find all the journal articles you need. The great thing about Google scholar is that you are able to see both the articles that the journal has cited as well as all the journals that have cited that journal article after it was published. Th is is such a great research tool that I only wish was available when I was studying at university!

There are a range of other great tools available on the left hand side of the search page. My suggestion to you would be to set aside some time to play with these tools and discover the wealth of information available to you. If you would like a step by step guide to better using Google search to increase your grades you can go to www.teacherstraining.com.au/google-search

Mike Reading is a Google Certified Teacher who draws on his extensive experience motivating and engaging students in a diverse range of teaching environments. Mike regularly provides training to thousands of teachers each year and is the author of the series of guides on how to use Google in the classroom. You can find more information on the Teachers Training blog at www.teacherstraining.com.au

Listen to this chapter at HowToLearn.com/amazing-grades-audio

How To Prepare for the SAT Exam

As an educator, I know the final years of high school can be ***daunting*** for students. Graduation looms along with college applications, navigating the **labyrinth*** of financial aid applications, and, scariest of all for some, the dreaded SAT exam. The SAT though, doesn't have to be terrifying. With a few simple tools in your belt, you, too, can **slay*** the SAT dragon.

★ **Know the test.** There are a few quick ways to improve your score, even if you don't do another thing to prepare:

☆ Many students don't know that you actually lose ¼ point for every wrong answer and gain a full point for every correct answer. That means that you should just leave some questions blank, but it also means that educated guesses can work in your favor. Eliminating just two choices narrows your shot to one in three, which are better odds than the ¼ penalty for blind guessing.

☆ Still fewer students know that the SAT questions progress from easy to hard. The first third of the questions in any section (except critical reading) are easy, so if an answer looks right early in the section, it very likely is right. The next third are of medium difficulty. Use process of elimination to narrow your choices, and then make educated guesses. The final third are hard questions, designed to be answered correctly only 10% of the time. That's right – just 10% – so don't be afraid to skip these!

☆ Knowing exactly what the scorers are looking for (for instance, specific, detailed information and choosing a definite position on the essay) will help you to do better on the test.

★ **Don't stress.** Stress has been scientifically proven to negatively affect the brain, which can, of course, negatively affect your test scores! Preparing will make you more comfortable going in, and that will help your brain to function better. How can you de-stress? Well first of all, lean in… I have a secret for you. Don't tell anyone I told you this, but… are you listening? The SAT is NOT the most important thing that will ever happen to you. Shocking, right? Well it's true. The SAT is just ONE factor for college admissions. Colleges look at a variety of factors, including SAT scores (I didn't say they didn't matter at all!), grades, extracurricular activities, application essays, and letters of recommendation. So do your best, but don't think that the whole rest of your life is riding on this one morning. Just relax and do your best.

★ **The math questions aren't that hard.** SAT math is approximately seventh to tenth grade material; there's nothing there higher than Algebra II. That's right – no trig, no calculus… not a logarithm in sight. So you probably don't have to learn anything new; just review what you already know and use the strategies in this book to learn and remember it.

★ **Read, read, read.** One enormous factor on the reading and writing portion of the SAT test is vocabulary. The best way to gain vocabulary and fluency in reading and writing is by… yup, you guessed it – reading. Makes sense, right? But what if you've only got a few weeks before the test and you just don't think you can get through *Frankenstein*, *Jane Eyre*, and *Crime and Punishment*? All is not lost. Read what you can, and familiarize yourself with the Latin and Greek roots, prefixes, and suffixes that make up the English language; they will help you to decode unfamiliar words. (By the way, have you noticed the asterisked words throughout this article? All of them are SAT-level words.)

★ **Practice, practice, practice.** Are you a musical ***aficionado*** or the fastest kid on the track team? You didn't get that way overnight – it took practice, and so does succeeding on the SAT. Taking an SAT prep course is a great way to prepare. These courses will familiarize you with the test and give you some of the test-specific knowledge and skills that will maximize your score. You can also purchase an SAT test review book or visit the College Board website (SATcollegeboard. org), which has practice sections and daily SAT practice questions.

★ **Sleep, eat, breathe.** Once again, stress is a major factor in student performance. Proper nutrition and a good night's rest will help ensure that you're at your peak on test day. Having your ticket, ID, and sharpened pencils (plus a sweater/layered clothing – you don't know if the room will be warm or cool) set by the door and ready to go before you go to bed the night before will eliminate the stress of rushing around in the morning, trying to gather everything you need. Once you're in the test, remember to breathe deeply – it's a great way to reduce stress. If you need to pause and stretch during any of the sections, it's okay to do so, as long as you stay in your seat.

★ **Work the whole time.** Yes, this test IS important. (Life or death? No. Important? Yes.) Pace yourself – make sure you're not rushing at the end, but don't waste any time on any section, either. If you finish before time is up, go back and check your answers. Try the harder questions – maybe all you needed was time, and now you have it. Whatever you do, don't let minutes lapse, even if you think you're "done." You're done when the proctor says, "Pencils down."

With all of this advice and **_diligent_*** preparation, you should do **_stupendously_*** on the SAT!

He who opens a school door, closes a prison.
- Victor Hugo

Beverly Stewart, M.Ed. is President and Director of Back to Basics Learning Dynamics, Inc., a leader in 1-on-1 tutoring for children and adults in over 60 subjects since 1985. Back to Basics is also a Delaware Department of Education approved Private School for K-12, Business and Trade School for ages 16+, and supplier of translating and interpreting services for schools, businesses, and government. You may contact Beverly at BackToBasicslearning.com or BeverlyStewart.com.

Listen to this chapter at: HowToLearn.com/amazing-grades-audio

Vocabulary Vibes:
The Key to Mastering New Vocabulary

When you're reading and you come to a word you don't know the meaning of, what do you do? Do you skip the word in hopes that it won't interfere with your comprehension? Do you try to figure out the meaning of the word by using the meanings of the words that surround the unfamiliar word?

Skipping a word works out well – some of the time. Figuring out the meaning of a word based on the meanings of the words that surround it works well if you know the meanings of words that surround the unfamiliar word. There is a more dependable way to figure out the meaning of an unfamiliar word. All you have to do is look for the units of letters in a word that carry meaning. The fancy word for a unit of letters that carries meaning is *morpheme*. A *morpheme* can be a *prefix* (a unit of meaning at the beginning of a word), a *suffix* (a unit of meaning at the end of a word), or a *root* (a unit of meaning in the middle, end, or beginning of a word).

Believe it or not, you use morphemes all the time. Think about the word *microscope*. *Micro* means *small*. *Scope* means *view*. A *microscope* allows you to *view* things that are *small*. Now, try *telescope*. *Scope*, of course, means *view*. *Tele* is a morpheme that means *from far away*. A *telescope* allows you to view things that are *from far away*. So, if *phone* means *sound*, what is a *telephone*? Right, it is sound *from far away!*

Let's try a longer, more difficult word, like *aberration*, which means *something that is not normal or something that is not what you would expect*. The morpheme *ab* means *away from*. If you are *absent*, you are *away from* a place or an event. If someone *absolves* you, he or she takes guilt or responsibility *away from* you. Wow! The next morpheme is *err*, which means *to wander*. An *error* is that which *wanders* from what is correct. And *erratic* behavior is behavior that *wanders* from what is expected. Cool! The single *a* is a connector syllable that helps with the pronunciation of the word. OK! lastly, *tion* means *the state of* as in *relaxation*, the *state of* being *relaxed*, or *determination*, the *state of* being determined. Literally, *aberration* means *the state of wandering away from* what is correct or expected. Amazing!

There are 14 valuable morphemes that can unlock the meanings of lots of words. Just by knowing the meanings of these morphemes, you can expand your vocabulary right away. When you start noticing these morphemes in words, you'll begin to notice others as well, and pretty soon you'll be a *wordsmith* (someone who knows and uses words well)!

Here are the 14 valuable morphemes with five examples of words created by adding other morphemes. See if you can guess the meanings of these words:

cept – to take or receive (exception, conceptual, accept, acceptable, acceptance)

duct – to lead – (abduct, product, production, deduct, conduct)

fact – to make or do – (benefactor, factory, manufacture, satisfaction, faction)

fer – to bear, yield, or carry – (circumference, aquifer, differ, infer, refer)

graph – written – (autograph, phonograph, geography, choreograph, graphic)

mit – to send – (admit, emit, omit, commit, intermittent)

ology – study of – (geology, anthropology, biology, astrology, neurology) plic – fold or weave – (duplicity, duplicate, explicable, explicit, implicit)

pos – to put or place – (position, compose, depose, disposal, expose)

scrib – write – (inscription, description, postscript, manuscript, conscription)

sist – to stand – (insist, insistence, consistent, assist, desist)

spect – to see – (inspect, suspect, respect, spectator, prospector)

tent – to stretch or strain (contentious, intention, tent, pretentious, distention)

ten or tain – to hold – (content, tenure, contain, detain, unattainable)

In addition to the morphemes there is an additional visual strategy on mastering vocabulary in this book. Be sure to use both of them.

All words are pegs to hang ideas on.
- Henry Ward Beecher

They can be like the sun, words.
They can do for the heart what light can for a field.
- Juan de la Cruz, *The Poems of St. John of the Cross*

Suzanne Carreker, Ph.D. is the Vice President of Programs at Neuhaus Education Center in Houston, Texas. For more information visit neuhaus.org., She is a certified academic language therapist (CALT), licensed dyslexia therapist and qualified instructor.

Barbara Conway, Ph.D. is the director of virtual learning at Neuhaus Education Center. See neuhaus.org for more information. She is a certified academic language therapist (CALT) and licensed dyslexia therapist in the state of Texas.

Listen to this chapter at HowToLearn.com/amazing-grades-audio

Best Learning Stategies for Kinesthetic Learners

Kinesthetic learning style is one of the three main ways people prefer to learn new information. It is known as a learning style preference and kinesthetic learners love to learn through more tactile or hands-on methods.

The other two learning styles are visual (pictures) and auditory (listening) learning styles. People who are kinesthetic learners are generally active, like to move around and learn best by physically doing something. Many kinesthetic learners today are labeled as disruptive students and get frustrated because it's tough for them to sit down and learn the material the same way other students do.

I didn't realize that I was a kinesthetic learner until the end of my sophomore year in college. Before that, I was struggling through school because I figured that was how it was supposed to be. I had decent grades and didn't get into any trouble but I dreaded going to classes and didn't feel like I was really learning anything.

When I learned how to study for my learning style, I actually started enjoying school because of all the interesting things that I learned. I went from the girl who would sit in the back of the class spacing out to actually being able to be engaged in the topic and learn things in class.

My grades improved dramatically and I thought school was so interesting that I wanted to continue my education and today I attend graduate school.

You might be a kinesthetic learner like me if you feel like you can't sit still and focus on something for long periods of time and get frequently distracted. You might get in trouble for being disruptive and or just have trouble listening when someone is trying to tell you how to do a new skill. You would rather just get out there and try it yourself. A lot of kinesthetic learners excel at sports or are considered athletic.

I want to share with you some of the tips that have helped me succeed in school.

★ First of all, I have trouble just reading textbooks and retaining any information, so whenever I need to read an important book I have a sheet of paper that I paraphrase the main points of what ever I am reading.

★ Then I go through and color code the notes with highlighters. This actually ends up coming in handy when it's time to study for a test or write a paper because now you will have a condensed version of the book to study from or use as an outline for your paper. Plus, as a kinesthetic learner, the act of writing down the information helps you to focus and remember it.

★ I like to make my own flashcards when studying and group them together by topic to help me learn groups of words together. Flashcards are nice for kinesthetic learners because they are something you can physically hold onto and move around.

★ Also, anytime I am studying a process or trying to figure out how something works I always try to draw out my own flow charts or diagrams. This is especially helpful for history or science classes where events happen in a certain order. Again, just the chance to write things in your own words helps kinesthetic learners with remembering information. One of the best investments that you can make is getting a small whiteboard. This way you can write things over and over, draw pictures or whatever helps you to remember the information. This strategy saves paper and keeps your room a lot cleaner.

★ Whenever I plan time to study, I let myself take a short break at least every half hour. I've realized that this works for me because if I don't take a break then I will keep getting distracted and won't get anything done anyway. The break doesn't have to be long. All you really need is a couple minutes. I usually use these breaks to get up and get a drink or walk to the other room and have a short conversation with someone. The key is to allow yourself to take these short breaks, but remember to go back to what you were doing before.

★ Some other ways that I help myself focus when studying are chewing gum and acting out what I'm learning. Chewing gum is helpful because as kinesthetic learners movement helps us to remember things. That's why many kinesthetic learners tap their feet, pick at their nails, or click their pens without meaning to during class, which can be very distracting to everyone else. Chewing gum is more discrete (be careful not to chew loudly or smack your gum) but can still give the same positive effects. I recommend sugar free gum so you won't get dental problems.

★ When I was studying for the SAT I didn't know that I was a kinesthetic learner and I felt like I was wasting my time. My score didn't improve whether I studied or not. However, last year when I took my GRE, which is like the SAT but for grad school, I figured out some study tips that worked for me. First, find a way to access practice tests, either in a study book or online. Before you do anything else, just take a test and see how you do. What questions did you do really well on? What questions did you not do as well on?

★ Then, read strategies for how to answer specific question types and make sure you do practice questions to help learn the strategies. This strategy works for the math as well as critical reading questions. You may also want to try making flashcards for any vocabulary words that you are not familiar with. Practice making outlines for sample writing prompts and most of all, feel free to write all over your test. Cross out answers you know are incorrect. Make notes to yourself. As you jot things down, you may trigger a memory to help you answer the questions correctly. The more you practice doing practice questions the easier it will be to do well on the actual test.

Angela Harter is a graduate student in nutrition at California State University, Chico. Her undergraduate degree is in kinesiology from Fresno Pacific University where she graduated with honors. As a kinesthetic learner who has used strategies in this book successfully, she wrote this chapter specifically to help kinesthetic learners succeed in school.

Listen to this chapter at HowToLearn.com/amazing-grades-audio

5 Foolproof Ways to Remember What You Read

No matter what your grades have been in the past, you can begin to boost your grades across the board by focusing on just one simple objective—improving your reading retention.

While you've most certainly heard of reading comprehension, the word "retention" may be new to you. Reading retention refers to how well you are able to remember what you read. This skill is one of the greatest predictors of academic success. When it comes time for a test it is critical to be able to effectively leverage your memory. Thus, if you want to improve your grades quickly and efficiently, it's only logical to focus on enhancing your ability to memorize and recall the information you've read. To help you do so, here are 5 foolproof ways to memorize and recall what you read:

★ **Picture It**

They say a picture is worth a thousand words, and when it comes to your memory, they're exactly right. Luckily, we all have imaginations capable of producing vivid mental pictures, and research has proven that these images are far more memorable to the human brain than written text. Forming pictures in your head as you study can make the material much easier to recall on a test or an assignment. For example, during history class, rather than try to memorize a boring list of facts and events in isolation, try making a mental video of the events and include the facts that you need to commit to memory. Then, replay this "film" in your head, focusing intently on the images in your mind as the event unfolds. Using this technique, you'll be much more likely to remember the details of the historical narrative when test day arrives.

★ **Create New "Absurd" Images To Really Enhance Memory**

Our brains are naturally wired to pick up on and remember things that stand out as abnormal or shocking. This is known as the Von Restorff Effect. We can use this ability to identify distinctions to help us recall even the most mundane things. How? Take the normal and make it abnormal. For instance, if you're attempting to remember state capitals, you can make the names of the capitals and their states sound like something weird or silly. For instance, you could remember that the capital of Virginia is Richmond by visualizing a girl named Virginia marrying a man with pockets stuffed with money ("rich man"). Or to remember that Ohio's capital is Columbus, you visualize someone calling out to you "Oh, Hi". You look up to see that it is Christopher Columbus.

★ **Make Associations**

Our mind is constantly trying to make connections and associations among the events that occur in our lives in order to try to make sense of the world we live in. Since we are naturally predisposed to linking things in our minds, our brain recoils when presented with a list of seemingly random items to remember. Yet, many times, this is exactly what teachers ask of students. For example, you may have to recall a list of literary terms for English class, the periodic table of elements in Science, or a series of formulas in Geometry. While these lists may seem unconnected at first, and thus very difficult to recall, if you simply take the time to create associations among these items, then memorizing them will become signifi cantly simpler. To give you a real world example, imagine having to memorize the U.S. Presidents in order. Using the association technique, you could remember the third and fourth president in sequence by imagining Thomas Jefferson lecturing his son James with a mad look on his face. This would help you recall that James Madison ("mad"-i-"son") was the next president in the series. Creating such a story line for all 44 presidents would help you to create a linked sequence of events that you could recall easily using this association technique.

tinyurl.com/7yae8uo

★ **Vault of the Loci – Connect Locations to Items You Need To Remember**

Loci, pronounced low-sigh, is another word for location. This technique allows you to recall a long series of items you read. Basically you decide on a place in your mind that you are very familiar with such as your house, school, neighborhood, etc. You then mentally walk through that place, associating items that you are trying to remember with locations in that place. For example, if you are memorizing the works of Shakespeare you could associate it with locations in your home. As you mentally enter the house you associate Romeo and Juliet with your front door (Romeo knocks on the door to visit Juliet), Julius Caesar with your living room (Caesar is assassinated using the fireplace poker), Hamlet with kitchen (you visualize a large ham being sliced on the counter), and so forth.

★ **Focus**

This last tip is the simplest of all, but may in fact be the most helpful in terms of memorizing material and recalling it quickly in order to ace your tests in every subject. When studying for memorization, it's important to devote all of your focus and attention on the task at hand. Eliminate all distractions such as television, email, phone calls, and music with lyrics. In addition, be sure you are alert and fresh during the study session, free from fatigue.

Break up your study session into sprints. People remember what they read first and what they read last more easily. This is called the "primacy and recency" effect. Spend 15 minutes focusing on material that needs to be memorized, followed by a five-minute break, and then repeat. One can repeat this pattern of bursts (concentrated study, then rest) for several hours. Although these may seem like insignificant measures to take, you'll be surprised to see the powerful impact they will have on your ability to later recall what you've been studying.

As you're implementing these strategies, keep in mind that the idea that some people have a better memory than others is largely a myth. Anyone can sharpen their memory skills using some simple, fun techniques like these. The best part is—these study methods can help you recall material for the long term, not just for the test; therefore, they promote real and lasting learning!

Teena Kamal, B.A. is a study and life skills expert on effective learning for students in middle school through college. She works with top universities to develop resources that prepare students to thrive and lead in the global economy. Learn more at www.Edu-Nova.com.

Listen to this chapter at HowToLearn.com/amazing-grades-audio

Colossal Comprehension Clues:
How to Understand Everything You Read

Imagine that you are on a ship headed to Spain. Everything is going along fine, so you think, but you find out that the captain accidentally entered the directional course at 44° instead of 45°. Your arrival day comes but instead of arriving in Spain, you arrive in France. That mistake, that small 1° variance has caused you to go off course and totally miss your destination.

So what does that have to do with reading comprehension? When you are off course by just 1°, reading comprehension can be hard for you. But, just changing by 1° can get you back on course to being able to comprehend what you read with ease.

What do you need to do to make that 1° change? Learning and implementing the 3 colossal comprehension clues to being a successful reader is all you need to do to make that 1° change and you will be a successful reader who truly understands what you've read.

Comprehension is all about utilizing what you read, not just regurgitating (memorizing and spitting out), what you read. True learning happens when you use what you read. You use what you read when you think about what you've read and then do something with it. Because it is critical to use what you read to really comprehend, it is critical that you write – take notes or draw pictures – while you read. Writing is the doing part of thinking. You can't write without thinking.

The 3 Colossal Comprehension Clues in a Nutshell:

1. Improve Comprehension Through Note Taking Easily
2. Improve Comprehension By Knowing What to Listen For in Lectures
3. Improve Comprehension Through The Magic of Color-coding

★ *Clue I: Improve Comprehension Through Note Taking Easily*

Do you take really good notes or do you miss the important parts of a reading assignment? Do you ever read over your notes and wonder why in the world you wrote that note and missed the important part of the reading assignment? Were you just writing anything down so you could say you were finished? Did you even think about it?

There are specific ways to write notes from what you read or listen too. For example, everything you read will either have a beginning, middle, and end (narrative) or be informational (expository). Take your notes accordingly. You can use graphic organizers like those in *Ten Minutes to Better Study Skills* to make note taking extremely easy because it is just fill-in-the-blank. Most textbooks typically have the same basic format, so understand and utilize the format and you will improve your note-taking skills.

Textbooks have main topics, sub-topics and highlighted words. Use these categories in your notes. If something is **bolded** it is important! So when you are taking notes, write down the topic, the sub-topic and highlighted words. Then define the highlighted words *(Hint: The definition will be in the words either right after the highlighted word or right before it.)* Then write the next sub-topic down and its highlighted words. If you do that for the whole chapter you will be able to answer the questions at the end of the chapter with a minimum of 70% accuracy and you will have a study guide to use when you are preparing for a test. If you want 90% to 100% on your tests, read the chapter in addition to taking the notes.

tinyurl.com/7avmrjq

★   *Clue II: Improve Comprehension While Listening to Lectures*

When you are taking notes from a lecture, think in the same terms as when you read. Write down the main topic the presenter is talking about and then write down the sub-points and any important specific detail that the presenter mentions. You can even use the same graphic organizer. If dates, numbers, people, or terms are mentioned, write them down with what they are connected too. Those are important! Think in terms of who, what, where, when, how, and why. You can also add size, shape, number, color, background, movement, mood, perspective, and sound.

★   *Clue III: Improve Comprehension Through The Magic of Color-coding*

Brain studies have shown that simply using color will improve retention by 25% so use different colored pens, pencils, or highlighters. You can also use removable highlighter tape. Highlight in the margin of your notes using different colors for different types of topics. For example, highlight in blue people and what they are connected to. Highlight places in red. Highlight dates in orange. You can place a green stripe next to the beginning section of a selection, a yellow stripe for the middle section, and a red stripe for the ending. The use of colored stripes will make it easier for you to remember what happened at the beginning, middle, and end of a selection.

★   *Bonus Tip: Practice Visualizing What You Read*

Visualizing what you read is not daydreaming. Visualizing is making pictures in your mind that go with what you read or are listening too. When you make pictures in your mind while you read and then color-code them into a simple sketch you will improve your ability to use what you read or listen too. These pictures or sketches may even look like doodles, but if you do them consciously, placing colors or shapes for particular points that are being made you will retain and then be able to use the information more readily.

The brain thinks in pictures and colors so use the graphic organizer for your notes. Color code specific points-joining the connections with color, write the information in your own words. That is the key to success! Writing is the doing part of thinking. Making pictures or using the fill-in-the-blank graphic organizer forms with color will magnify the results and your comprehension will rapidly improve. You can see that a few simple changes, implementing the 3 colossal clues to reading comprehension success, the 1° shift can really make a difference. In fact, that 1° shift using the 3 clues to colossal comprehension can truly turn you into a successful reader that comprehends well. See an example of a text-book note taking graphic organizing form from *Ten Minutes to Better Study Skills* and see bonus videos: http://bit.ly/GS35qZ

Bonnie Terry, M. Ed., BCET, is the author of *Five Minutes To Better Reading Skills*, *Ten Minutes To Better Study Skills* and numerous others books and reading games. She is a Board Certified Educational Therapist and Internationally recognized as America's Leading Learning Specialist and the founder of BonnieTerryLearning.com. Terry is an expert in identifying students' learning disabilities/learning difficulties. She is also host of Learning Made Easy Talk Radio that airs every Sunday morning: http://amazingwomenofpower.com/radio/. Ms. Terry coaches teachers and parents so they can give their child a 2 – 4 year learning advantage in just 20 minutes a day. She is a frequent media guest and speaker.

Listen to this chapter at http://bit.ly/GS35qZ

Reading in College:
Overcoming Three Major Challenges

Freshman college students are literally blown away by the amount of reading required in college. 50 to 100 pages or more a night, per class, isn't that unusual! And seeing that most **college students haven't had any formal reading training** since learning how to read in elementary school, they are quite under-prepared for their massive reading workload.

So what do college students do? Many struggle trying to do it all, some do just some of it and many others just throw up their hands in disgust and don't even try. Unfortunately, this is one of the reasons that only around half of students who enroll in college actually end up graduating with a bachelor's degree.

There are **three major reading challenges** all college students face, which when better understood and overcome, could make a huge difference in their ability to succeed in college. The **first challenge** is figuring out **how to concentrate and stay awake while reading**. Many students make the mistake of saving their reading for last, doing it at the end of the day when they are most physically and mentally tired. It's no wonder that they fall asleep while reading or spend many more hours than needed trying to absorb the content. If you are trying to read and you are really tired, it may be a better use of your time to take a short nap (give your brain a rest) or if it's already late at night, get up early the next morning.

★ **Don't save your reading for the end of the day.** Find pockets of time earlier in the day to get your reading done: between classes, earlier in the morning, before dinner, first subject of the study session.

When students tell me they get sleepy when they read, I ask them where they are. Many say "on my bed", "on the couch", or in some other comfortable place. Well common sense rules that if you are in a comfortable place, your brain is thinking "relax," not "work." So better positions to read are those where the body is sitting upright at a desk or table and your mind is thinking work, not relax.

★ Though a library study desk is a better place to study than your dorm room, **the BEST place to read and study is . . . in an EMPTY CLASSROOOM!** It's where you learn, the seats aren't too comfortable, and you don't want to stay long. You tend to concentrate better and work faster there.

Another way to gain concentration while reading is using speed reading strategies. When you learn to read faster, you have to concentrate. The slower you read, the more time you have to daydream.

★ **Read with your hands or white card.** There are more than a dozen effective ways to place your hands or card on a printed page. Though you may feel uncomfortable at first, **these methods will force you to concentrate better, keep your place and most importantly, read faster.** My favorite one to get you started is called **the White Card Method**. Take a blank white card (3x5 card or back of a business card or piece of white paper), and place it ON TOP of the words you are reading. When you read with the card ABOVE your eyes, your tendency to go back is less and you are more focused with what's coming up, not what you already read.

★ **Take a speed reading class** (or read a book on the subject) when you are not taking classes (during the summer or on a school break). You will learn who you are as reader and what strategies you can choose from to become a better reader. *Download our free resource called **Discipline Your Eyes** to get your eyes and brain started.* (revitupreading.com/free-resources)

The **second challenge** student's face **is dealing with the sheer quantity of material that is required.** With students reading both fiction (story material) and non-fiction (factual material), it seems non-fiction is harder to read and remember. The best way to get a handle on any non-fiction reading assignment is to understand that all non-fiction reading material starts from an outline. And what you are reading is just the fleshed out outline.

★ **Find the writer's outline in non-fiction to introduce you to the material, to review or to weed out unnecessary material.** You can find the meat of the material in the FIRST SENTENCE of every paragraph, the introductory paragraphs and the concluding or summary paragraphs.

The **third challenge involves remembering what is read.** With the sheer quantity read, remembering what you read can be quite the challenge. Using some note making strategies while you read will help you to trigger your memory later on.

★ **Highlight your notes** *effectively.* Too many students use their highlighters like a coloring stick highlighting more than 25% of a page. **Highlighting just key words and phrases is more effective** when you review **than entire sentences and paragraphs.** Take a look at this chapter. Read through just the bolded or italicized words and you will see they reflect the essence of this chapter. No one wants to re-read an entire paragraph and then wonder why they highlighted it! Whatever you highlight needs to reflect what is most important about what you read.

★ **Read the entire paragraph or section before taking any notes;** otherwise you will think everything is equally important, which it is not. Though there are more academic reading challenges, these three seem to be the most common. Figure out the best conditions that encourage your concentration and reduce your quantity by learning some speed reading techniques. Remember to find the writer's outline and take effective notes which will save you time reviewing later. There is nothing glamorous about pulling an all-nighter to read. These tips will help you get your reading done AND get your sleep too. What more could you ask for?!

Abby Marks Beale has taught speed reading for over 25 years and is America's #1 Speed Reading Expert. She is the author of *10 Days to Faster Reading, The Complete Idiot's Guide to Speed Reading* and *Success Skills: Strategies for Study and Lifelong Learning.* She is also the creator of the popular online course Rev It Up Reading that gets readers up to speed with what they read. For more, please visit www.RevItUpReading.com.

Listen to this chapter at HowToLearn.com/amazing-grades-audio

How To Write a Winning Essay in Three Easy Steps

In this chapter my goal is to show you a simple, three-step process of writing an essay of any length and on any topic - even if you're totally confused about writing and even if you don't like writing. So, let's begin. The three steps for writing a winning essay are:

Step 1. Take a Stand
Step 2. Write your Thesis Statement
Step 3. Write the Body of the Essay

Now, I know what you're thinking: "But what about Introductions and Conclusions? Besides, I was taught to structure my essays this way: Introduction, Body, Conclusion. What happened to that?" Well, there's no other way of saying it, and I'll say it bluntly. This old and ineffective way of teaching essay writing is responsible for your frustration with writing and for your teacher's frustration with reading what you wrote.

And here is the main problem. Most of the time you are advised to begin your essay with some sort of a 'hook' to grab the reader's attention. Then, after you've done that, you present your thesis, which is your main point. This thesis can be placed at the end of the first paragraph or, if your introduction takes two paragraphs, then it should appear somewhere within those two paragraphs.

This doesn't help you or your reader, for several reasons. First, this doesn't help you develop your essay in the quickest and easiest way possible. Second, after reading your introduction, your reader may miss your main point in the shuffle of other statements that are kind-of-sort-of related to your topic. And finally, you may actually lose your reader's attention by taking too long to get to the main point.

tinyurl.com/72m4r7l

So, what do you do instead and how do you solve these problems? You simply follow the three-step formula above. Let's do an example. Let's say that we want to write an essay about high school life. And here would be your teacher's essay question:

"Being a high school student is a wonderful experience. Do you agree or disagree?" So, your first step is to take a stand.

Step 1. Take a Stand

You simply need to decide firmly whether you agree or disagree with the essay topic in question. And, of course, both you and I realize that high school life has its ups and downs, its own excitements and disappointments. And you could certainly write a statement in which you agree or disagree only partially. But let's keep it simple for our purposes here and let's assume that you are totally thrilled with being a high school student. Then you should state it as early as possible. The first sentence is a perfect place: *"Being a high school student is a wonderful experience."* Great - step 1 completed. Let's move on to step 2:

Step 2. Write the Thesis Statement

I would like to teach you a simple but very effective technique I call the Power of Three. Here is how you can apply it to write a great thesis statement: *"Being a high school student is a wonderful experience for three reasons."*

Now - you may be asking, "Why three? And not five or ten?" And the answer is that three is the easiest largest number for the human brain to deal with effectively. We simply think better in terms of three. One doesn't help you, because only one reason that high school rocks provides little information to fill up your pages. Two is better. But three is best. And anything more than three is simply unnecessary, at least in a simple essay such as this one. Let's keep it at three. (And, by the way, with practice, you can use the Power of Three to develop any topic.)

Now, a full thesis statement consists of two parts: Thesis and Statement of Support. The first part - thesis - is the first sentence that we just wrote: "Being a high school student is a wonderful experience for three reasons." And the second part of the thesis statement should simply outline every reason briefly. Let's see what this looks like in practice:

"Being a high school student is a wonderful experience for three reasons. First, meeting new people and making friends is an exciting part of high school life. Second, high school provides for an opportunity to explore college courses, which may help choose a major earlier rather than later. And finally, high school students have an opportunity to learn how to drive a car through driver's ed programs."

Do you see what we just did? The Power of Three pretty much forced us to come up with three reasons that make high school life great. This makes our life easer, because we already have a paragraph going - we're not starting from zero anymore. And now all we have to do is devote a paragraph or a section to each of the three reasons. When we're done doing that - guess what - our essay is finished (unless you want to add a conclusion, which your teacher may require you to do - more on that later). So, now that we've completed steps 1 and 2, we are ready for Step 3:

Step 3. Write the Body of the Essay

Let me mention here that the hardest part of writing an essay is really done. This is because writing a thesis statement the way I teach it requires you to think in a very clear way. And clear thinking is challenging. Now - according to our thesis statement, our essay must have how many main parts (or sections)? If you answered 'three,' then I'm proud of you - you are getting this very quickly. And here are our three main parts: Part I - Making friends, Part II - Exploring college courses, Part III - Learning how to drive.

Depending on your word count requirement, you may use this structure to make your life writing this essay even easier. Let's suppose that you need to write 500 words. Well, our thesis statement takes up 67 words. Let's do some math. 500 minus 67 is 433. Say, you need roughly 450 words in the body of the essay. Divided into the three sections we came up with, we now need only about 150 words per section. Now, that should be really easy to accomplish. If you write three paragraphs, and in each paragraph you provide just one specific example that supports your point, then - guess what - your essay is finished.

Now, of course, your teacher may require you to write a conclusion. No problem. Conclusions simply repeat what you've already stated. So, why don't you simply reword your thesis statement, attach it to the ending, and call it a conclusion? Very easy.

Philip Saparov is an e-learning professional at TutorPhil.com. He teaches college students all over the world how to achieve academic success and enjoy the process. His expertise ranges from writing research papers and reading difficult texts to achieving higher levels of confidence in the academic setting.

Listen to this chapter at tinyurl.com/7ueq5og

How To Unleash Your Creative Genius When You Write

The pressure to write and write creatively in a short amount of time might seem uncomfortable at first but just like anything new there's always some resistance.

Toss your inner critic aside and focus on the experience of writing for the sake of writing, unconcerned with the end result.

If you shift your focus around you might be surprised. You could very well have the end beginning of something great. In my experience, the following two exercises have yielded a wide range of stories, poems and slice of life paragraphs. Students have produced the first chapter of short story, and/or a few strong stanzas which gave birth to a beautiful poem.

The goal is to keep an open mind and let your emotions guide the pen and just keep writing. Your hand stays connected to the pen, the pen remains on the page and your free association will guide your hand. Please try not to edit or censor your thoughts as you go, the whole idea is to generate the creative genius inside and let the ideas flow!

The One Sentence Slip Exercise:

1. Tear one strip of a lined notebook piece of paper about 4" wide.

2. The class needs to agree upon by a theme which can be an emotion: joy, anger, sadness, humility, shock or a situation say, "We started driving down Vail's Hill when the car suddenly…"

3. Everyone writes one sentence on the theme or situation and then folds their sentence written on a slip of paper in half.

4. Switch your slip of paper with the sentence you wrote with another student.

5. Using the other student's sentence rewrite this sentence and take this sentence in any direction you want.

6. Write until you have filled an entire page of a notebook.

7. Everyone writes/creates as differently so some of you most likely can fill up a page faster than others. This is fine. Please allow for at least 15-20 minutes for this part of the exercise.

8. Each student reads the sentence they were given and states: "This is the sentence I was given" and then proceed to read what he/she wrote. (It is very important to listen actively while each student shares what they wrote.)

After everyone has read their piece aloud to the class, each student comments on one other student's piece in a constructive, positive light. This exercise is guaranteed to surprise and entertain your class because a new door or window of perception will reveal itself through your classmates' examples. You may use this example and continue working on it for a homework assignment in a creative writing class. Sometimes the best stories, poems and creative non-fiction have been developed from writing in groups. Students in my college classes and basic skills classes have been able to break their writer's block after participating in these exercises.

The Four Seasons Exercise:

This exercise can be done any time of year and is meant to look at the specifics of each distinct characteristics of each season. Unlike the one slip sentence exercise; this exercise will increase your vocabulary quickly. Do not worry about nouns, pronouns and adjectives; they will surface as you focus on words from your memory bank of that season. Go around the classroom and each start with **summer**, the next student has **autumn**, the next **winter**, the next student **spring** and so on until each student has a season to work with.

1. Tear out one sheet of notebook paper, and write as many things as she/he can about the season designated to her/him.

2. For example: **Summer**: warm nights, potato salad, ocean, beach, iced tea, watermelon, wild flowers, Baseball, picnics, vacation, camping, humidity, shorts, soft breezes, 4th of July, longer days, fireworks, swimming, fishing, sun tanning, heat stroke, haying, star gazing, hiking, hot dogs, ice cream, red, white, and blue.

3. After you have a list, tear out another sheet or two and start a paragraph using as many words from the list as you can. Once you have used one of the words, cross out each word and keep going until all the words are crossed off the list. If you need more time, say about 15 minutes or so, revise what you have so that it makes some sense.

4. Add sight, sound and touch and 20-34 words on your list. Add or subtract some more words to round out your paragraph.

5. When you are finished, each student takes turns reading their list they came up with and the revised paragraph.

These exercises stretch your imagination by starting with a memory, and then using the list to brainstorm a solid paragraph which expresses a creative memory narrative in a short amount of time.

Susan M. Sanders teaches English and Humanities classes for The Community College of Vermont. Her true calling is writing and revising poetry, and short stories. Her work has appeared in *The Green Mountains Review, Lucidity, Flying Horse, Rattlesnake Review, California State Poetry Society, The Lucid Stone, The Mountain Troubadour, Conversations at the Hearth, Soapbox, The Vermont Literary Review, The Green Mountain Trading Post, Innervisions* and several others.

Listen to this chapter at HowToLearn.com/amazing-grades-audio

Easier Ways to Read Your History Text, Make it Come Alive and Get Better Grades

Remember when you were in elementary school and learning history seemed like so much fun? You would learn about events such as the First Thanksgiving by making those funny Pilgrim hats or Native-American headdresses out of colored paper and then reenacting it by bringing in food and having a real feast.

Sometime between elementary school and now, your love and interest for history might have slipped away. Now, history seems like it's all reading about a bunch of dead people who mean nothing to you. It doesn't have to be that way anymore. The key to studying history and social studies is to make it come "alive" again.

Learning history means reading – there is no way around it. However, you can make the reading of history interesting and by so doing, your studying of it so much more effective. First, before reading the chapter assignment in the textbook, page through it and see what you will be dealing with. Always read any chapter previews that are provided. They will provide the broad overview you need to read more effectively. You will know the reason for reading.

Think of ways in which what you are about to read relates to your life. Next, read all the graphs, charts, sidebars and captions to pictures and photographs. It is in these textbook aids that the interesting stories, facts and strange tidbits of history can be found. It is this information that will peak your interest to want to know more. From this information, start to develop questions that you want answered when you start to read.

As you are reading, make sure to stop at a logical point and analyze and review what you just learned. History should always be read and studied in small segments. What you just read is going to connect to what is coming so you can't move on until you are sure this new information makes sense. Do not move forward until you are convinced you understand.

Creating a visual study aid for yourself – some sort of graphic organizer - will go a long way in helping your understanding. I particularly like semantic webs (there are many different terms for these) and Venn Diagrams. Create a central topic and list all the relevant details that are needed to create understanding. When you resume reading, you can add to your diagram at the next stoppage point. These will be very easy to study from when it comes quiz or test time. If you are artistic, you could even sketch or draw what you just read. By creating visual aids, you are also able to make connections between the various information you are learning. History is all about connections and the visualization of history is SO important in your ability to connect the dots!

History more than any other discipline, is about humans and their lives. It is real people, in real places doing real things. Since it is real, then attack studying of history in human terms. To learn history you need to "see" it, "feel" it, "taste" it and "hear" it in order to learn it. When reading a book, listening to a lecture or studying for an assessment, put your self into the event. Relate to what the people must have been feeling. Ask yourself, "What would I have done?" See the scene, smell the smells. You have a wonderful built-in study tool that does not get used enough by students. It's your imagination. USE IT! Make studying come alive again.

Perhaps the best way of all to study history is to actually go to where it happened. To follow in the footsteps of the history makers and immerse yourself in their world is a powerful tool to understand social studies. However, we cannot all just get on a plane and fly to Rome. We can, however, go to museums, libraries, battlefields, and national parks not that far from our homes. These places are a goldmine of valuable information and experiences. And now, through the wonders of technology, we can bring Rome to us. There are hundreds of wonderful websites dedicated to the social studies which can be viewed and examined at your leisure. You can see what things look like, read the stories and meet the characters of history through these websites. Some of these websites are even interactive to make the experience even more exciting.

A valuable tool which is often overlooked is the people right in your own backyard. You can just talk to neighbors, family members or people in your area who have lived through particular events. They can bring you that first person experience which can open your eyes to different ways of thinking. Visit a local V.F.W. and the people there would be more that happy to share their experiences. Retirement homes are a wealth of information. Use these resources and you will broaden your social studies knowledge beyond your expectations.

Finally, when it comes time for that assessment, there is one trick which you will find invaluable. Remember, history events are real. With that in mind, when you come to a question which is giving you trouble, don't say, "I don't know." Instead, ask yourself, "What DO I know?" Use that wealth of knowledge you have accumulated in your lifetime as a social creature to think through a problem. You will be surprised how much you really already know.

Following these suggestions will open up a whole new world for you. History will again be interesting, relevant and fun.

History cannot give us a program for the future, but it can give us a fuller understanding of ourselves, and of our common humanity, so that we can better face the future.

- Robert Penn Warren

Robert Kuhn, B.A. is a certified Social Studies and Special Education teacher in Pennsylvania and Delaware with over 15 years of teaching experience. He also teaches study skills and SAT preparation.

Listen to this chapter at HowToLearn.com/amazing-grades-audio

How To Turn Your Subjects into Games and Create Faster Learning

Most of us will agree that playing games alone or with others is more fun than studying, taking tests, and getting grades. What if you could add fun games and healthy competition into your studies to make learning fun and interesting? This can change the whole dynamics of learning for you. My goal is to make learning fun and interesting so that it will also stay with you longer than just until the test is over.

You can learn to study for subject knowledge and good test scores just like you play games to win and with the same intensity and excitement. We all like to win or we just like to have fun playing together. You can make learning fun if you look for the ways and be creative. I am proposing some methods in this chapter to get you started. But you will find even more ideas on how to do this that you can share with others on your favorite social media site and blogs.

You can also post your ideas and links to follow to your groups or projects on the Non-Trivia Quest game blog at http://non-triviaquest.blogspot.com. We will use your great ideas and contributions in an online addendum to this chapter.

Self-study and using games to make learning more fun and exiting can work for you. An example can be to set goals for yourself and challenge yourself to win by reaching and exceeding those goals as you compete against yourself. You can also make subjects more interesting and relevant to today's world and to learn why you need to know the subjects in our lives.

For instance, in history you can find how events affect the way people and countries act and react in the world today. In math you can see how this material is useful to your life today and tomorrow. In geography you can see how it is important to know where the countries are in the world with their neighbors and their demographics. In the world today, we are all closely united as part of a small planet and need to know more about each other.

You can also keep track of your time to complete your homework in each subject and try to beat your previous time. You can test your reading speed and comprehension scores on a bar chart over time. You can test yourself to beat your own scores in each subject through the year. Then study the rules for how the test scores are judged to improve your chances. This could be just like a video game or your favorite sports to win by honing your skills within the rules and with a lot of practice. You play against yourself for topping your best scores and watching the results.

Group studying and brainstorming using games in a contest together can be a great experience similar to team sports and playing games with friends. Student members can develop the game rules and motivation to participate as they develop questions and answers (Q&As) of your studies. This can include a description and discussion on each Q&A to help understand and better retain the subject material instead of just memorizing answers. It can also help give you confidence of being prepared for the tests that can be an advantage with much needed rest and less stress.

Each member of the group can pick a subject to study that they feel strong in and mentor the others as the moderator for that subject. The moderator for each subject may be responsible for the group's preparation and devise the extra study material where needed. Each month the group may want new moderators for the subjects as a way to help get out of your comfort zone with your favorite subjects.

Online group studying using games can be a valuable extension of a small local study group. Again, making a game of the study group can help stimulate interest and longer lasting learning. Today we have many tools that we can take advantage of on the Internet and through our smart phones and tablets. You can make a bigger study group and brainstorm through your social networking friends on Facebook, Twitter, and others.

You can also join or start your own study group in blogs and forums, plus make the study and game playing more rich in content and interactive with podcasts and your webcams. You may name a blog or forum for each subject and invite others that have interest to join, play, compete, or just follow your group discussions. Then you may compete for recognition as the top guru on the blog or forum subject.

You can also make a game and contest of who can get the most relevant hidden treasures beyond the textbook or workbook from the Internet for a wider perspective and relevance of interest and background.

Math, history and geography examples of making games for learning may include a contest to see who can get the most answers to a question that covers a subject category. A geography example question could be, "Who can list the most countries that border the Mediterranean Sea?" A history example question can be "How many presidents of the US can you name?" A math example question can be "How many ways can you describe the ratio of 1 part of 4?" Some answer examples can be in a fraction = 1/4, a percentage = 25%, a decimal = 0.25, a $\log_{10}$ = -0.602, and in scientific notation = $10^{-0.602}$.

The debt we owe to the play of the imagination is incalculable.
- Carl Jung

Douglas Arduini, BSEE, is an electronic engineering consultant and award-winning game maker. For more information visit his site at Non-TriviaQuest.com.

Listen to this chapter at HowToLearn.com/amazing-grades-audio

Use Speed Reading, CLEP, DANTE, and DSST to Finish College in Just One Year

In the time it takes you to read this sentence, I can read this entire page-and another as well. Acknowledged as the world's quickest reader, I managed to finish a 4 year Psychology program within only one year applying brain-based learning. Let's discover how to read very quickly to help you do the same.

Revealed: The Solution For Extremely Fast Reading

Why is it simpler to read the road in a vehicle moving at 70 miles per hour, than it is to read a book in just one direction at 200 wpm? The solution to this query holds the solution to extremely fast reading. In an automobile, your mind processes the information just like looking at a film. When reading a book it appears like a tiny individual is reading every word out loud: One…Word…At…A…Time. You listen to a book using your eyes when reading, and that's exactly what slows you down. Let's practice an effortless technique that can substantially boost your reading speed.

tinyurl.com/6lq66x5

To boost your reading speed use an easily grasped non-fiction book. What follows is a effortless strategy to calculate your higher reading speed. Read for just one minute making use of your book, and after that put a pencil mark in the margin on the line where you finish.

Next move your right hand across the copy, one line at a time, as fast as you can fully grasp. Make your eyes go along with your hand at your maximum comprehension speed. Rehearse this process for 5 minutes. In order to calculate your brand new reading pace go back to the page that contains your pencil mark. Commence reading utilizing your hand to advance your eyes across every line of copy at your maximum reading pace for just one minute. At the conclusion of the minute you'll be very impressed with just how much more you're able to move beyond the initial pencil mark and this will help you learn to finish college in a fraction of the time.

You can view a free speed reading lesson video at http://www.FreeSpeedReadingLesson.com

Revealed: The Five Keys To Understanding

Are you aware there are just 5 things you need to understand to learn any kind of topic? You need to understand the new words, names, numbers and statistics, five primary concepts, and answers to questions. Allow me to explain.

About *80%* of mastering a completely new topic area is understanding its terminology. Develop a set of 3x5 index cards that have a vocabulary phrase on one side, and the meaning on the other half. Create a list of the names of individuals talked about in this book, and identify what they achieved on the back of the card.

Record any number, date, statistic, or formula, and jot down its importance on the card's back. For every heading and sub-heading in your text make a card, and identify the five primary concepts present in each part on the flip side. Lastly, write each question on a card, and get the exact answer on the reverse side. Never ever duplicate the content straight from your text. Always write down the information and facts utilizing your own words. This hassle-free action can lead to mastering the meaning as well as relevance of important information instead of memorizing incomprehensible words.

Revealed: How To Remember And Recall Essential Information

Take a look at any question, and say the answer out loud. If you make an error, you'll use a brain-based learning solution found in this book to master the material. Doesn't it make sense that the senses you use while learning, the more brain you stimulate, and the simpler it becomes to remember and recall later. This is exactly what you'll be doing.

Put any improperly identified card on a do-over stack. After that write down the accurate answer 25 times, while saying aloud. Rather than just examining the right answer, you're writing it down, stating it aloud, hearing the information, and seeing it. This involves you to utilize much more of your brain's sensory faculties to learn. When done reshuffle the cards you inaccurately observed, and repeat all these simple steps until you get every last card right.

Leveraging The Power Of CLEP, DANTE and DSST Exams

Now that you know how to learn anything faster, here is the final power secret. Taking CLEPS. CLEPS are advanced placement exams that many schools accept in lieu of taking courses. You can pass out of a class and get the maximum credit the college allows by taking a CLEP exam. Among the subjects you can fulfill using CLEPS are science, math, social sciences, and humanities. You can Google the term CLEP to see all the different courses. Remember though: each college or university will only allow you to CLEP out of a certain number of courses, so you need to find out how many of those they will allow. Some colleges will also allow you to simply take the final exam in a course to pass it, rather than going to class.

DANTE's are like CLEPS, but are produced by the Defense Department. DSST exams are similar (see more about them at http://www.getcollegecredit.com/

Most schools accepting CLEPS also accept DANTE exams. Google the term DANTE, and you will find many additional credits for subjects available by taking this exam.

By speed reading your material, targeting the precise material to learn, using the power memory strategy, and applying it to CLEP and DANTE exams, amazingly it is possible for you to complete a four year program in a single year.

Howard Stephen Berg is recognized as the world's fastest reader thanks to the cutting-edge accelerated learning techniques he developed. These learning techniques have been proven over decades to turn information over load into information assets. Respected internationally for his contribution to the learning process, he has the unique distinction of being listed in the *1990 Guinness Book of World Records* for reading at more than 25,000 words per minute and writing more than 100 words a minute. Mr. Berg is a presenter and has authored two best selling books including his Nightingale-Conant program, "Mega Speed Reading."

Listen to this chapter at HowToLearn.com/amazing-grades-audio

Learning Differences:
The Advantage of a Disadvantage

I have heard it said that, "Sometimes our greatest strength comes from our greatest weakness."

If that is so then the inverse can be true as well. Our greatest weakness can also be our greatest tool in the pursuit of progress. In fact, Ralph Waldo Emerson once said, "Our greatest strength grows out of our greatest weakness."

This is true in my case, as well as the millions of others who attend school and are diagnosed with a learning disability, learning difference or struggle with some type of disadvantage.

When I was younger I was diagnosed with dysgraphia along with the poster child of all learning issues: ADHD. For those of you who are not familiar with dysgraphia, LDonline.org says it is a learning disability that affects writing abilities. It can manifest itself as difficulties with spelling, poor handwriting and trouble putting thoughts on paper. Because writing requires a complex set of motor and information processing skills, saying a student has dysgraphia is not sufficient. A student with disorders in written expression will benefit from specific accommodations in the learning environment, as well as additional practice learning the skills required to be an accomplished writer.

Dysgraphia affects small motor skills, neatness, clarity and sequential writing. Plainly put, my handwriting looks like what you might expect Captain Hook's bad hand to produce in the 3rd grade and my spelling and grammar are atrocious. Overall, putting words on paper is an all-around painstaking task.

I also cannot draw (although I am creative) or make/interpret graphs of any kind. So as you have probably pre-disposed, math and grammar were the 'really fun' subjects of mine in school. To add to all this, the ADHD hasn't really helped the situation. I cannot focus or concentrate on much of anything, even the things I am passionate about or find the most interesting.

These hurdles are somewhat ironic because I love to write. I write professionally and for pleasure, so somewhere along the way I learned, well, I am still learning really, how to turn what seems like a curse into a gift.

School was for me, and probably for many of you, where the problems first began to manifest themselves. This is actually really good because the earlier your learning difficulties are discovered the sooner you can turn them into an advantage. In fact, the challenges help you become more self-aware and stand out in the classroom.

If remedial tasks in the classroom are frustrating or difficult you may ask why others seem to do them easily without distress. Side-note: the answer is boring and never helpful or productive. If you're a parent reading this, it's not easy for a child or adolescent to understand why things are difficult, so make sure to notice and to ask what is difficult for them. Then you will know what the areas of struggle for your child are. Remember they are still learning who they are and what their potential is, and as they age, their self-awareness improves over time.

Initially, I thought I was just not cut out for some subjects in school and most people were just better than I was. This was a mistake that harmed me for years, both and in and out of school.

Once you find out that the reason you 'just don't seem to cut the mustard' is the result of a disability or learning difference, you can start to observe your weaknesses and plan ways not only compensate but use them to give you a leg up.

My Errors Because of Dysgraphia In
The First Draft for This Chapter

The Advantage of a Disanvantage.

A popular cliché tells us that our greatest strength can be or our greatest weakness

if that is so then the inverse can be true as well. Our greatest weakness can also

be our greatest tool, if not at least the awareness of such a weakness can be one of

our biggest allies in the persuit of progress. In my case as well as millions of other

children and adults ours a learnig disability or Learnig disinvantage.

My personel disadvatge are Disgraphia and everyones favorite poster disability

ADHD. Disgraphia is the inability to process and formaulte words

in to writing. It effects small moter skills neatness and calirity and sequential.

Writing. Plainly put my hand writing looks like a 3rd graders. My spelling and

grammer is otrociase and putting words on paper is a allarund painstaking task. I

also cant draw make or interpit graphs of anykind. Math and grammer were real

fun subjects of mine in school. To add to all that I have ADHD. I cnat focus or

concentrate on much of anything even the things I find most interesting.

My own weakness was processing my knowledge and getting it onto paper, so my first foe turned ally was time.

As I got older and went through many sleep deprived nights in high school and college and I finally learned that I needed almost double the time it took my peers to complete assignments or tasks.

Once I learned that I was able to schedule the time I needed, ideas come very quickly to me. As you begin to realize you can get the accommodations you need you will find new ways to ease up on yourself and focus more on how your disability can serve you. For me, I don't need to allot much time for brainstorming. I do however need to schedule my time to allow for editing, breaks, procrastination and burnout.

Even writing this chapter, I've paced around my house, played with my pets, surfed the internet, reread my writing, and questioned my ability to put out any coherent thought.

© Istvan Csak

The planning for the thing I am doing right now needs to be very specific. 20 minutes for this, an hour for that, etc. Test-taking was also something where time played a huge factor. I always felt the stress of the time limitations especially when there was an essay involved. My hand would cramp, my mind would drift and the page blurred.

I was always too stuck in my ways to ask for any kind of extension and it was a mistake. I failed and got lower scores on countless tests because I never asserted myself and asked for more time.

I almost had to repeat whole semesters in college because of it. I know I had to repeat classes because of it, and I could have passed tests for credentialing programs the first time because of it.

The times I did suck it up and request more time I did great. The test taking process was less stressful and I learned to use my resources.

My 'favorite' advantage of having a learning disability is the ability to stand out in the classroom and form a helpful and positive relationship with the teacher or professor which ultimately helps you achieve more success. Standing out and asking for help will keep you accountable for your assignments and also give your teachers the confidence they need to teach to any type of student in the classroom.

The stigma of a learning disability or learning difference is a myth. Nobody actually cares about the fact that you have a learning disability but people do care about results and grades. Remember grades correlate in people's minds to achievement. The higher the grades, the more people think you can achieve in life.

The last advantage I want to talk about is having resources. This includes computers, dictation, note-takers, tutors, or other people who will help you succeed. My best resource was the computer. It was helpful not only to write papers but when taking tests as well. It also familiarized me with a keyboard at a young age and gave me skills I constantly use today. Figure out which resources help you the most and ask for them.

I made countless mistakes in school even when I knew I had learning issues. I tried to cover them up or use them as reasons to do less work. It took me a while to accept help and I paid for it in grades, jobs, going to college and countless hours of stress.

Once I was honest with myself that my learning troubles had nothing to do my intelligence and self-worth, I greatly advanced in my school and professional life.

I got one of my first jobs out of college because I told the interviewer about my dysgraphia. She thanked me for my honesty and hired me on the spot. I write these words to any student or parent who is discouraged or feels 'less than' because of a learning disability or learning difference. Please put that idea out of your head because it's not worth it. Remember that the smartest people don't always know the answer, but they do know how to find it.

John Patrick Mavredakis, B.A., QMHP, is a qualified mental health professional who works with special needs students in a residential treatment center. He is also a fiction novelist and musician living in northern California.

Listen to this chapter at HowToLearn.com/amazing-grades-audio

How To Advocate for Yourself if You Have Learning Differences

To *advocate* is to argue for or support a particular cause or policy. To *self*-advocate, then, means to ask for support for YOURSELF!

If you have any type of learning disability, you will want to ensure you get the best services offered. First, if you are attending a public school, you have rights to reasonable accommodations for your disability. Knowing what your rights are, and what you need for success, will help you make informed decisions about your learning. More importantly, when you reach 18, your parents can't legally advocate for you any longer, so you need to know how to do it!

How do I know? I am a special education professor AND a parent of a son with a disability. We have done everything I have written about here. My son went from being an extremely shy high-schooler who was afraid to say anything during his annual IEP meetings to a successful college student who not only advocated for himself with his teachers and the Office for Disabled Student Services (DSS), but graduated from Community College with Honors! He will tell you it really paid off for him in the end.

The first step in becoming a good Self-Advocate is to find out all you can about your abilities; you need to know YOU: your strengths and weaknesses, your desires and interests, and how your disability affects your learning.

/tinyurl.com/83ltugr

Notice I didn't say DIS-abilities? That is because I want you to think of what you are GOOD at first! Talk with your parents and teachers, especially your special education teacher. Ask to see your IEP, the Psychologist's report, Speech and Language Report, and any other information available in your file. Ask about your abilities and strengths, and then ask for a complete explanation. In my son's case, he was diagnosed with disabilities in spoken and written language. Speech improved over the years, but writing continues to be hard for him. However, he is good with animation and film editing, so in college, he looked for a field that supported those strengths. He is now studying special effects and animation, both of which don't require a lot of writing.

Second, take what you learn about your disability and write down what helps you learn best: Could it be a quiet room? Strict schedules? Someone nearby to ask for help? More time on a test or writing assignment? Next, ask your parents and teachers what accommodations you were given over the years to assist with your learning, and how these accommodations affected your achievement. Ask if there were accommodations you should have been given that weren't, or propose an accommodation yourself, then ask why it was not or could not be provided. Knowing what did and didn't work will help you know what to ask for when you begin to advocate for yourself.

The next step is to know your rights and responsibilities. In your meeting with your special education teacher, ask about the difference between IDEA (for students in K-12) and ADA (for students and adults). More on this at: http://nichcy.org/laws/idea and ADA.gov. In general, you are covered by IDEA until you graduate from high school. In college and in the workplace, you are covered by ADA, but your rights will be a little different. Have your teachers and parents explain the difference to you, and the differences in your rights and responsibilities as you go past high school. This is especially important if you are planning to go onto college! There are important things that YOU must do for yourself, because you will be an adult, and on your own.

YOU will need to contact the DSS office and let them know everything you have learned in Steps 1 and 2 above. YOU will need to talk to your teachers about needed accommodations. And YOU will need to decide whether or not to talk to a potential employer about your disability. Don't worry, though. You can bring a parent to the DSS if you give the college permission. My son insisted that I come with him for the first meeting, and gave the college permission to talk with me. However, over the next 5 years, he did most of the communicating with DSS himself until he became very good at it.

Finally, ask your teachers and parents to help you practice for meetings with people like the DSS office and your teachers. Find out who the key people are at your high-school or college so you know who to go to when you need something. You need to be firm but flexible in communicating your needs and preferences, and you need practice in how to problem solve if the person does not agree with what you are asking.

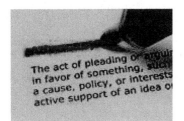

It helps to think of a situation where you need to negotiate with a teacher who is not providing the appropriate accommodation. For example, could you be successful if you have written copies of orally given instructions or lectures? How could you ask for that in a way that is calm, assertive, and clear? Also, be willing to ask questions when something is unclear to you or you need clarification something. Teachers like it when you ask for clarification rather than doing something poorly because you are afraid to ask!

My son started slowly at the Community College. THAT IS OK! Take your time and go at your own timetable through college until you can do everything on your own. No one will think poorly of you! My son earned an AA and a Certificate in Animation and is now attending a 4-year University. I am so proud of him! More importantly, he is proud of himself, and you will feel that way, too!

Never give up
No matter what is going on around you
Never give up
    - His Holiness The Dalai Lama

Dr. Barbara Glaeser is a Professor of Special Education at California State University, Fullerton and author of *Preskills for Learning* at www.preskillspackets.com.

Listen to this chapter at HowToLearn.com/amazing-grades-audio

Dyslexia is Your Strength:
5 Strategies That Will Help You Get Better Grades

What if you are smarter than you think? Dyslexia is just a description and certainly not your destiny. Take a look at the list of remarkable people (just like you) who have dyslexia:

Jay Leno   Thomas Edison
Salma Hayek   Winston Churchill
Walt Disney   Leonardo da Vinci
Tommy Hilfiger   Alexander Graham Bell
Anthony Hopkins   General George Patton
Henry Ford   Whoopi Goldberg
Cher   Muhammad Ali
Albert Einstein   Orlando Bloom
Woody Harrelson   Henry Winkler

The Grand Secret of Dyslexia

The grand secret of dyslexia is that you already make images of words and their meaning in your mind. Therefore you have the ability to create a physical manifestation of any word so it is meaningful for you and once you do that, you can read easily. As Albert Einstein said, "Imagination trumps knowledge."

For most dyslexics, the letters, words, and phrases are simply black marks on a piece of paper. Therefore they don't have any meaning unless you assign meaning to them. The good news is that there are five ways to make reading more meaningful to you.

Strategy #1 to Triumph Over Dyslexia: Make Clay Models of Letters

Clay has long been used by dyslexics to give meaning to words like 'the' and 'and' and other words that have no physical meaning when they are first read.

It is necessary first to get the letters of the alphabet into a physical form that you can recognize. Use modeling clay to make large clay models of each of the letters of the alphabet, plus punctuation marks. Make models of capital letters first, in order, and then small letters next, in reverse order (the sequence of the letters is reversed, not the letter itself.) Feel the letters with your fingers, say the letters out loud, and feel them again and again, until you get a picture of that letter in your mind and it becomes meaningful to you.

Strategy #2 to Triumph Over Dyslexia : Make Word Pictures

Learn to "photograph" a combination word/picture, where the word is printed right on its picture (not under it or near it, right on its picture showing what the word means). Start with things (nouns) as they are easier to do at first. Then go on to do action words (verbs).

For example, draw a large duck quickly on an index card. It doesn't matter how the duck looks. Your mind can make a perfect realistic picture of a duck when it sees what you have drawn.

Print the letters of the word "duck" quite large right on the picture of the duck (not under the duck, or near the duck, but literally right on the duck). Then hold the duck straight out in front of you with one hand and trace each of the large letters of the word "duck" with one of your fingers. Do this several times. Then print those same letters of the word "duck" on the back of your hand or bare forearm.

Holding the printed duck straight out in front again, look at it with "soft focus," seeing the whole duck complete with printed letters on it, one picture, duck with word. Your mind will automatically "photograph" the duck (with embedded letters) together in one picture in the mind's eye. It's all one picture, duck/word, word/duck.

Close your eyes and see if you can still see (in your mind's eye) the duck. If you can't see the duck in your mind, just open your eyes and look at it again ("photograph" it again and change the color if this helps). Do this "refresher" look as many times as you need to in order to be able to see the duck when your eyes are closed.

If you can't see the duck in your mind's eye when your eyes are closed, just pretend that you are seeing the duck. It works just as well. To test yourself, put the printed "duck" picture out of your sight, and pretend it is out in front of you at eye level or higher. Look at your pretend picture of the printed duck, and copy the letters onto a blank sheet of paper. Compare with the original. If you make a mistake, good, good, good!

Strategy #3 to Triumph Over Dyslexia: Love Mistakes!

Learn to love mistakes! They are your friends. If the letters don't come out right when you compare them with your original, then do something silly or funny with the erring letters. If a letter is missing, paint the letter in the original bright red with an imaginary paint brush, dipping it in an imaginary can of red paint. Or paint imaginary little furry lines on it to make it stand out. You "get it." If a letter is out of its right order, draw an arrow on it to show the "lost one" the way to go. Repair mistakes in outrageous ways and your mind will love to remember the repair. If all else fails, burn the letters in with a hot branding iron. Imaginary of course!

Strategy #4 to Triumph Over Dyslexia: Be Calm and Alert

With physical labor, the harder you try, the better it works. With the brain, the harder you don't try, the better it works!

Learn to calm yourself before trying to do mental tasks such as word recognition, or reading. Find any relaxation method that works for you. Pay attention to your breathing for example (take three deep breaths, letting each out with a long slow sigh). Make a fist, very tight, and say to yourself, "Open fist," and clench all the tighter. Feel the tension all the way to your elbows. Then, without thinking, just let your hand fall to your lap and the fingers will fall open naturally. Relax.

Strategy #5 to Triumph Over Dyslexia: Energize the Body, Energize the Brain

A failing university student with dyslexia sat still in the library, concentrated hard, made great effort, and learned little. She put a "study table" (board) on top of the handlebars of her exercise bike at home. She peddled her way to success in university. She later learned to just pretend she was peddling her bike while sitting still in the library. She got studying success just cycling in her mind.

J. Collins Meek, Ph.D., is a neurological learning specialist in Edmonton, Alberta, Canada. He has worked with dyslexics and others to help them successfully read and learn. For more information visit his site at DocMeek.com

Listen to this chapter at HowToLearn.com/amazing-grades-audio

Overwhelmingly Overwhelmed: How to Tackle Studying One Night at a Time

OK – so you feel overwhelmingly overwhelmed. The test, the paper, the massive homework assignment looms in front of you, and your attention is at an all time low. How can you reign in your attention long enough to get through just one more session of study?

Here are a few steps toward getting through another night of the drudgery… when your brain feels like it's in an uncooperative mode.

© ArenaCreative

1. Catch of the Day

What study method will work for you today? The brain is consistently inconsistent in the way it chooses to focus. Figure out your modus operandi of the day. Come up with a learning strategy that fits your brain at that minute. It could be reading while standing up or working out on an exercise bike. Maybe it's turning your notes into pictures. It might be reading out loud, or letting someone else – or following along visually while someone else or a book on tape reads to you.

2. Ready, aim, fire!

Don't shoot blindly in the dark. Know exactly what you have to learn. Use your study guide, syllabus, or the questions in the chapter to help you know your target. Define what you need to learn and by when.

3. Back to basics.

Make sure you have the foundation of what you are learning. You can't learn to divide until you learn to subtract. Find a concise overview of your material and build from it. Use chapter headings to make an outline. If you don't have that, try the outline in an old fashioned encyclopedia or (dare we say this?) Wikipedia.

4. 555-5555.

Divide your material into chunks. There's a reason telephone numbers have dashes. Take breaks. Move. Make sure your breaks are temptation free, which means you're not going to fill the breaks by playing a video game or getting on Facebook.

5. What was that again?

Review as you go. After each break, go back over what you've already studied. Your brain remembers the first and last things it learned much easier, so keep reviewing your learning. Use your outline and study guide. Ask yourself questions. Visualize each study card. Recite each poem or song you've made up.

6. Zoning Out.

Minimize distractions. You may need to go to the library, sit in your car, or make a fort on the bottom bunk, but block out those things that will distract you. If noise bothers you, try noise canceling headphones. Turn off your cell phone and your computer screen. Regulate the temperature. Eat. Your brain doesn't want to study, so it will choose to focus on anything else it can. Take away as many of those things as possible.

© tomwang

7. Help! Help!

Get the right kind of help. You probably can't do all of the above by yourself, so ask for help! Don't be afraid or embarrassed to ask a teacher, that 'smart' kid, or even your mother. Find the person who can help you organize, define or chunk your learning. Let someone else proofread, or correct your spelling. You may just need someone to keep you accountable.

So – are you ready? You *can* do this. You're learning - and you're learning to work and improvise and beat the odds. As a result of the effort you're putting forth, you are building your character and your work ethic, which will take you a lot further in life than making an A on a test.

Remember, you're not just studying to learn about derivatives and Taoism and phospholipid bilayers. You're practicing for life. For just a second, back up and see the big picture. See tonight's homework as one stepping stone that leads you closer to becoming what you were designed to be. And then get back to work.

Kayla Fay, B.A. is the author of the publisher of *Who Put the Ketchup in the Medicine Cabinet?* You can get more information at ADHD-inattentive.com which is a website about ADHD Inattentive Type. Fay's four very ADHD inattentive sons are the inspiration and source of knowledge behind *Focus Pocus - 100 Ways to Help Your Child Pay Attention* at http://pay-attention-secrets.com/

Listen to this chapter at HowToLearn.com/amazing-grades-audio

Literacy Strategies for Secondary Special Needs Learners Across the Spectrum

This chapter contains tips I use for my secondary special needs students to help them reach their full potential. I write this in the hope that these tips may benefit you in the same type of teaching setting. Working in a school with students who have Additional Support Needs (ASN), I have strived over the years to find ways in which to make the curriculum accessible to all my students who portray a very wide spectrum of abilities and learning challenges.

I created and adapted many courses and indeed wrote the Access 2 courses (the level below Standard Grade) in English for my local authority. I also created and delivered Access 3 courses (equivalent to Standard Grade Foundation level) As I was doing this, the pupil population of the school had Moderate Learning Difficulties (MLD) and my courses were moderated and passed by the Scottish Qualification Agency's (SQA) moderator.

Just as yours is, my challenge as an English teacher is to find an alternative route to reading since the traditional methods failed to make an impact on many of my students. I want to share my methods with you hoping that they will inspire you to create your own. My course which involves active learning for teaching phonics helps poor and nonreaders achieve success. Also, a very welcome side effect to this approach is the high level of student motivation.

http://education.skype.com

I begin by using some party ideas. The first step is to use large jigsaw letters to make various phoneme sounds (beginning with 'oo', moving to 'ee' then 'ea' and playing pass the parcel (to age appropriate music). When the music stops the student has to provide a word containing the phoneme. Once I am confident that the class is secure in all three I then introduce the phoneme island game mixing up the three phonemes. When the music stops, the students have to jump on an island then say a word containing that sound.

I make up flash cards with words containing the three phonemes. The students use the cards first in a matching game. The tasks are differentiated by size of cards and pupils are grouped according to ability.

The higher reading group receive the smaller cards with more difficult words and the lower reading group use larger cards with simpler words. The next stage of learning is the introduction of differentiated bingo boards containing a mix of the three phonemes. (If there is a more able reader in the class then I employ him/her as bingo caller). I then assess learning by having a whole class spelling bee.

The next step in the process is the word dominoes. I organize the class into several ability groups and I lead the least able group. My teaching assistant leads the middle group and a pupil leads the most able group.

At this stage I assess learning by holding a spelling competition between the groups. I then ask each group to self-assess using the Traffic Light System.

The last part of the program is an interactive hangman game on the smartboard. Students particularly enjoy this game and I find that it consolidates their learning. Learning is assessed at this stage with a paired spelling competition and again students self-assess using the Traffic Light System to gauge their own achievement.

Following all these steps, I then assess students individually on a one-to-one basis using word checklists and have been really pleased with the results.

I then repeat the whole process using a different range of phonemes. Once the students are secure in at least six phonemes I introduce the dice game where each side of the dice contains a different phoneme.

Pupils throw the dice and provide a word containing the phoneme that the dice lands on. As students work through the different sounds I add them to the hangman game so that the game becomes more challenging. This helps to prepare the students for the summative individual assessment at the end.

Following this program I introduce the class novel beginning with a DVD version followed by a quiz to ensure that pupils understand the text. I consolidate learning by making up a board game and cards containing questions about the text. Once I judge students to be secure in their knowledge of the text, I use the book version to make up bingo, domino and hangman games based on the vocabulary from the text to develop reading skills.

Active learning is a real feature of this type of teaching. You can use your school grounds to make learning come to life. For characterization, I instruct students to work cooperatively to find words in the book that describe a character. They underline the words then bring them to life in a drawing. They then use the words to label the poster. This is followed by a similar exercise for setting. Depending on the ability of the class or group, the words from the poster are developed into sentences. I usually model this first.

Plot is covered by differentiated storyboards or comic strips. I have used the drama convention of 'Collective Drawing' to support a class in devising a storyboard which allows or the fact that there are only a couple of able writers in the class. The other students take on the other tasks including drawing, layout, resources and coloring, which allow each student to contribute his/her particular skill or talent.

My courses have been devised, adapted and added to over the past few years to meet the range of student abilities I am faced with. Perhaps we can connect on Education.Skype.com and learn more strategies to share with our students!

Maire McLeod, Post Grad Diploma, is a master teacher who teaches secondary students in Cumbernauld, Scotland.

Listen to this chapter at HowToLearn.com/amazing-grades-audio

Conversations About Making the Educational Experience Better for Students with ODD

Students with Oppositional Defiant Disorder (ODD) struggle terribly this chapter is meant to help bridge the gap that may exist between teachers and students with ODD. Students, if you have ODD, it may be helpful to read this chapter knowing that your teachers, professors and parents work to make your educational experience better. There are some specifics in this chapter that relate to language usage that may be helpful for both teachers and students with ODD.

ODD is term used to describe a person who displays a certain pattern of behaviors that includes losing their temper frequently, defies authority, is easily annoyed and deliberately annoys others.

The key elements of ODD include the following characteristics: argues with adults; refuses and defies; angry and defensive; spiteful and vindictive.

In essence students with ODD display a "counter- will "against authority especially when frustrated or stressed. They are often completely inflexible in these situations and the more pressure which is applied to make them conform the greater the opposition. These are often the students who will say "you can't make me", "it's not fair" and "get out of my face or I will sue you"...

Th e reasons and origins of this condition are difficult to clearly detect but often the pattern will indicate frustration and intolerance as a result of a range of issues.

This could include learning and behavioral needs including unrecognized ADHD or Dyslexia. Other reasons can be lack of structure and attachment in early development, low academic performance and low self-worth or a combination of the above.

Douglas Riley, in his excellent book *The Defiant Child*, defines some of their behaviors students with ODD as

★   They live in fantasy land where they can defeat all authority figures
★   They are optimistic and fail to learn from experience
★   You must be fair to me no matter how I treat you
★   Seek revenge when angered
★   Need to feel tough
★   Feel you will run out of moves eventually
★   Feel equal to their parents
★   Emulate the behavior of their least successful peers
★   Answer most questions with "I don't know"
★   Logic revolves around denial or responsibility

Students with ODD want more power and are extremely good at pushing other people's emotional buttons. Thus, here are some tips to help your students with ODD be successful and counterbalance their struggles.

Sending a student out of the classroom is not helpful. However, simply provide them a space to cool down until they are calm and collected. Arguing in public is not at all helpful, thus talk with your student one on one privately.

As a teacher, it is best not to be drawn into arguments. It takes 2 people to conduct an argument...if the student "says this lesson is boring and I hate you"...it is better to respond...yes you may think this lesson is boring but please finish questions 1 to 5 before the break."

Overall the key to helping your students and yourself is to use language effectively and not make things personal. An example would be, "I need you to finish the assignment" as opposed to "will you" or "can you" finish the assignment being prominent.

Begin other sentences with: Let's: in five minutes you will have; when I return I will see; today we are going to, you will be, I expect you to, I know that you will, thank you for.

Additional Information About ODD

ODD is diagnosed in the same way as many other psychiatric disorders in children and adults which involve a multi-modal diagnosis including a review of the family and medical history.

Over 5% of children have ODD and although in younger children it is more common in boys than girls, as they grow older, the rate appears to roughly equal in males and females.

It is exceptionally rare for a student just to have ODD as usually they generally also have ADHD. It is important to know that ODD is characterized by aggressiveness and not impulsiveness. With ODD the behavior can often be premeditated while it is usually not so purposeful in ADHD.

General strategies and approaches to make the school experience more positive:

★ Keep reading the mood of the child
★ Always focus on the incident not the child, don't personalize
★ Try to provide a "save face" option in front of peers/siblings by providing a choice of outcome
★ Remove the audience factor, try and talk to them quietly on a 1:1 basis where possible and remind them of past successes and capabilities - try to find something positive to say first for example.

"Do you want to move closer to the board or remain where you are?" "Do you need me to help you or can you get on with things on your own?" "Is that what you want? What are you going to choose?

Other options include:

★ Be prepared to go into the "broken record" mode at times and don't get into drawn into smokescreen behavior
★ Use of humor if appropriate and try to fi nd the positives in any situation
★ Give them a responsibility
★ Isolate them to avoid peer reinforcement and embarrassment and let them have their say
★ Give clear messages about negative behaviors and costs
★ Ask moral questions

Focus on moving forward but also dig for an apology. The key to buying a house they say is location, location and location. For successful management of children with ODD the principles would be patience, patience and patience…

Fin O'Regan MA, PGCE BSc, is an author and one of the leading behavior experts in the UK and Europe. He is currently a Behaviour Consultant for the SSAT and an associate lecturer for Leicester University, the National Association of Special Needs, the Institute of Education and the Chairperson of the European ADHD Awareness Taskforce. His books include T.E.S. award wining book *Educating Children with ADHD, How to Teach and Manage Children with ADHD; Surviving and Succeeding in SEN and ADHD; Impact and Intervention: Troubleshooting Challenging Behaviour and Challenging Behaviours* and *The Small Change: Big Difference series Inattention, Hyperactive and Disorganised.* Find out more at his website, Fintanoregan.com

Listen to this chapter at HowToLearn.com/amazing-grades-audio

Asperger's and Better Grades

If you have Asperger's it means you have many strengths that can help you be a really good student and get better grades. Using your natural visual learning strengths and style makes getting terrific grades easier. Here are some special tips to use in school.

★ **Discover your personal strengths**

Learn more about yourself. Make a list of things you are good at. Sometimes students are really good at math or science. Other students may be good at spelling or working on a computer. Which classes are easiest for you? Which ones do you like best?

If you are not sure what your strengths are, ask your parents or a teacher to help you figure out what they are. Sometimes you get to choose which class to take or which project to work on. You will usually get better grades when you choose activities that use your strengths.

★ **Know what is harder for you**

We all have some things that are easier and some things that are harder for us. When you know what is harder, you can do things to help yourself. For example, Alex can type really well on the computer, but it takes him a lot longer to do his school work when he has to write with a pencil. If he uses the computer to do a lot of his school work he will do it better and it won't take him as long to finish.

Here's another example. Dan loves to read science books but the books in English class are more difficult for him to understand. He is not getting good grades in English class. English is harder for him. He might need to get extra help from his teacher so he can do better in English and if, when he reads, he turns the words into images, it will be easier to recall the text.

★ **Find an advocate or a special person**

An advocate is a special person who will be able to counsel you and ensure you have all the things you are entitled to so you're successful in school. Be sure and talk with your advocate if you're having any problems in your classes. Sometimes your advocate will help you get tutoring or extra help with your school work if you need it. Your advocate can also help you if you are having problems with other students. This is a good person who can answer questions when you need more information.

Talk to your parents and have them help you ask for a special person to help you at school.

★ **Learn when to ask for help**

Everyone has good days when school work is easy. Everyone has days when school work is hard for them. If you have schoolwork or homework that you don't understand, be sure to tell your teacher that you are having problems. Most teachers will help you, but you usually need to tell them you need help. It's OK to ask for help.

★ **Keep organized at home and at school**

Every student has a lot of stuff like books, paper, assignment sheets, folders, pens and pencils. Put your stuff in a special place so you can find it when you need it. That means putting things away in your locker or desk or backpack so you will know where it is. If you have to take your school things home, pick a special place to put them so you will remember to take them back to school the next day.

Do you go home from school and forget to take your homework with you? Try writing a note or having your smart phone remind you. It can be very frustrating when you don't have the stuff you need. Keeping your school supplies organized will help you be a better student so you can get better grades.

★ Write it down

There are lots of things to remember at school. Writing things down can help you remember. Here are some ideas. Use a calendar to keep track of special events and when your assignments are due. Some classrooms have special rules or special routines the teacher wants the students to follow. Writing them down will help you remember and schedule your smart phone to remind you too.

It can be hard to remember all the homework that your teachers give you. Just write it down so you don't forget anything and if your school allows you to use your smartphone or tablet, be sure and plug all the information you need to remember in it.

★ Find other tools that will help you be successful

If you have a smart phone, it may have some other tools that can help you with your school assignments. For example, use the camera to take photos to help you remember what something looks like. Use a timer or a stop watch to keep track of how long you are practicing something. Set an alarm to remind you when it is time to start or stop an activity. Talk into a recorder to remind yourself of something you need to do. Make a little video to help you remember what to say or what to do in a certain situation.

★ Take care of yourself

Taking care of yourself will help you be a better student so you will get better grades. Be sure to use good hygiene and get enough sleep so you are not tired at school. Be sure to eat a good protein breakfast to give you energy. You will get better grades when you look good and feel great.

Linda Hodgdon, M.ED., CCC-SLP is a Speech-Language Pathologist and consultant for Autism & Asperger's Syndrome. She is the author of the best seller, *Visual Strategies for Improving Communication*. Sign up for her FREE newsletter at UseVisualStrategies.com to learn more tips for students with Asperger's Syndrome.

Listen to this chapter at tinyurl.com/7hktfsz

SAT and ACT Strategies for
Students with Learning Differences

Standardized test scores play an important role in many colleges' admissions processes. Unfortunately, the SAT and ACT can be particularly challenging for students with learning differences. Luckily, there are some strategies and techniques that will help level the playing field for students with learning differences, helping them get into the colleges of their choice.

Media accounts often give the impression that getting into college is impossible. You shouldn't panic: most colleges still accept a majority of their applicants. Standardized test scores are often essential to the admissions process, but their importance depends on the college or university you are considering. A growing number of schools are "test optional," not requiring students to submit SAT or ACT scores for admission; these schools place greater weight on your other credentials.

College Planning Strategies

If you are a student with learning differences, two overall strategies will be important to your college planning efforts:

tinyurl.com/7alqomx

★   **Select colleges that are right for you.**

Every student needs to find a school where he or she is able to be happy and successful. This is even more important for students with learning differences! If your test scores are far below your grades and class rank, consider adding some test-optional schools to your list.

★   **Take both the SAT and the ACT.**

Not that long ago, students applying to hard-to-get-into schools were required to take the SAT. Today, all colleges and universities—even Ivy League schools—accept either the SAT or ACT. Interestingly, many (but not all) of my students with learning issues say they prefer the structure and format of the ACT. Take both tests at least once during your junior year to determine which one is best for you.

SAT and ACT Success Strategies

Keep in mind that the SAT and ACT are challenging for everyone! Many students with top grades make average test scores; students with learning differences may find the tests even more demanding. It is possible for you to improve your ACT and SAT marks, even if you face unique challenges along the way.

1. Focus on accuracy.

Stop worrying about finishing the section, and start focusing on getting questions right: slow down and concentrate. If you struggle with focus issues, processing speed, or difficulty reading, taking more time is essential. Some students only need to answer 60% of the questions with reasonable accuracy in order to see significant score improvement. Focus on getting the questions you attempt right!

2. Determine whether you would benefit from extra time or other accommodation(s).

Seeing-impaired students can take Braille tests. Hearing-impaired students need to test in a setting where they can see the time signals given by proctors. My student with extreme arthritis couldn't bubble in her own answers.

Extended time is the most common accommodation offered on the SAT and ACT, but for some students it can be a curse rather than a blessing. Currently, the SAT is a four-hour long exam. With extended time allowed, students can sit for six hours. Students with ADD/ADHD may struggle with four hours; six hours seems like an eternity.

Work with your guidance counselor and special education coordinator to determine if you would benefit from testing accommodations. Be sure to begin the application process early, because approval for accommodations can take six to ten weeks.

3. Familiarize yourself with the format and scoring structure of each test.

Obtain official practice test booklets from your school's guidance office. If you understand how each test is structured, you can pace yourself to maintain appropriate focus over the allotted time. The SAT has ten timed sections of reading, math, and writing mixed throughout. In contrast, the ACT is more predictable: English, then math, followed by reading, and finally science.

It's also important to recognize the unique scoring method for each test. On the SAT, you are penalized ¼ a point for incorrect answers, so it is better to leave a problem blank if you don't have time to solve it. However, on the ACT there is no guessing penalty, so you should pick one guessing letter and use it for every question you do not have time to complete.

4. Focus.

I tell my students that the ACT and SAT are like marathons of test taking. I can run a couple of miles, but unless I begin training in earnest, there is no way I will complete a marathon. You need to train to develop your ability to maintain extended focus on admissions tests. Begin by taking one timed section at a time and dedicating your attention to the questions for the entire duration. Then do two or three sections at a time until you have built up to the entire test.

If your learning difference involves trouble focusing, consider the role medication has in your learning plan and the difference it could make on your ability to focus for the prolonged testing period.

5. Review content.

Admissions tests focus on math, reading, grammar, vocabulary, and writing content. No amount of strategy or focus can help you solve that geometry problem if you have forgotten basic rules of triangles! If you have significant gaps in your knowledge, you may need to work with a teacher or tutor. Remember, you are working to improve your score, not to get every question right. Do not panic if you don't know how to answer the hardest questions.

Above all, set realistic expectations!

My final suggestion for students with learning differences is to set realistic expectations. You already know that some academic areas are more difficult for you than they are for others. Set scores and college admissions goals based on your abilities. Understand that the SAT and ACT are challenging for everyone. Practice. Focus. And do your best.

Megan Dorsey, M.Ed. is a nationally recognized expert in test preparation and college admissions who has helped thousands of students earn the scores they need and get into the colleges of their dreams. For more information visit CollegePrepResults.com

Listen to this chapter at HowToLearn.com/amazing-grades-audio

Vision is More Than 20/20!!!

Read this chapter if you get tired when you read, struggle to remember what you read, skip lines, lose your place or generally feel that school is the last place you want to be. Many of your feelings can easily be explained by undetected visual skills and the problems that causes.

Achieving in school and receiving AMAZING GRADES is a great goal. In order to accomplish this goal you will need to attend class and understand the material presented to you verbally and visually. This sounds simple but in fact is quite complex. I am an optometrist and want you to realize that the visual demands placed on you as a student are very high because you have to read more and more books plus use a computer.

Have you ever thought about how much you use your eyes for reading, computers and other close up work, yet you get your eyes tested by an eye chart that is 20 feet away?

Most people think "20/20" means seeing a letter about 9 mm. high (less than ½ inch), on an eye chart 20 feet away, and equate this with perfect vision. Do you read your books at 20 feet away? The Snellen Eye chart is the "Classic Big E" chart you see hanging in most medical offices. This chart was invented in 1842 to test the sight of soldiers to determine if they could see across the battlefield. The same chart is still used today in our modern world, but again, it only tests for "sight" which is the mere ability to see at 20 feet away.

True "VISION" is really the result of a person's ability to understand and interpret (get meaning from), the visual information that comes to him/her through their eyes. The majority of this VISION is within our arm's reach, this is NEAR VISION.

WOW, this new definition of "VISION" really means that vision takes place in the brain, and that the eyes are just the sensory organs that gather the visual signals and send them to the brain for interpretation.

Unfortunately, many parents and teachers still think that if their student measures "20/20" on the eye chart, their vision is "perfect" and therefore, if material is presented to them in a book, there is nothing to prevent them from "seeing" it correctly, comprehending the words, and learning the material rapidly.

This assumption is false! It has been demonstrated that in most classrooms, learning involves looking from desk to front of room; then, changing focus "back and forth" or, maintaining sustained reading at approximately 16 inches from the eyes. These "near vision skills", such as tracking, focusing, and eye teaming, are not tested by an eye chart at 20 feet. Near vision skills are "learned" and both parents and educators are generally unaware of the potential problems that stem from poorly developed visual skills.

Have you ever seen a student write letters backwards? Do you know someone that loses their place when they read? Ever heard a student say that after five minutes of reading their eyes feel tired or they can't remember what they just read?

Near Vision is Still Not Widely Recognized as a Causative Factor in Learning Problems

It is really best to assume that all students have different levels of vision and this affects their personal learning style and their ability to reach their potential.

Visual functions occupy a large portion of the brain; it is amazing how complex human vision is. Vision is learned; so as the brain develops, so does vision and perception. Good near vision skills are a foundation for learning; poor near visual skills usually result in frustration or anger being expressed by teachers, students and their parents if they are unaware of the effects of poor eye tracking, focusing, eye teaming, and vision perception skills. The consequences of failure in school when basic learning abilities are not developed are well known:

- ★ "I'm Dumb" (low self-esteem and guilt)
- ★ "The teacher and other students don't like me" (assumed feelings of inadequacy)
- ★ "Reading is Boring" (loss of motivation to learn)
- ★ "I hate school" (I'm a failure; I don't like to be where I fail)

These feelings can result from a failure to learn because a system which does not test vision skills at nearpoint too can set kids up to fail. This can cause serious emotional or social problems in otherwise intelligent people. These are the students who are "smart in everything but school." Do you know someone like this?

These students were assumed to have the near vision skills necessary to visually learn but, they did not possess the needed near vision skills to read well, and were not even tested for them. So, they struggled with reading, got left behind, and ultimately got frustrated with themselves and did not reach their true potential.

Research has shown that the majority of students that fail the Snellen eye chart test are "nearsighted", myopic, and are the best readers in school. However, the students that see very well far away, and measure 20/20 or 20/15, are hyperopic, have more difficulty reading and are more likely to be in Special Education. The juvenile delinquent population has a very high percentage of near vision problems.

The **GOOD NEWS** is that this behavior can be prevented if sufficient "near vision skills" are developed so that successful learning can take place.

Visual Function
★
Cognitive Visual Abilities
★
School Achievement
★
AMAZING GRADES

Kristy Remick, O.D., is a Developmental Optometrist, and Assistant Professor at Western University of Health Sciences in Pomona, CA. She is the Director of Community Outreach at the College of Optometry and is the author of *Eyes On Track: A Missing Link To Successful Learning*. Dr. Remick has appeared on numerous radio and television shows and speaks at multi-disciplinary conferences and seminars on the topics of vision and learning, optometric visual therapy, vision problems related to brain injury and stroke, and the relationship between juvenile delinquency and vision. Please visit her site eyesontrack.com.

Listen to this chapter at HowToLearn.com/amazing-grades-audio

Smart Fats:
How Omega-3s Enhance Your Brain For Better Grades

Success in the classroom includes not only strong learning strategies but brain health and nutrition as well. Proper nutrition helps lay a strong foundation for optimal brain health and functionality throughout life. In fact, there is good evidence linking consumption of omega-3 fatty acids to improved attention, learning, memory, behavior and higher test scores.

Omega-3s for a Better Brain

Your brain is dynamic and continues to develop long after birth. In fact, the brain nearly triples in size in the first year of life! By age 3 the brain has grown dramatically, producing billions of cells and hundreds of trillions of connections, or synapses, between these cells. A child's brain is super dense and will stay that way throughout the first decade of life.

Beginning about age 11, a child's brain gets rid of extra connections in a process calling "pruning," gradually making order out of a thick tangle of "wires." If a pathway is not used, it's eliminated based on the "use it or lose it" principle. However, science has shown us that not only is it important to "use it", but to nourish it properly as well.

Recent research suggests that the brain's frontal lobe, which is associated with impulse control, planning, organization, and decision-making abilities, continues to grow well into a person's twenties. We need all those skills to succeed in life, but especially to succeed in school. Studies show, and clinical evidence supports the use of the omega-3 fats Eicosapentaenoic acid (EPA) and Docosahexaenoic acid (DHA) to help nourish the brain by offering key benefits in these functional areas.

Both omega-3 and omega-6 fats are considered essential fatty acids, or EFAs. As their name implies, EFAs are nutrients that your body depends on for good health and functioning but cannot manufacture itself. Instead, you need to get these fats from diet or through supplementation. Unfortunately, Americans tend to consume too many omega-6 fatty acids—typically in the form of vegetable oils like soy and canola—and not nearly enough omega-3s (found in salmon, sardines, and other types of fatty fish).

This imbalance in the ratio of omega-3 to omega-6 fats can promote inflammation and may contribute to a variety of health problems, including attention deficit/hyperactivity disorder (ADHD), dyslexia, autism spectrum disorders, and other behavioral and psychological issues. The good news: A growing number of studies suggest that omega-3 fatty acids can have powerful positive effects throughout the body, including the brain.

Omega-3 fats literally make up a part of every cell membrane in your body. Your brain is comprised of 60% fat with gray matter making up approximately 45% of total brain fat, and of that gray matter, approximately 30% of it is made of DHA. It makes sense, then, that omega-3s, and DHA in particular, are crucial for proper development and function of the brain and the nervous system. But that's not just lip service: A wealth of research continues to reveal links between omega-3s (usually in the form of fish or fish oil supplements) and optimal brain health in children and teens.

Here are just a few of the impressive findings:

Attention and Behavior: Researchers from the University of South Australia looked at 132 children between the ages of 7 and 12 who had ADHD and were not on medication. Among this group, they found that children who took fish oil capsules were calmer, less impulsive, and showed improvements in attention, behavior, and vocabulary. Another study showed that, after five months, unruly children who took fish oil supplements showed improved behavior, concentration, and bonding, as well as the equivalent of nearly nine months' improvement in expressive language ability.

Grades and Test Scores: Research has found that students who eat fish more than once a week have higher grades and score better on tests of intelligence than those who consume seafood less often. And, in a British study, 184 teenagers at a school for the behaviorally challenged were given fish oil supplements for twelve weeks prior to taking the usual standardized test for this age group. On average, they exceeded the results predicted for them by one grade.

Learning and Literacy: In one 2007 study of 355 children between the ages of 6 and 9, those who regularly took fish oil supplements saw their verbal learning and spelling ability improve, retained information better, and were even less likely to take sick days from school. More recently, a study of 90 children with ADHD between the ages of 7 and 12 found that taking DHA supplements was linked to improved reading and spelling, as well as reduced behavioral issues.

Memory and Problem Solving: It's never too early to start getting adequate omega-3s. Researchers have found that children whose mothers consumed enough of these healthy fats while pregnant are more likely to score higher on tests of memory function, while other evidence suggests that babies who receive formula supplemented with EPA and DHA do better at problem-solving tasks than their peers.

Lasting Benefits: The cognitive benefits of omega-3s don't diminish with age either. One study on nearly 4,000 adolescent boys tracked their consumption of fish and cognitive performance. After accounting for education level, boys who were eating more fish at age 15 demonstrated significantly higher scores on tests of combined intelligence, verbal performance, and visiospatial performance at age 18.

Studies like these demonstrate just how important it is to get omega-3s throughout childhood and adolescence. Yet most people aren't getting anywhere near what they should. That's probably because few people eat enough fish like salmon, sardines, mackerel, and anchovies, often because of concerns about contamination with mercury and other pollutants.

This is why I and many health care experts recommend supplementing with omega-3s in the form of fish oil (algae oil if you're vegetarian). However, you shouldn't take just any omega-3 supplement. Instead, look for products that have been processed and purified in a low-heat, nitrogen environment to eliminate oxidation. These steps help to ensure that the oil is fresh, pure and great tasting, and contains low amounts of pollutants like mercury, commonly found in wild fish. Also look for fish oil that is in the triglyceride (TG) form, which is easily utilized by the body because this is how the fat naturally exists in fish. A Certificate of Analysis is available from reputable companies to ensure that you get the highest quality product.

Recommended omega-3 dosage varies with age, and you may want to consult your health care provider for more information. There's nothing fishy about how to succeed in school, and omega-3 supplements are an important addition to any savvy student's toolkit. So be smart and nourish your brain.

Keri Marshall, N.D., is a licensed Naturopathic Doctor who specializes in pediatrics, women's medicine, chronic disease management and integrative health. Dr. Marshall currently serves on the Natural Medicine Journal Editorial Board, the AANP Board of Directors, the Alternative Medicine Review Editorial Board and as Chief Medical Officer at Nordic Naturals. For more details visit NordicNaturals.com and Omega-Research.com.

Note: No portion of this chapter is intended to diagnose or treat any medical condition. See your health care provider.

Listen to this chapter at HowToLearn.com/amazing-grades-audio

Conversations with a Doctor About ADHD

Despite the staggering growth of ADHD diagnoses, every parent whose child is struggling to get good grades in school may wonder if their child really has ADHD. In the year 2000, 6.2 million kids were diagnosed with ADHD while, a decade later, 10.4 million were given the diagnosis, with many being prescribed psychostimulant drugs.

In this chapter, I want to discuss various aspects of ADHD and share my thoughts on parenting and other aspects of ADHD.

Here is a recent case I had where the parents disagreed about whether their child actually had ADHD. It may be of some help to you as you make decisions about your child. (Names are changed for patient privacy). Dan and Sarah are divorced with split custody of their child, John. Sarah's pediatrician diagnosed John as ADHD and Dan disagreed. He felt that John had attention-seeking behaviors instead. Against John's wishes, Sarah's pediatrician placed John on a drug called Concerta. Sadly, this family's problem is all too common, and it leads to two key questions:

tinyurl.com/77ab9t5

First, does this child *really* have ADHD? And the second question is, no matter what the diagnosis, NOW what? When their parents divorce, kids are stressed. Does the official diagnosis take this into account? Yes. Th e criteria medical doctors use to define all disorders, the DSM-IV, (a V version will be released soon) includes this item: "the symptoms are not better accounted for by another mental disorder." In a divorce, the child's problem behaviors are often better accounted for by a diagnosis of Situational Anxiety Disorder.

In John's case, it's likely the anxiety of his situation is distracting his attention at school, and John needs to be reassured that his parents still love him and will not abandon him. John eventually adjusted to his new world. The medicine was stopped and John's grades improved to the A-B status. His behavior became more focused as time progressed. These changes wouldn't happen if his ADHD diagnosis were correct.

If the child is only displaying ADHD behavior *according to the mom*, and only when he is with the mom, can he still be diagnosed as ADHD? Hopefully not. The DSM-IV, which is clear on this issue, states the behavior must show up in *2 of 3* environments—home, school and community. Moreover, "There must be clear evidence of clinically signifi cant impairment in social, school, or work functioning."

However, John's mom still is insistent that her son be on medication, and the courts might well side with her, despite the medical standard. No doctor could listen to Dan and look at John's report card and make the diagnosis of ADHD stick in an unbiased court of law. What did I recommend to John's dad? Print out the DSM-IV criteria and copy the report card. Take them to John's doctor and have an informed conversation.

This family's problem also illustrates the common phenomenon that the doctor still prescribed the drug, and the mediator still approved it, even though the child didn't even come close to meeting the criteria for ADHD. Th is happens all too often.

ADHD is considered to be a genetic disorder as research in the Lancet medical journal among others indicates. This means its rate of increase should match the increase in population. However, several decades ago, the federal government started providing schools and parents' money for children with ADHD. Since then, the diagnosis of ADHD has been increasing at a rate *three* times that of the population. This means that *at a minimum 70%* of those children getting labeled ADHD don't have the disorder.

This also means that most of the *research* on the disorder is done on children *that don't have the disorder.* Oregon Health and Science University has reviewed over 5,000 studies and shows *no proof that the drugs used to treat ADHD work.* When I mentioned that statistic in a workshop recently, a mom I'll call Linda said to me, "You're wrong. Drugs *do* work. I have my son on the meds and he is excelling in school. Without those drugs he was failing every subject."

This mom illustrates the common myth that if the drugs work, it confirms the diagnosis of ADHD. Please don't shoot the messenger. I'm just reporting the facts. This mom had her heart set on the "one pill solution." Therefore, what I couldn't bring myself to say to her is this: The theory behind ADHD drugs is that there is a biochemical imbalance that the drug counterbalances. But *drugs* don't counterbalance; *nutrition* does.

Of course, if the drug is really correcting a biochemical imbalance, then the child would not need to take the drug for the rest of his life. William Walsh, Ph.D., founder of the Walsh Institute, notes that a better approach is simply to add the vitamins and nutrients needed to help the body create the balance it needs. After testing some 6,000 children diagnosed with ADHD, Dr. Walsh says they have a pattern of deficiency —for example, two-thirds have a relative zinc deficiency. He has had success in using nutrient supplements to help the children control their behavior.

Moreover, putting *anyone*—ADHD or not—on stimulants will create more focus for a while until they develop a tolerance to the drug, and then they will need more. Eventually, they could need such a high dose that it becomes deadly. Usually the doctor changes drugs before that point, but as current standard of care is to keep the child on medication for 60+ years, your child will be switching drugs until he runs out of options long before he runs out of life.

What's the future for Linda and her son? Another mom I'll call Bonnie, a mom of a now-adult ADHD man, could illustrate that. Bonnie is an extraordinarily well-informed mom. She used meds, books and behavior therapy to ensure her son graduated from high school. On his 18th birthday her son ran away. He stopped taking his meds, and has been in trouble with the law (speeding, not paying tickets, etc.), and living on and off the street ever since. He is now an adult--and he's retained no coping skills. Somehow his excelling in school wasn't the end goal Bonnie really needed. Excelling in life might have been a better goal.

To pursue that goal, Bonnie would have needed to feed her son's passion. His passion would have given him the *incentive* to control his behaviors. This combination of passion, which creates the desire to own his problems, and all the other approaches Bonnie tried, would have solved the ADHD behaviors. But for 18 years, from the viewpoint of Bonnie and her son, the problem behaviors associated with ADHD were the fault of the drug, the label or anyone else besides him.

Without ownership of the problem, the drugs will fail. This isn't my opinion. It's just the facts. So, no matter what the diagnosis, the question we as parents really need to answer is this: Do we want our child to take ownership of their behavior now while they are young and the consequences simpler, or when they are older and the problems more complicated?

Stephen Guffanti, M.D. is a practicing physician, author and parent. He offers a unique background and tremendous insight and communicates with warmth and humor. Not only is Stephen a physician, but he's also dyslexic and ADHD, and from this unusual perspective he brings hope and understanding to families. Born with a passion for education as well as medicine, Dr. Guffanti has served as the medical director of a clinic specializing in learning disorders and has studied nutrition and its effects on learning. Dr. Guffanti's books include *Rocket Phonics, The Purpose of Passion,* and *Does Your Child Really Have ADHD?* For more information visit his sites at adhdoractivechild. com and rocketphonics.com.

Listen to this chapter at HowToLearn.com/amazing-grades-audio

How Bullying Affects Academic Achievement

A shocking report in 2012 says that 37% of secondary students in California report that they have experienced some form of bullying at school. New studies revealed on MSNBC show that nearly 13 million kids are bullied throughout the United States.

Victims of physical, emotional, and cyber-bullying feel less safe, are more frequently absent, and perform lower in academic areas as compared to their non-victimized peers.

Some forms of bullying account for up to a 1.5 letter grade decrease in any academic subject.

How is School Bullying and Student Academic Achievement Related?

A recent meta-analysis of 43 studies concluded that students who are bullied are more likely to receive lower grades and scores on standardized achievement tests (Pacer Center, 2011).

tinyurl.com/7nrhezs

The personal and emotional toll that bullying has on students is all-too-apparent in today's classrooms across our nation as recent tragedies of student suicides verify. Many of these students see suicide as their only outlet in an effort to find peace.

Efforts to address this serious and ever-growing problem needs to focus on two areas: 1) educating our parental community, students, and staff about the signs and negative effects of bullying, and how to deal with each effect; and 2) promoting a greater awareness of bullying in our schools, creating a safe and supportive school environment which include safeguards against bullying.

Greater efforts must be directed toward reducing school-wide bullying and its devastating effects, while creating a positive school climate that has clear expectations and an evaluative process of the school's bullying program…not just the school's bullying policy.

What Can We as an Educational Community Do to Help Stop Bullying in Our Schools?

There is no one simple answer or quick fix to stop bullying. It is not enough to write anti-bullying policies or designate one school staff member to deal with bullying issues.

Although school-size reduction might help, this is not feasible in the current economic structure. However, research has supported the value of implementing a constellation of components to improve the social climate of schools and protect all students, including our high-risk populations.

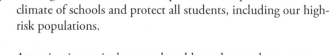

Attention in particular must be addressed toward two areas — training and strengthening all school-based and community relationships.

★   **Training**

Schools need to pro-actively take action to create more engaged learning classrooms, and supportive school environments involving all students, parents, and our law enforcement officials. At least one positive relationship with a caring adult at the school needs to be fostered as this also provides a "safe place" for students. Caring peer relationships are particularly important (e.g., through a peer mentoring program), especially when students transfer to a new school during off-times.

★ Strengthening Relationships

Staff, students, and parents need to be educated about the signs of bullying, its negative effects on emotional well-being and academic achievement, and how to deal with it, including establishing and consistently following anti-bullying policies.

★ How to Create a Clear Bullying Policy and Vision

An effective strategy to reduce bullying is to create a school-wide policy that defines bullying, outlines how teachers and school staff should address the issue of bullying in the classroom, and delineates how incidents are to be dealt with after they occur.

All students need to be aware of the consequences of bullying. The school policy must clearly define all forms of bullying behavior.

Bullying behavior can be classified under four main headings: physical, verbal, relationship and cyber-bullying.

Many bullies try to pass off acts of aggression as roughhousing between friends, or just having fun.

However, there is a difference between playing and bullying. An episode of bullying has three identifying characteristics: A power difference between the individual being bullied and the bully; a negative intent on the part of the bully to hurt, embarrass or humiliate the other and repeated behavior—with others, with the same person, and/or with the same person over time.

★ The Power of Student Body

Mobilize the masses of students who are neither victims nor bullies to take action against bullying.

Students can take action in many different ways: Refusing to watch bullying, reporting bullying incidents, initiating conflict resolution strategies, using distraction with either the bully or the victim.

The message here is to collaborate, as an educational community, while promoting a unified vision and mission for Anti-Bullying.

Claudio V. Cerullo, Ph.D. is the founder of TeachAntiBullying.com. Dr. Cerullo is the co-creator the Teach Anti Bullying software, TAB 1.0, with Vel Micro Works, Inc. As a former school principal and a higher education faculty member for over 20 years, Dr. Cerullo is focusing his efforts on reducing bullying in America. He is a presenter and the author of six children's books, two of which are on bullying, two educational videos on bullying, and one computer software application on bullying to be used in the classroom.

Listen to this chapter at HowToLearn.com/amazing-grades-audio

How To Stop Bullies in Their Tracks

It's pretty hard to concentrate on good grades when you feel threatened by bullies. This chapter, by international bullying expert, Dr. Kathy Seifert, provides steps to help you stop bullies in their tracks.

I was a great student, but not very good at games and sports as a child. That was OK for my mother and my best friend, but the bully in my class thought it was hilarious. My feet turned in when I ran. I was so embarrassed. He made fun of me any time he could. I did not tell anyone because back then, you were supposed to just "suck it up and take it". Thankfully, those days are almost gone and I want you to help us all eradicate bullying forever.

★ **There is Power in Numbers.** Under the hard exterior, bullies are often cowards. If someone more powerful deals with them, they will back down. So don't expect to deal with a bully on your own. You may need someone older at your side to tip the power scale in your direction. It is OK to ask for help. (See the Yellow ribbon project, YellowRibbon.org).

tinyurl.com/722yy5s

★ **Respect Everyone.** We are all similar yet different and it is easy to like people who are just like us. It is a little more difficult to be kind and respectful to those who are different from us. However, that is how you become a strong, happy, healthy adult in a community where everyone counts.

★ **Talk About Your Problems.** Learning to talk about problems, conflicts, and disputes is one of the keys to stopping bullying. Some schools have peer mediation, and one great program is "Operation Respect" with the song from Peter Yarrow, "Don't Laugh at Me" at DontLaugh.org

★ **Child Bullies Grow Up to Be Adult Abusers.** Bullies who are not corrected will continue to bully. Bullies grow up to be very unhappy and sometimes violent adults unless they learn to solve their problems by talking. They may end up being abusive toward their children, who then, also become bullies. Nobody wants that.

★ **Don't be a Bystander.** Students that are being bullied may be afraid or too embarrassed to try to get help. They may need someone to stand up for them and stop the bullying. If you are watching a bully, there is something called the "bystander effect" where each person watching the bullying assumes that someone else will do something to help. However, often, no one goes for help. Be the one that tells a teacher or a parent about a bullying problem.

★ **Bullying is NOT Normal.** Some people think that bullying is just a normal part of growing up. Bullying is not normal and is wrong and harmful. Many bullies come from homes where there is violence. That's what makes bullies think that violence is normal and OK. Violence is not normal and needs to be stopped by someone who is in charge of a class or a school. A great program to suggest to your school is the Olweus Bullying program at Olweus.org.

★ **Bullying is a Problem for Adults to Solve.** If you report bullying to your teacher and nothing is done, ask your parents to go to the school. Bullies don't stop unless a teacher or parent intervenes and then they must watch for retaliation against someone who reports bullying.

★ **See Something, Say Something.** (http://goo.gl/3ofOy) Most of the school shooters you hear about felt they were bullied or rejected by their peers. Sometimes bullying is just the tip of the iceberg for a much larger problem. There is no way to tell unless someone evaluates the bully and the victim to see if there are larger problems and risk of violence. Counseling can keep a school bully or victim from becoming a school shooter. Instantly report any bullying you see.

★ **Ask for Help as Many Times as You Need To And Document All Bullying.** Fighting may solve an issue for the minute, but only talking can solve the problem for the long term. Therefore, continue to ask for help until you are finally safe at school. If the teachers don't act, go to the principal, the school board and even the newspapers. Google the story on a young man named Sawyer Rosenstein. A New Jersey school district recently paid him $4.2 million for his injuries from a bully because they were wrong not to listen to him and protect him. Thus, it is important when you report a bully or being bullied that you also document everything in writing and send it to the principal.

★ **Stop Bullying Before It Gets Out of Hand.** Stopping bullying may prevent a tragedy from happening later. Let me give you an example. Phoebe Prince committed suicide after being teased and bullied by her peers in a Massachusetts school. Six students who bullied her have been charged with felonies related to her death. It is also alleged that the school did not intervene to stop the bullying of Phoebe and one other student. Schools need to take the lead to stop bullying.

★ **Cyber Bullying is Becoming More Frequent.** Share your cell phone activity and social networking sites with your parents if you see bullying taking place. Bullying is an important topic to discuss with your peers, parents and teachers and the goal is to protect everyone from bullying. Schools cannot stop it without your help too.

Kathryn Seifert, Ph.D., is a psychologist in Maryland, Executive Director of Eastern Shore Psychological Services, the founder of PreventBullyingNow.info and author of *How Children Become Violent* and *Youth Violence*. She lectures internationally, appears on CNN and FOX, and provides training on "Assessing the Risk for Violence," "Attachment Disorders," and "Attachment Violence & Assessment." Dr. Seifert also developed the CARE 2 Assessment, an instrument designed to assess the risk for violence and to determine the appropriate level and type of services that risk youth requires.

Listen to this chapter at HowToLearn.com/amazing-grades-audio

How To "Acquire" English as a Second Language

Steven Krashen and Tracy Terrell have the most significant research known about acquiring a second language. Their book, *The Natural Approach*, shows that language cannot simply be memorized in a high stress environment but must be acquired naturally, just as your first language. They call it 'language acquisition.' Their techniques help anyone learning English as a second language and enhance the quality and outcome of their learning.

How To Make Learning A Natural Process When Learning English

When you learn your first language you have a long listening period before anyone expects you to speak. During that time, you have a significant number of physical interactions such as holding and playing with objects, throwing and catching a ball, turning the pages in a book, etc. You listen to your family every day and acquire a solid receptive understanding of the language well ahead of the time you learn to express yourself.

You want your English as a second language experience to mimic your first language acquisition process as much as possible. Therefore, you will want to immerse yourself in the culture, listen and become familiar with the language as often as you can. Even though you may be in a classroom environment learning English, do everything possible to surround yourself with the English language outside of the classroom.

When you're in the classroom you will want to talk and interact with your teacher and your friends as much as possible. While doing so, have an open mind about corrections you might receive regarding your pronunciation and grammar. Make sure you respond positively both to your own attempts as well as those of those around you. Everyone is doing their best and you want to make sure that the classroom activities are cooperative and collaborative.

Using Word Definition and Picture Cards

Cards with words, pictures, definitions and sound can be very helpful. You can print them out from internet sites such as audioenglish.net, do2learning.com and 1-language.com/. Making your own cards can also give you associations or connections to words and their meaning and help you remember them easier.

More importantly than the cards themselves are using the cards in games and low stress activities that you enjoy with your friends. Create as many games as possible with words and their meaning.

Common W ords

The 1,000 most common words in any language form 80% of day-to-day used words. They are greetings, inquiries, basic information about you, names of retail items etc. Th e best people to learn these with are your friends, teachers and others around the school or university.

Reading, Writing, Listening and Speaking

Writing: As a beginner, do not write long sentences using too many connectors or conjunctions. Use simpler sentences to avoid making too many grammatical errors.

Reading: Choose books that you are interested in to read. This will help you sustain your interest for longer periods of time.

Listening: Watch and listen to programs on television and the radio as much as possible. Th e language on the news, cooking shows, in advertisements and sitcoms will help you quickly acquire new words as you will see the body language that goes along with them.

Speaking: As you learn to speak English, it is helpful in the initial stages to repeat words you hear from your teacher to acquire pronunciation and meaning of the words. If you will also role play various situations with your friends it helps you immerse yourself in the more 'physical' part of the language. Krashen and Terrell refer to this as total physical response. Topics for role play should be based on real life situations like ordering food in a restaurant, grocery shopping, eating a meal, etc. Every situation you can practice in English has something more to teach you and very soon you will find you've solidly acquired the English language.

To have another language is to possess a second soul.
–Charlemagne

Meenakshi Sriram teaches English for corporations in both mid and far eastern countries. She also teaches English to IGCSE students and also trains foreign students in ESL at the APL Global School in Chennai, India. Sriram has also been a journalist for the national newspaper in India.

Listen to this chapter at HowToLearn.com/amazing-grades-audio

How English Language Learners Manage Writing Anxiety in College

Asupportive educational environment flexible enough to meet the differing and changing needs of students is essential in a multicultural classroom.

English as a second language writers endeavor to better understand the linguistic and/or contextual gaps writing in English. However, the anxiety of not knowing English well enough to express their ideas in writing, is always present in their minds. Like anything else in life, different students deal with this obstacle in different ways. Yet, if the students are encouraged to see themselves as potential writers in English rather than struggling students, they may deal with the challenges in a more creative way.

As a second language speaker, reader and writer of English myself, I can attest to how difficult it is to attain a level of native-like proficiency in speaking, reading but particularly in writing at the high school or college level.

Students who come from all over the world to get a degree from institutions of higher education in the United States, are well aware of the pressure they have to endure in order to show that they are able to compose in English and complete the requirements of the English as a Second Language programs so that they can be admitted in regular English classes where they have to compete with native English speakers.

Although some of these students are highly educated in their countries, the overwhelming concern of not being able to express their thoughts in English that is understandable, creates a level of anxiety, which sometimes can be debilitating and may compromise the students' self-perception. Some students may pursue more basic grammar knowledge while others may think the writing topics are so difficult. In fact, they may not be equipped to deal with some writing topics because they are not fully acquainted with the American culture. In their view, though, not knowing enough grammar or not having a large English vocabulary feels like an insurmountable obstacle.

Anxiety increases not necessarily because some students do not know enough English, but because they are too focused on what they do wrong, rather than to value the wealth of creative ideas they bring from their countries.

Others, however, use their inventiveness to tackle new tasks. Their perceptions about writing in English determine their level of anxiety. Some students who have taken writing classes said the following:

"English is my Second Language, so writing is quite difficult for me. I'm afraid of making grammatical mistakes and of peoples' opinion. I need to learn more grammar before I can feel confident writing in English. I avoid writing in English as much as possible. Although writing is part of my work, I always find a way to delegate it to someone else. I'm too frightened, so I write very little in English."

Another student said, "When I was in the writing class, I felt very scared. I hated that feeling, but I wanted to continue with the class to improve myself and do better. The writing assignments were a torture, but when I got my paper with the teacher's comments and corrections, my self- confidence improved.

I began to learn from my own mistakes, which was so much better than memorizing grammatical rules. Learning to write paragraphs and essays was a nightmare for me. I couldn't do it at first because I wanted to use sophisticated vocabulary to impress my teacher, but I wrote sentences which were not very clear at all. A teacher I will never forget told me to be patient with myself, start with the basics and that I would have great potential. So, I paid careful attention to the process, and began to understand how to do it. Once I got it, I thought to myself, it's not that difficult. I just have to practice it."

A third student commented, "When I start writing in English, I get anxious when I think about grammar and vocabulary. Although I know I have to write grammatically correct in English, I think having interesting and engaging ideas is more important. After I finish my writing assignment I feel so empowered because I can now share the knowledge, ideas and concerns I bring from my country, with people from all over the world, writing in English. It wasn't easy at first, but I always ask questions in class when I don't understand something. Also I value my teachers' willingness to help me and give me feedback anytime I need. My favorite and most helpful activities in class have been when all students, including me, discuss our fear and difficulties in learning English, so we help one another making this journey more enjoyable. We want to write better in English. We learn from our mistakes. I think it is so wonderful to be able to write my ideas in two languages now."

Creating spaces where students can engage in self-reflection, share their concerns with each other and with their teachers and become comfortable with who they are as they struggle to convey their thoughts in written English, dispels their fears and lessens their anxiety. Getting amazing grades writing in English begins with having students acknowledge their infinite possibilities. Students are educated when they feel empowered.

If you talk to a man in a language he understands, that goes to his head. If you talk to him in his own language, that goes to his heart.

−Nelson Mandela

Francesca Armendaris, Ph.D. is a professor teaching English as a Second Language at Golden West College in Huntington Beach, CA. She is the author of *A Guide for English as A Second Language Writers Volume* available at tinyurl.com/7pdlljs.

Listen to this chapter at HowToLearn.com/amazing-grades-audio

How To Handle Peer Pressure and Get Higher Grades

Peer pressure is fairly common among students and deals with the evergreen issue of subtle psychological pressure you may have to face in this so-called competitive age.

The fact that students are old enough to understand that others may gossip about them, or try and get them to do things they otherwise would not, is no less daunting than when making good choices. Students experience pressure from parents, peers and teachers all asking them to conform to things that may not be consistent with who they really are. Young people are, by nature, highly vulnerable to expectations set upon them especially by their peers.

When these expectations are based on the true appreciation of the 'individual capacity' of a person, they serve as motivational elements. When pressure is applied in other ways, it can serve as a deterrent to being the best one can be.

Baha'u'llah, the Prophet Founder of The Bahai Faith – wrote: *"Every child is potentially the light of the world."* Education, right admonition and practical expectations are some tools that can educe out this 'light' hidden in each child. However, if the expectations are over demanding and beyond the 'individual capacity' of a child, they break him and such a breakage remains irreparable for his entire life. For example, if the same child who has the potential to be a great mathematician is expected to be a William Shakespeare it will be an erroneous expectation on the part of teachers, parents or friends.

Yet...students do grow up knowing that such "expectations" exist. A parent who wants their child to become a doctor or an engineer without considering the inherent talents of the child is trying to satiate some inner desire of their own through the behavior of their child. Peer pressure can also be an expression of deformed desires of envy, fear, etc. For example, a student can 'envy' or 'fear' that his friend may do better on an exam and he will be the loser. Driven by this sense of envy, he may start ridiculing his friend that in fact, it is the friend who is going to fail or that the questions will be too difficult. It stands to reason that the peer pressure is grounded in the student's subconscious mind and will weaken his confidence level, eventually leading him to perform badly if he has no conscious way to combat it.

When students understand that each individual is unique and appreciates themselves for their intrinsic value they have a system built in to handle peer pressure in a positive way. As **Bruce Lee** quoted *"I'm not in this world to live up to your expectations and you're not in this world to live up to mine."* Respecting the individuality of one's self is the first and foremost strategy to handle peer pressure to get high grades.

The friends you see everyday around at school and at your home make up your "peer group." They're sympathetic to your situation towards parents, teachers, and siblings because they're going through the same things you are. Having a peer group means that you get to hang out with people who share the same likes and dislikes as you do and give you some independence from adults. A peer group can encourage you to do good things like group study, doing projects together, prepare for a test or even play a game together. Who doesn't love hanging out with their friends but you must remember your peers can just as easily convince you to do things that you would never normally do and could potentially harm you.

One of the best strategies is to be prepared for peer pressure and ask yourself, in advance, how you will handle the situation? When you've done this, well ahead of the actual circumstance you have planned out your behavior and are not subject to the "passion" of the moment.

One of the easiest strategies to deal with difficult peer pressure is to avoid it altogether. Surround yourself with friends you trust, who have strong values, like to study and get good grades and you'll be far less likely to become a victim of peer pressure. Next time you say 'no,' you can say something like, "I've already told you I don't want to be disturbed during my study hours. I want you to stop trying to get me to change my mind." Hopefully, she or he will apologize and stop. If not, you might want to give your friend a little space. It's not worth it to hang around with people who don't treat you well or respect you and your decisions. To do the smart thing when your pals are pressuring you, look at both sides and weigh your options. Your friends may make a convincing case to skip class for example, but you need to ask yourself if it is really worth the consequences in the end.

One very important element in handling peer pressure is to realize that what you do may affect someone else in ways you never thought possible. You actually have the capacity to be a role model and an inspiration to someone else and not even realize it. Being assertive and honest means doing what you want to do, not what someone else wants you to. Your your peers will look up to you, rather than give you a hard time if you express your own opinions. There are several ways to get out of a sticky situation. Tell the person no and remain firm on your decision. If it continues, simply walk away.

While this sounds easy reading here in this book, but it may not actually feel as easy at the time it actually happens. It's best to know ahead of time what your values and beliefs are and express them often to friends and peers. If they know where you stand, they are less likely to pressure you to join in, and may even feel compelled to model your positive example.

It can be often be hard to go against the grain and resist peer pressure. The best advice is to firmly believe in yourself. Others cannot belittle your value if you hold yourself in high esteem. Peer pressure cannot make you less than you are if you don't give your friends or family permission to do this. This is the very strongest defense you have. You don't have to give anyone permission to make you feel badly or do something you know you should not do. My best advice is to be the best you can be and keep yourself around others who have the same values.

Children are influenced by their friends, just as adults are. That influence can be helpful or harmful. It can help children do better in school...or cause real problems. The good news is that by following a few simple tips, parents can help children deal with peer pressure—and even make it a positive influence in their lives.

Few Tips for Parents

- ★ Help your child develop self-confidence. Students who feel good about themselves are less likely to give in to pressure from others.
- ★ Encourage your child to take part in co-curricular activities at school.
- ★ Listen to your child. Your willingness to listen and not just lecture will show your child that you respect his opinions.
- ★ Spend Quality time with your children during their Examination days. Be there for them when they need you.
- ★ Encourage your child not to fall in the trap of wrong peer pressure. One of the best ways to deal with, handle, and just avoid peer pressure is to stay away from it. You child can do this by choosing who they decide to hang out with - know who their true friends are. Tell them not to hang out with the "cool group" if they do drugs or pressure your child to make bad decisions.
- ★ True friends are a good group of students who will help your child make the right choices.
- ★ Get to know your child's friends. See who they hang out with .
- ★ Turn peer pressure into positive pressure. Encourage your child to befriend those students with positive behavior and good grades.

Students if you follow these helpful tips on how to handle and even avoid peer pressure at school, you will find yourself staying out of bad situations and trouble. Sometimes the most important part of saying no to peer pressure is simply standing up for who you are and what you believe in. Though dealing with and avoiding peer pressure, especially in school, is not easy, you will thank yourself in the future when you look back and know that you made the right decision and see the good grades you achieved in life by handling Peer Pressure.

Tina Olyai, M.S. is the award-winnng Founder Director of Little Angels High School in Mahadji Nagar, India. She has been honored as an outstanding and visionary educator and has launched numerous empowerment programs for youth. She regularly appears in the media for her remarkable innovations in education and for more information visit: lahs.org.

Listen to this chapter at HowToLearn.com/amazing-grades-audio

Feeling Depressed or Anxious? Here are Tips Which May Help

Before you read this chapter, be advised that it is not intended to diagnose or treat any symptoms you have. If you experience feelings noted in this chapter, consult your healthcare provider. Two common mental health issues that can interfere in schoolwork and success in learning are depression and anxiety. Both of these can be identified by an awareness of symptoms.

What is depression?

Often people connect sadness with depression. Clinical depression is more than feeling occasionally down in the dumps or sad. It is often referred to a whole body illness because it affects so many parts of a persons functioning. It affects: sleep, eating, feelings, thoughts, energy level, motivation, ability to concentrate/focus, ability to enjoy activities that you enjoyed in the past.

How is depression diagnosed?

There are no special blood tests to diagnose depression. Diagnosis is made through assessment of symptoms, severity of symptoms and duration of symptoms. Nine areas of functioning are assessed and people who are diagnosed with depression have a minimum of four of them for two weeks or longer. Here is a summation of symptoms to begin a depression assessment:

★ Appetite - disturbance in normal pattern, eating too much, not eating at all, unexplained weight loss not due to a medical condition.
★ Sleep - change/disturbance in normal pattern, sleeping too much or difficulty falling or staying asleep.
★ Mood/feelings - persistent sadness, anxiety, irritability, numbness, or a combination of any of these.
★ Speed - your body may feel sluggish, lethargic or sped up. Your thoughts may also be affected in a similar way.
★ Self-worth - feelings of worthlessness, helplessness, persistent guilt, negativity in thought patterns.
★ Perspective on life - feelings of hopelessness, pessimism towards the future, thoughts of suicide or preoccupation with death.
★ Focus/concentration/memory - difficulty thinking clearly, staying on topic while reading or studying, trouble making clear decisions or combination of above.
★ Energy level - feelings of restlessness or frequently low energy/fatigue.
★ Loss of interest/motivation - decreased interest in activities, people, things that used to bring happiness or pleasure; decreased motivation in daily tasks, less interest in sex.

Causes of Depression:

The most common cause is stress however many other causes are listed in the DSM IV manual. Stress can be defined as an emotional overload or a series of taxing events. This overload eventually depletes the neurotransmitters (chemical messengers) that are critical for cells to communicate with each other in the brain. Genetics also play a role in being predisposed to depression. Sometimes stress is not a contributing factor. The changes in brain functioning may be related to hormonal shifts, medical conditions, seasonal changes or side effects of medications. Chronic or serious medical/health conditions frequently contribute to making the brain more susceptible to imbalance.

Anxiety

Anxiety is a state of uneasiness and apprehension usually accompanied by a cluster of physical symptoms. These include:

Physical: nervousness, dizziness, increased heart rate, shortness of breath, clammy hands, muscle tension, nausea, lump in throat, choking or smothering sensation, faintness, sweating, shaking/trembling.
Thoughts: "I am going to die", " I am losing control", "I'm going crazy", "This will never go away", "I'm having a heart attack", "I can't cope with this", "I'm going to faint", "I'm making a fool of myself ",

"Something terrible is going to happen".

Feelings: terror, fear, worry, nervousness, shame, irritability, humiliation, vulnerability, embarrassment or weakness.

Behaviors: agitation, restlessness, distractibility, inability to concentrate, pacing or fidgeting, avoidance, repetitive behaviors.

Causes:

Most people experience mild/moderate anxiety throughout their life. These symptoms can heighten your ability to focus your attention, energy and motivation. However, overwhelming severe anxiety that interferes with daily life/functioning is not normal. Many external factors can contribute to anxiety:

- ★ An overload of stress from work/school
- ★ Stress in personal relationship
- ★ Financial pressure
- ★ Emotional trauma - death of a loved one
- ★ Medical illnesses i.e., stroke, heart attack or hypoglycemia
- ★ Use of illicit drugs i.e., cocaine, crystal meth
- ★ Excessive use of caffeine
- ★ Stress from chronic or acute medical illness
- ★ Medication side effects

A mental or physical condition, the effects of drugs or a combination of these can cause anxiety. Sometimes the cause is unknown, some say they have felt anxious/nervous their whole life. Anxiety can occur at any age.

Types of Anxiety include:

1. Generalized Anxiety Disorder: Often experienced as daily symptoms of persistent anxiety in a variety of situations that does not go away.

2. Panic Disorder: Episodes of intense terror or panic, which seems to "come out of the blue". During a panic attack many people experience extreme body sensations/symptoms. Despite the "attack" being brief in time and lasting only a few minutes it creates a dread and worry about the next attack.

3. Phobia: Attacks are associated with specific situations or objects. This results in a tendency to avoid this situation thinking it will be triggered again.

4. Obsessive-Compulsive Disorder: Obsessions include recurrent distressing thoughts, images or impulses that create extreme anxiety. Compulsions include routines or rituals a person repeats to reduce anxiety. Most commonly washing, checking or ordering things. If these symptoms are a source of stress or significantly interfere with functioning, help from a mental health professional is often needed.

5. Post Traumatic Stress Disorder (PTSD): PTSD patients have a history of feeling helpless based on a traumatic life event i.e., rape, war, kidnapping, serious accident, robbery. Common symptoms include: repetition of the event over and over again, feeling numb, ongoing low level of anxiety, nightmares, panic attacks, exaggerated startle responses, difficulty falling or staying asleep.

Treatment:

You will want to seek out a mental health professional to fully assess symptoms and assist in developing an appropriate treatment plan. Often, treatment plans include a combination of the following: regular exercise; cognitive/behavioral treatment; medication; relaxation/meditation practice; psychotherapy, counseling; planning and following through with enjoyable activities on a regular basis. Once identified both depression and anxiety are treatable conditions. The key is often pushing past feelings of personal failure or weakness or stigma of a mental health condition. Rather, it's best to see them as heath conditions that can be treated over a period of time. Skills are taught to cope more effectively with symptoms so they do not interfere in having a successful productive life.

Robin J. Kastner, ACSW, LCSW is a therapist in an outpatient psychiatric clinic providing individual and group therapy. She also teaches a class on overcoming depression. Kastner is licensed to practice in Michigan and California and has worked for over 25 years with adolescents and families.

Note: No portion of this chapter is intended to diagnose or treat depression or anxiety. Please contact your health care provider for more information or help if needed.

Listen to this chapter at HowToLearn.com/amazing-grades-audio

How To Inspire Students to Believe They Can Achieve Their Goals and Dreams

Motivation is one of the most important, most influential, and most neglected aspects of a teacher's lesson plans. We take the time to plan homework assignments, instructional activities, and assessments of all types, but we seldom write down what we intend to do to motivate our students to want to do their work—and want to do it well.

When you take the time to consider it carefully, it is odd that we seldom take time for one of the most vital aspects of successful instruction. No lesson, no matter how beautifully planned and organized can succeed if our students simply choose not to do it. The short-term result of this lack of motivation is harsh. Instead of a pleasant hum of engagement, students busy themselves in unproductive and destructive ways. The long-term result is even more heart-breaking. Adults who can't read, write, or function successfully in our increasingly complex society lead miserable and desperate lives that are a drain on national resources.

Research tells us what practicing teachers have known for years: there is no magic bullet, no one quick fix that will transform our students from uncaring children into avid scholars. Instead, we use as many techniques, strategies, and activities as we can to appeal to our students as often as we can. Of all of these options, though, there is one that is the most important. It is the one that is the foundation of everything that we do as teachers: we must never lose faith in our students' ability to succeed.

Although most teachers are aware of their responsibility to serve as counselors and advocates, we tend to underestimate the effect that we can have on our students because we work in a formidable flux of constant decisions, difficult demands, and hard-to-manage problems. With all of these facing us as soon as the bell rings, it's not always easy to remember that our attitude about our students can really change everything.

You have enormous power over the lives of your students. In fact, you can make the children in your classroom into successful students or you can make those same children into failures. You constantly communicate your beliefs in many subtle ways such as though your body language, the assignments you make, and how much time you spend with individual students. If you act with a calm assurance that conveys your belief that the students in your class are capable of good behavior and academic accomplishments then your students are highly likely to behave well and strive for success. You will be able to inspire them to dream big and then to work hard to achieve those big dreams.

If you doubt this power, consider the alternative. Why would students struggle to learn, to behave, to come to school without a caring adult who appears glad to see them succeed? For some students, a teacher is their only lifeline.

How can you use your belief in your students to inspire them to be the very best they can be? How can you help them reach their dreams? Every day, you transmit your belief in the abilities of your students in a variety of different ways. Here are just a few of the most basic ones that good teachers use every day:

★ Start each unit of study with assignments that students can achieve with ease. Success builds upon itself. When students see that they can accomplish what you ask of them, they will want to continue that success. After students realize that they can accomplish the tasks you require of them, their willingness to persist as the work grows more difficult will improve. They will work harder for longer periods if they know they will be successful.

★ Celebrate often with your students. After all, their successes are your successes. You do not have to dedicate lots of time to formal celebrations. A simple posting or display of good news, a signal that allows classmates to acknowledge each other in positive ways, or a quiet word with individual students will all encourage them to keep trying.

★   Reward effort as well as achievement. It is important to make sure your students see the link between success and effort.

★   Be as consistent and as fair as you possibly can. Students of all ages are quick to react negatively when they detect even a small hint of suspected unfairness. They will shut down quickly when this happens. Consistency and fairness will make it easier for you to build a relationship of mutual trust that will make sure students stay focused on the big picture—their own successful futures.

★   At the end of class ask students to share what they have learned. Often, they are not aware of how much they have really actually achieved until they have the opportunity to reflect.

★   We all know that open-ended questions and assignments can serve as sparks to deepen critical thinking skills. Open-ended questions and assignments are a respectful way to demonstrate your faith in your students' ability to tackle tough work.

★   Teach your students how to handle the failures that everyone experiences from time to time. Help them understand that they can learn from their mistakes as well as from their successes.

★   Tell your students about your confidence in their ability to succeed. You just can't say it too loudly or too often. Tell them over and over. When they start believing what you say about them, then they will start believing in themselves.

Believe you can and you're halfway there.
- Theodore Roosevelt

 Julia Thompson is the author of *Discipline Survival Guide for the Secondary Teacher, The First-Year Teacher's Survival Guide,* and T*he First-Year Teacher's Checklist.* She is also the founder of juliagthompson.com, juliagthompson. blogspot.com and has been a teacher for more than 30 years. You can also follow her on Twitter at TeacherAdvice@Twitter.com.

Listen to this chapter at HowToLearn.com/amazing-grades-audio

How To Create an Emotionally Intelligent Classroom

There can be no doubt that students learn most effectively and are most likely to achieve their potential within an environment in which they can thrive. An emotionally intelligent (EQ) classroom is just such an environment and as such should be the aspiration of all educators no matter what the grade level.

"OK, I get that", you say to yourself, but how do we go about it? What can we do specifically? And what happens in an EQ class anyway? Well, the first thing that happens is that the teacher accepts that his/her own behavior is the most significant. What we model establishes the culture in our class so it is vital that the way we manage our class reflects the qualities of EQ and helps meet the innate needs of students. Here is an overview of those key emotional needs and some strategies for meeting them:

A Sense of Achievement:

Students need to feel successful. They need to feel they are making progress and the best way to do this is to give regular and frequent feedback on their learning. The mantra is "catch them being successful" as often as possible.

- ★ Establish a ratio of around 5:1 - positive comments : negative ones
- ★ Focus on effort more than being clever or smart. This allows them be in control over their progress and reinforces that effort and attitude take you further than just being smart. *"The effort you put into that assignment has earned you a great grade Jake"*
- ★ Use more feedback than praise. *"This table has shared the resources, allocated jobs and have planned their presentation. Great job!"* rather than, *"Great job you guys at this table"*. The more you emphasize what they are doing, the more you boost self esteem.

A Sense of Autonomy:

Nobody really likes getting bossed around right? We all prefer when we feel we are in charge of things. Give students as many opportunities for making choices and in this way help them develop responsibility for their success. Also make sure they understand that actions have consequences.

- ★ Use the language of choice in positive and negative contexts.

  "If you choose not to complete your work in class Tony, you'll be deciding to stay back at recess and do it then. Is that what you want? You decide." "That picture looks great Ruben. Should we display it in class or the corridor? You decide." "You can decide whether you work on the questions first or the diagrams. It's your call."

A Sense of Security:

It's pretty obvious that your students cannot learn if they don't feel safe. The presence of anxiety and stress cause us to have a very narrow, one dimensional view of the world. Bullying is just one example of this.

Neurologically, stress inhibits our ability to think clearly and rationally and to hold wider and alternative perspectives. And it will definitely inhibit the process of risk taking which in essence is exactly what the process of learning is – doing stuff you haven't done before and maybe getting it wrong.

- ★ Make it an overt part of your classroom rights to protect safety – both physical and psychological. Explain, use role play, drama, art work, integrate it into the curriculum with choosing stories, human rights issues etc to emphasize why it is important. And make it part of whole school policy.

★ Be OK with getting things wrong yourself. Model the safe thinking that goes with it. Make getting it wrong an integral part of the learning process.

★ In other words it's a phase we all go through. No one learned to ride a bike first time!

★ Stay calm! Shouting and using negative language or showing students up in front of the class is an absolutely certain way to create anxiety and fear.

★ Have fun! Sharing fun activities, using humor appropriately and responding spontaneously to events sometimes all help to make the classroom a safe and enjoyable place to be.

A Sense of Belonging:

Students need to feel part of their class – to have an emotional connection to their teacher and other students in order to feel most comfortable. There is a strong overlap with the sense of security here.

★ Learn names as quickly as possible and use them with respect. When correcting students, ensure you make a distinction between them and their behavior.

★ Ensure they play a part in class decisions wherever appropriate

★ Encourage feedback *"On a scale of 0 – 10, how comfortable do you feel about being in this class?*

★ *What things would allow your score to be just a little higher?"*

★ Use positive language as a default. *"I need you to get back to work now Kerry"* rather than *"Stop goofing around when you should be working!"* *"Remember to put these papers on my desk before you go out to lunch"* rather than *"Don't forget to hand in your work"*

★ Discover their interests and hobbies and be curious about them. People like to be considered knowledgeable.

★ Talk about "our" classroom and how "we" do things.

★ Keep parents and guardians informed. Send letters and make calls home about their progress (and not just when there is a concern). Let parents know about the qualities you see in their child that you admire – respectful; sense of humor; leadership; persistence etc.

A Sense of Hope and Optimism Using Reframing:

Life in the classroom has its challenges and not everything will always go smoothly. Helping students remain optimistic that things can get even better and getting them to make sense of these challenges in ways that maintain hope and resilience is vital. One huge skill in this area is "reframing" or creating more empowering perspectives. A few examples are:

STUDENT: *"I can't ever do equations."* TEACHER: *"Sometimes they can be a little confusing at first. Let me show a cool way of working with them."* Adding the words "sometimes" and "a little confusing at first" is more empowering that "can't ever" and respectfully challenges the limiting beliefs. Reframing things usually involves one of the following: Making it a phase or a stage – yet, so far, up until now; diluting strong language – never becomes sometimes, always becomes occasionally.

Andy Vass is the author of *The Behaviour Management Pocketbook*, along with six other books and was described in the Times newspaper as the "foremost presenter on behavior in the UK." He is a coach, author and trainer specializing in developing emotionally intelligent workplaces. Find out more at andyvass.net

Listen to this chapter at HowToLearn.com/amazing-grades-audio

The Tools of Success for Every Teacher

What amazes me time after time, year after year, in dealing with my students, is that a lot of them really don't know how to achieve success. School should be a great place to teach children the methods to achieve success.

One concept that I introduce very early are the simple, yet very effective principles of goal setting. Some students in the early grades have heard about the importance of goals. By their high school years, virtually all students have heard about the need to set goals. Few students however, are taught how to achieve their goals.

One day my principal walked into my class as I was teaching about goal setting. I had just asked my class the question, "How can you eat an elephant?" After a long pause I asked my principal and he answered, "One bite at a time!" After another long pause, my students start to get it. At that point, I elaborated that the statement was accurate no matter how huge the goal may be.

A journey of a thousand miles, begins with the first step it is said. At this point that I tell students that everything is incremental. I give them the example of me and my weight. I didn't put on 20 extra pounds all at once. Over the years, I exercised less and less and ate a bit more and more until I started to put on an extra pound (or two) a year. Over 20 years, those pounds add up! Since it took me 20 years to gain the extra weight, I'm not going to lose it all at once.

How To Set Goals

Most goals are reached one step at a time. The most important thing is to get started. I made a conscious effort a number of years ago, to get back into shape and exercise. Since I'm often too tired to exercise before and after school, I started to exercise with my students by running and doing stretches with them during our physical education classes. I not only show students how goal setting works in theory, but also in practice.

Early in the year, I distribute a goal-setting handout to the students. I also make a transparency for the overhead. Then I explain each point to the students.

When I first started this practical goal-setting exercise with my students three years ago, my goal was to run 5 minutes non-stop by the end of the school year in June. That was no easy task. I tried all summer, before school started to get into shape by running. For some reason, although I ran all the time in high school and partly throughout university, I couldn't run more than one and a half minutes! For some time, I just couldn't break that barrier. So, I went "public." After telling my students my goal, writing it down, then posting it publicly for all to see, I was determined to show my students how to implement a goal.

I am happy to write, that before the year was over I did achieve the goal of running 5 minutes without stopping. The next year, I doubled the goal to 10 minutes and showed those students how to achieve their goals while I modeled how I achieve mine. Again, I succeeded. Flush with success and confidence, the following year, I doubled the goal to 20 minutes. That was definitely a year long goal, which I succeeded in achieving. The following year, I continued with the goal increasing it to 30 minutes. That goal was also achieved. Next year, I'm looking at doing 60 minutes!

I tell students that their goals don't need to be school goals. Over the years, their goals have included doing more reading, to becoming a better soccer goalie, getting an advanced yellow belt in karate, earning more "I Did It Awards", scoring a goal in hockey, and watching less T.V. Some students duplicated my goal of running. Knowing these students' goals and what's important to them, gives teachers a great opportunity to help students to connect them to success. If I know that a student is looking for a babysitting job and I know parents who are looking for a babysitter, I can connect them. It's the same for students looking for jobs or places on the school team. If I know of someone who can help them, I will connect them. This approach also shows students the power of networking and getting to know other people. Each of us has just 86, 400 seconds every day to use. How we use them determines our success.

If you want to build a ship, don't drum up people to collect wood and assign them asks and work, but rather teach them to long for the endless immensity of the sea.

- Antoine Saint-Exupery

Don't sell the steak, sell the sizzle.

- Dale Carnegie

Instruction does much, but encouragement does everything.

-Johann Wolfgang Von Goethe

Marjan Glavac, M.A. is an award-winning teacher, the best selling author of four books, a speaker and classroom teacher with over 29 years of teaching experience. His books are: *How To Make A Difference: Inspiring Students To Do Their Best; The Busy Educator's Guide To The World Wide Web; How To Make A Difference: Inspiring Students To Do Their Best: Teaching Is... Moments That Inspire And Motivate Teachers To Make A Difference*, and he is the co-author of *How To Thrive and Survive In Your Classroom*. For more visit TheBusyEducator.com and TeachingIs.com

Listen to this chapter at HowToLearn.com/amazing-grades-audio

Two Simple Ways to Get Students Interested and Involved in Lessons

Just imagine your formerly bored and disinterested students coming to your lessons with broad smiles, actually *wanting* to be in the classroom. Imagine not having to bribe or coerce them into action and instead having a happy, positive start to lessons in which they are eager to learn new concepts. Just imagine them *radiating* enthusiasm about the activities on offer. How enjoyable would teaching be if you knew how to *invite* the undivided attention of your students instead of having to demand or force it?

A pipe dream, you say? Well it doesn't have to be. All it takes is a highly engaging and appealing lesson which encourages students to 'buy-in' to the topic. Here are two types of activities you can use to pique students' interest and get them raring to go and ready to learn.

1. Use curiosity.

Curiosity has tremendous motivational power. It represents an intense, passion-driven thirst for information, a state which can't possibly be created with traditional teacher motivators like rewards and punishments, and to which *all* your students will respond. It's human nature and your students will want more of your lessons. My inbox is bursting with emails from teachers telling me how their classrooms have been transformed by the various applications of 'curiosity'. They write to tell me how much their students *love* their lessons, how much *fun* they have, and how participation and interest in learning have improved dramatically. With some creativity, when you bring curiosity to the teaching process you can have students literally *begging* to take part in your lesson.

So what can you do to get your students curious? The easiest way is to just make an unexpected change. Here's a great example:

Some time ago I sat in as observer on a Year 7 science lesson. The main task was a simple information retrieval exercise. Students arrived as normal expecting to find the usual cold, clinical science lab. What they saw was a room in darkness save for the orange glow of an up light in one corner, and the strains of a Jean-Michel Jarre track wafting round the gloom. The mood was set perfectly and as the bemused students crept into the room the teacher handed them each a nicely designed 'Star Ranger Fact Card' on which to record details about planets in the solar system, and a 'Mission Sheet' explaining that they would find these answers at different locations around the room under a poster of each planet. The same results could have been achieved of course by leaving the strip lights on and asking the students to 'fill in a table using the text book' - but you don't have to be an Einstein to know which approach the students preferred. Instant enthusiasm!

2. Use the right type of questions.

Most teachers ask questions at the start of lessons to either introduce a new topic or gauge students' prior knowledge, but invariably these questions do little to stimulate student interest. Let's say the lesson topic is 'the circulatory system'. The opening question might be: *"How many of you can explain what a blood vessel is?"*

This approach is unlikely to create a flood of student interaction because the teacher is relying on *volunteers* - those students who are *always* eager to take part in lessons. To get the *non*-volunteers taking part you have to have a question that they can *relate* to, something connected to their interests or their experiences. Think about it: why would these students even care about blood vessels? Where is the relevance to real life? See if you can spot the difference between the following styles of question:

A) Who can tell me how blood gets round the body?
B) Who knows what a blood vessel is?
C) Can anyone tell me what a blood capillary is?
D) When did you last cut your finger badly?

A) Give me five differences between Macbeth's character before and after he kills Duncan.
B) How does Macbeth change after he kills Duncan?
C) What words would you use to describe Macbeth at the start of the play?
D) When was the last time you did something really terrible that you later regretted?

Can you see why 'D' in both cases would be far more likely to get the non-volunteers listening and switched on? Those questions hook them by giving them opportunity to think about events that are *relevant* to them or have had a direct effect on them.

I know what you're thinking. Yes, it's all very well asking a question about their real life but how are we supposed to move on to the lesson focus? Well, once we've 'hooked' them, they'll naturally *want* to talk. Suddenly you're met with a forest of hands in the air, and an eager crowd of students attached to them, desperate to share their personal stories. It's no longer about 'how do I get them involved?' It's about tempering their enthusiasm and steering them towards the lesson topic.
Follow-up questions might go something like this:

When did you last cut your finger badly?
How long did it bleed for?
How did you stop the bleeding?
Do you think it would it have stopped if you had just left it?
Where does the blood come from and how does it get to the cut?

Well done - you've just explained what a blood vessel is.

For more ideas like this to motivate your students and get them engaged in lessons visit www.lesson-ology.com

Rob Plevin, B.Sc (Hons), PGCE in Secondary Science, is a former principal (deputy head teacher) and relentless optimist with the practical experience to help teachers in today's toughest classrooms.

He now runs the websites Behaviourneeds.com, Lesson-ology.com and Classroomexpert.com which provide teachers with videos and downloadable resources to help with classroom management and student motivation.

Listen to this chapter at HowToLearn.com/amazing-grades-audio

How To Foster Achieving Resilient Students

Never doubt that a small group of thoughtful, committed people can change the world. Indeed, it's the only thing that ever has.
- Margaret Mead, Culture and Commitment, 1978

As teachers, we change the world every day, one student at a time! In our classrooms we have the opportunity to create a coherent environment, a climate so potent that it can override almost everything else in the lives of our students. Students today experience so many risks in the world including poverty, crime, racism, lack of healthcare, bullying, divorce, etc.

Think for a minute about one of your students who is highly successful in spite of these challenges. What has helped him or her succeed in your classroom? Your student has developed something called RESILIENCY.

Resilient students, stated simply, work well, love well, play well and expect well. They spring back despite risks. They are high performers in school and believe in themselves and their capacities! Resiliency researchers like Emmy Werner, Michael Rutter, Norman Garmesy, and Bonnie Bernard inform us, that not only do we have the potential to be that one significant adult who can make a difference in a student's life, but that we can build this resiliency in our classrooms and school environments.

What, then, as teachers, can we do to foster high achieving resilient students? What kinds of things can we reflect upon regarding our practice? I hope what follows will make a difference for both YOU and your students! Let's examine the profile of a resilient student in these three areas of practice.

★   **Provide Opportunities for Meaningful Participation**
★   **Set and Communicate High Expectations**
★   **Provide Care and Support**

Provide Opportunities for Meaningful Participation

1. A resilient student participates in helping others through cooperative learning, service learning, peer helping, and other avenues. Hundreds of studies on cooperative learning verify that academic success is created through properly facilitated team learning groups. In the "real world," a team approach is widely used in business and other organizations. Let's reflect here and ask some helpful questions. As a teacher how are you:

★   limiting your lecture time for more time to facilitate cooperative group learning?
★   teaching students the skills they need to work collaboratively? Make no assumptions that students know how to collaborate! This is a skill set. Teach them!

2. A resilient student believes his voice is heard in classroom and school decisions. We know that classrooms are to be inclusive. All voices are to be heard and, as we know, it's ok to agree to disagree. As a teacher how have you:

★   created a learning environment where every voice is heard, and respected?
★   promoted active listening skills? Again, these are skills to be learned.

3. A resilient student exhibits a sense of self-efficacy or confidence in taking on new challenges. In a safe, inclusive environment students feel free to take risks. As a teacher how do you:

★   provide students with a variety of learning challenges?
★   foster an "I can do it" attitude of confidence in your learners?
★   delegate empowering responsibility and leadership to students?

Setting and Communicating High Expectations

4. A resilient student believes that positive goals can be accomplished. In the age of standards and accountability, we know how important goal setting is. We live it! We set goals and establish learning objectives. How, then, do we assist our students in setting their short and long term goals? Let's reflect. As a teacher how do you:

★ establish and communicate clear expectations for both academic and behavioral performance? Do you include the "why" in your expectations?

★ assist your students in regular goal setting?

★ celebrate student success? This ranges from providing ongoing specific positive reinforcement to showcasing student work, to a class or school-wide celebration! When goals are reached, celebrate!

5. A resilient student encourages self and others to do "the best possible." Let's reflect upon how you foster this resilient quality in your teaching. High performance and doing our best go hand in hand. Here is where I believe you "reap what you sow" in terms of the kind of learning environment you have built. Time to celebrate YOU and YOUR positive learning environment!

Provide Care and Support

6. A resilient student feels that school is a caring place. Let's do some time travel! Looking back... who were your most memorable teachers? What do you remember about them and their teaching? Did they inspire you to achieve? Time, once again to reflect. As a teacher how do you:

★ demonstrate to students that they matter and that you care?

★ advocate for your students. This, to me, is part of our "job description!"

★ establish mutual trust?

★ continue to be a consistent and positive role model?

7. A resilient student has a sense of belonging. This is so important according to resiliency research! Reflect on what you do to:

★ know your students?

★ create a learning environment in which all students experience a sense of belonging?

★ establish community agreements and uphold them with consistency?

8. A resilient student experiences school as a community. We know that in campuses, large or small this takes conscious work on the part of all community members! What do you and your school do to:

★ create a cohesive community for students?

★ inspire student leadership and school-wide opportunities for participation?

★ contribute to the greater community?

9. A resilient student sees many ways to be recognized and rewarded. Too often students hear about what they have done wrong as opposed to what they contribute! I believe we can change this, one classroom and one school at a time! Reflect on what you are doing and what more you might do to:

★ recognize and celebrate student achievement?

★ celebrate student accomplishments and contributions?

★ let students know that what they do matters?

Let's build high performing students through continuing to reflect on the resiliency characteristics we've just explored. Remember, we have the power to build resiliency in our students and in our learning environments through our practice and who we are as caring professionals!

Ellen Jones, M.A. is a professor at California State University, San Francisco. She has taught at the school, district, county, state, and collegiate level.

Listen to this chapter at: HowToLearn.com/amazing-grades-audio 🔊

15 Ways to Become a More Effective Teacher

Here are several ideas that you may want to try using in your own classroom. They have made my life easier, and I am sure they will do the same for you as well! One of the best things you can do as a teacher is "arm" yourself with knowledge that will help you show your students how to get better grades, improve your classroom management skills, teach you how to prevent and deal with behavior problems, and help you plan lessons more effectively. Have a look at the rest of the suggestions below:

1. Create an atmosphere of mutual respect - coach a team, support an activity, lead a club, get involved with students in your school, show them that you care about things that they care about.

2. Have a sense of humor - it really makes a big difference for you and the students! Smile and interact with students... yes, even when some students challenge you.

3. Plan effective lessons - Make your lessons interesting, meaningful, and have them connect to personal experiences of students in your class. Help them link what you teach to what they already know. It will make learning and understanding happen, and students are likely to look forward to what you are going to do and say next!

4. Communicate with parents regularly - keep in mind that it is all about helping the student grow and learn. During interviews and contacts with parents, avoid unnecessary criticism and choose your words carefully. Point out what they can do before you tell them what they can't.

5. Offer praise - look for evidence of success and positive, constructive behavior...acknowledge it and praise it. Give out certificates, impromptu parties, brag about students, etc.

6. Incorporate hands-on activities - also use multimedia, show relevant films and videos that increase understanding of the curriculum. Note that even the book you're reading makes use of the latest technology so students have visual, auditory and kinesthetic (hands-on) strategies.

7. Make handouts and tests visually attractive - it maintains interest and sends a message that you care.

8. Keep your classroom, including own desk, clean, uncluttered and well organized. This will promote a similar organizational mindset among the students. Clean and organized classroom makes students feel you are in control and know what you are doing.

9. Exude confidence - in your body language, when you speak, and make discipline decisions etc., hesitant teachers invite behavior issues and possibly disrespect.

10. Plan a clear and effective discipline policy - before the first day of classes! This will help you know exactly what to do when things don't go the way you expect them to go. It will help avoid frustration and make quick and decisive decisions about behavior problems in the classroom. Present yourself as someone who handles classroom situations promptly and fairly.

11. Discuss your discipline policy and plans with administration - this will avoid unwanted surprises and give you appropriate support when you need it.

12. Take courses, buy resources, and go to conferences that teach you effective classroom management skills. This was always a priority for me, and I believe that it should also be in the plans of most other educators.

13. Use summer vacation to rest, but also prepare for the upcoming school year. Take courses, read professional material, plan future lessons and units, reflect on the previous year, plan improvements to your program, and organize yourself for the following academic year. This will give you a good start and the needed confidence for months to come.

14. Seek advice, share resources, and team up with other teachers to find ways to save time in the classroom. Sharing units, lessons plans, and receiving tips and advice, always help save time.

15. Make yourself available after classes or after school to assist students, answer questions, clarify, and encourage. Regularly remind and invite after-school visits, as some students may be a bit shy to ask questions in class.

You can't always change your situation, but you can always change your attitude
- Larry Hargraves

Stevan Krajnjan, B.A. B.Ed, OCT is author and founder of TimeSaversForTeachers.com and TeacherReportCardComments.com. Krajnjan received the Exceptional Teacher Award by The Learning Disabilities Association of Mississauga and North Peel in recognition for outstanding work with children who have learning disabilities. He was also inducted into the sports hall of fame in the city of Brampton and lives in Canada.

Listen to this chapter at HowToLearn.com/amazing-grades-audio

Engage, Engage, Engage

Given that technology in education seems to place less emphasis on face to face communication, it is timely to reflect on engaging students in learning. I believe that engaging the hearts and minds of students allows them to retain more without even recognizing that this process has occurred. Passion in teaching becomes the driving force in a better education.

Passion: Anthony J. D'Angelo says, *"Develop a passion for learning. If you do, you will never cease to grow."*

In my own school and university experience I remember both the disappointment and the frustration my classmates and I felt when faced with a teacher/lecturer, with brilliant academic credentials, who could not convey a passion for the subject or bring it to life in the classroom.

As a result, whenever I prepare to lecture I always look first at the subject and determine what level of passion I can bring to the delivery. My experience with my students fuels my passion in the classroom. This passion enabled me to bring the academic learning to life. Bringing passion into the classroom can be a powerful tool and one that must be tempered within the time constraints of the lesson but none the less is a critical ingredient in delivering a learning, growth inducing lesson.

The most humbling experience I have had as an educator came during this teaching assignment. One of the client groups I had during this time were final year high school students. I taught the mental health workshops to about 4000 students a year across numerous locations. Each month I would attend the organizations board meetings in the city. On one of these occasions, as we were waiting to start the meeting, a young woman entered the meeting and waved at me smiling broadly.

I did not recognize her and assumed that she was a new member of staff. During the meeting she was introduced as a student on placement. During refreshments, after the meeting, the young woman approached me and said 'I know you don't remember me but I just wanted to say thank you'. Puzzled I inquired why. Apparently, some years earlier I had delivered the mental health education package in her high school and she had been inspired to choose a career in mental health. This experience has become my most powerful motivation tool as an educator. It reminds me every day to leave my personal headspace at the door of the classroom and to remember that a passionate delivery has the power to change people's lives including my own.

Enthusiasm: Be enthusiastic people! Ralph Waldo Emerson said, *"Nothing is ever achieved without enthusiasm."* Irrelevant of what the subject matter is there is no excuse for a lack of enthusiasm. While working as sessional staff, on a theory based university unit, I made an effort to provide the students with current real world scenarios often drawn from my own experience. The students would then be challenged to apply theory, of their choice, to that scenario.

These challenges often generated lots of discussion in relation to varying opinion on what theory was the best fit. These discussions lead to enthusiastic deconstruction of the theories and lively debate. The proof of the value of this approach was the use of these deconstructions in exam questions relating to the theories. The in- class enthusiastic debate had cemented the elements of theory in their minds. When I have had the pleasure of bumping into some of these former students, they often, not only remembered these lively discussions, they referred to them with affection.

Curiosity: To open a door to a sense of curiosity in the mind of a student is a powerful tool. Galileo said, *"You cannot teach anybody anything. You can only help them discover it within themselves."* It is not our role to provide everything a student needs to know. It is our role to encourage, challenge, inspire and tempt them to search out answers for themselves. Each individual in the classroom will have a mind filled with preconceived notions in relation to the subject you are teaching. Some of what we say in class will confront and challenge these preconceptions.

Do not be afraid to acknowledge different points of view on the subject. Even controversial opinions have their place as tools in a learning environment. Challenge the students to seek out reputable research to support their varied arguments. Often the greatest learning experience can be achieved by encouraging the exploration of what we think and why. Open the door to discovery and they will venture in.

Fun: Bob Basso says *"If it is not fun, you're not doing it right."* Some of my favorite classroom moments have been fun filled learning events. When working with a group of undergraduate students I was explaining that their second assignment was to be a presentation. As a group we talked at length about the 'death by power-point' that we had all experienced at least once. I recommended to them that they think outside of the square and explore the many varied options available to them.

That discussion included, talk of using good quality information, being enthusiastic about the subject, challenging and questioning ideas and having fun. As a group they delivered a diverse and inspiring series of presentations. Some developed debates, workshops, question and answer exercises in the format of a board game. Others enlisted the assistance, in part, of guest speakers, movie clips, music. All of this for a class on Introductory Criminology, a theory based first year university unit. The one presentation that sticks in my mind that had the class on their feet was delivered by an unassuming pairing who had been quiet in class and were shy and needed prompting to contribute. They drew one of the presentation slots some weeks into the semester and often took copious notes during others presentations.

On the day of their delivery they arrived in bright yellow T shirts and baseball caps. From the moment they stepped to the front of the room the class was mesmerized. What followed was a polished performance of a rap song that utilized all of the criminological theories we had covered in class. I realized in that song they had met all of the criteria to varying degrees.

Interestingly, their exam responses reflected the self-learning they had achieved via this process. For me those theories, even today, often have a back beat in my head and that alone makes me smile. The exploration of varied methodologies in the classroom can provide unexpected opportunities for both student and teacher. I recommend letting go of rigid formats to move through the barriers into the **passionate, enthusiastic, curious** and **fun** world of education.

Alison Clifton, B.A., Cert IV in Training and Assessment, works as a Senior Trainer for the Western Australia Police in the Communications Infrastructure Program.

Listen to this chapter at HowToLearn.com/amazing-grades

Back to The Future with Mastery-Based Learning

Making good grades took center stage throughout my school days, college years, and even my post-graduate studies.

During high school, I recall playing a basketball game at a distant location, trying to catch a little sleep on the bus ride home, and arriving at our little single wide trailer knowing I would have to find a creative way to study for my first period biology exam that was scheduled the next morning. You see, my dad's work day started at 3-4 A.M., and he had no sympathy for late night cramming.

The solution I resorted to most often included crawling into my closet, positioning a small lamp nearby within proximity to an electrical outlet, then quietly closing the sliding closet door so I would not be discovered by either parent. By now you have probably decided I'm an overachiever at best or crazy at worst. The truth is neither.

Today, I'm convinced that my problem was one of uncertainty and ambiguity. Although I had teachers that were, in my opinion, the best my generation produced, the practice of stating clear learning targets, teaching to those targets, practicing to those targets, receiving both positive and corrective feedback consistent with my practice of those targets, being informally assessed, practicing self-correction, being formally assessed, and ultimately mastering those learning targets was not everyday teaching pedagogue.

Thus, being the slight perfectionist with a desire to memorize every detail, knowing my post-secondary education would be dependent upon academic scholarships and loans, and being totally unsure of what should be considered important or trivial, I resorted to late night cramming sessions that produced the necessary short-term recall for the next day's exam.

Because I am intrigued by the variety of learning theories, practices, and programs that contradict common sense, when I was introduced to mastery learning or competency-based instruction, as it's frequently called, after nearly 20 years of K-12 teaching, my tongue-in-cheek attitude inspired little more than a smirk. I simply wasn't buying one more first- of- its- kind concepts.

Then I saw it in action! The only problem was that it wasn't new; it certainly wasn't the first of its kind; but it did accomplish what it stated – MASTERY! Reintroduced into 20th century classrooms by names such as Bloom, Blank, Keller, Skinner, Piaget, and now BREWER, mastery learning has its roots in the blacksmith shop of early America and the teaching methods of the one-room schoolhouse.

The goal of mastery learning is for all students to learn at roughly equivalent, high levels. Course materials are broken down into incremental pieces with associated specific, manageable learning targets. When students are provided appropriate learning conditions, tailored to their individual learning styles and needs, not only do they learn, they master learning. Mastery learning assumes the natural ability of students to learn when nurtured in a learning climate that supports that learning. Principles associated with mastery learning focus on LEARNING RESULTS, not teaching activities; FLEXIBLE TIME, not fixed time; INDIVIDUALS, not averages; and TEACHER COACHING and STUDENT PRACTICE, not teacher telling and student listening.

For the mastery learning process to be effective, teachers must have a vivid understanding of incremental learning targets and these targets must be clearly communicated and reviewed with students. A brief pretest is administered to determine students' beginning knowledge. High quality multi-modality instruction follows the pretest, and students engage in carefully planned practice activities that embed the particular learning objectives for auditory, visual, and kinesthetic (or a blend of these three) learners. Formative assessment of learning directs subsequent learning experiences, and mastery is achieved when students meet the summative mastery goal. Most mastery programs require between 80 and 90 percent mastery of a learning target before allowing the student to advance to the next learning target.

Instructional planning that supports and accommodates varied student mastery in regard to required time, provides opportunities for teachers to schedule enrichment studies for some while allowing time for others who require the extra input to achieve basic mastery. A key component to this open-mastery approach is the school's attitude toward mastery and the administrative and instructional support that makes it possible for all students. Traditional learning holds time constant while mastery varies. Mastery learning holds mastery constant while time varies.

Mastery learning is the most empowering practice that I have ever applied in my classroom, both for my students and for me as their teacher. It focuses on learning, supports teaching, simplifies grading, encourages enrichment, requires mastery, and contends that performance results underlie the notion of mastery. In other words, mastery takes learning from thought to action. The WHAT, WHEN, HOW, and IF students learn in customized mastery programs distinctly separates them from traditional learning programs. I have watched proudly as students, considered lower functioning and basic, were empowered through mastery learning. Whether it was because they got a second or third chance to test or because they were instructed in a way that met their unique learning needs or because their grade was based on mastery and not an average of every test they had taken, seeing one of these students empowered to learn simply because I practice mastery learning in my classroom confirmed that it is the right thing for me.

In conclusion, I must confirm the absolute brilliance of my teaching ancestors. Preceding generations understood education to be a vehicle that would transport young people to chosen trades and occupations. Essential skills required to perform job tasks comprised the targeted learning and learning was incremental. Small tasks led to larger tasks and demonstration of learning was required prior to advancement. Although the mass of educational research and teaching jargon has multiplied numerous times since those simpler times, frustration with an obvious descent in performance-based learning that empowers the learner to step from knowledge to practice has led our present generation to take a serious journey "back to the future" in educational practice.

I hope my doctor's learning was mastery-based, and my dentist, and my hair dresser, and my car mechanic, and my nurse, and my anesthetist, and my counselor, and my house carpenter. Otherwise, they may have run out of time at the very unit that I need their expertise!

You've got to dance like there's no one watching;
love like you can never get hurt;
sing like there's no one listening;
live like it's heaven on earth;
and teach from the heart to be heard!

Jan Brewer, M.A. is a health and fitness instructor at Lewis County Middle School in Hohenwald, TN.

Listen to this chapter at: HowToLearn.com/amazing-grades-audio

How To Create Joyful Learning in the Classroom

As teachers, we always want to create joy in the classroom as it facilitates more learning and certainly faster learning. Th e challenge is HOW do we create joyful learning in the classroom? HOW do we infect our students with enthusiasm? How do we bring fun and JOY in the classroom?

Here are some simple techniques which will help us have the most joyful learning possible.

I remember my English teacher Ms. Kalha in college quite vividly and her wonderful statement "Education is what is left behind after the textbooks have been forgotten".

If this IS indeed so, then lets embark on the journey of making education a joyful experience. What happens inside schools has a deep and lasting effect on the mind-sets that children develop toward lifelong learning. A teacher affects eternity and one can never tell when his influence stops.

JOY 1: Find the Pleasure in Learning

If we want students to be charged with enthusiasm, if we want them to see school and learning as joyful, we need to rethink how and what we teach. Let them enjoy learning as well as they enjoy games. Find ways to increase laughter in the classroom.

JOY 2: Music and Rhythm

Many of the things I remember most easily were learned with song. Ask your students to create songs and rhythm when learning something new and they will remember much longer and have an easier time retrieving the information for a test.

JOY 3: Give Students Choice

I tell my students to decide on the topic they want to study for that week and then as "experts" they will teach the next week. Try this in your classroom.

JOY 4: Let Students Create Things

People like to create things. The list of what students can create across the curriculum is virtually limitless: newspapers and magazines, brochures, stories, picture books, posters, PowerPoint presentations, interviews, oral histories, models, diagrams, blueprints and floor plans, plays and role-plays, mock trials, photographs, paintings, songs, surveys, graphs, documentary videos etc.

JOY 5: Show Off Student Work

I tell my teacher education students that the walls of their classrooms should speak to people; they should say exactly what goes on in that space throughout the school day. I can tell what teachers value by simply walking into their classrooms and looking at the walls.

JOY 6: Towards Holistic Learning

The new challenges that we face in the 21st century with the advent of information technology necessitate a systemic change towards a model of holistic learning that is experiential and linked to real-life situations. Find situations that help students incorporate what they learned in their everyday lives.

JOY 7: Get Outside

We adults know all too well that fresh air, trees, and a sunny day can do miracles for the human spirit. In an era where recess and playgrounds are being taken away, get your classes, no matter what the age, outside to reinvigorate and rejuvenate their learning. As a teacher, I often take my students outside to read, write, or have a class meeting. It is delightful for a student to sit under a tree and read or for a class to sit in a circle on the grass and talk. Ecosystems are all around us.

JOY 8: Read Good Books

Everyone loves a good story. All students enjoy a good story so allow books beyond your texts simply for the sake of student enjoyment!

Teaching As Joyful Experience

A teacher is like a candle who burns itself to give light to others.

Here is an Indian scripture which personifies my view of teachers.

Even If I make the paper of Entire Earth;
And I turn all the forests into a huge pen;
And convert all the seven oceans as Ink for this pen;
I will not be able to THANK MY TEACHER ENOUGH!

Amita Puri, Ph.D. is a teacher and teacher trainer with Army Institute of Education, New Delhi, India. She has been conducting workshops for preservice and inservice teachers for the last 20 years and specializes in educational psychology and guidance counseling.

Listen to this chapter at HowToLearn.com/amazing-grades-audio

Education Technology:
Cutting Edge Meets the Classroom

Education used to be as simple as a book, a chalkboard, and a pencil but the current notion of education is evolving alongside technology. Is a person's education defined by the piece of paper hanging on the wall or is it more about the hands-on experience of problem solving and lesson feedback?

The issue at hand sees the education industry pulled in two directions. On one hand, the teacher-to-student ratio is growing across the board while classroom budgets shrink. Outside of K-12, college tuition is simply not feasible for some families. On the other hand, technology has made education more accessible than ever before. The internet revolution changed many things -- entertainment, news, communication -- but it took a good decade to trickle down to education. However, today's students can get qualified degrees online from major universities and technical academies; in addition to that, everything from textbooks to course notes and lecture videos can be found on the web.

So while the logistics of traditional education are becoming increasingly difficult for the would-be student, access to the actual material is greater than ever before. Technology has pushed this further and faster, aiding the learning process from top to bottom. With textbooks now on student iPads and college-level calculus taught online, has education reached a new plateau or is this just the beginning? For those in the Education Technology industry, recent achievements demonstrate the power of innovative thinking in a traditional field. But most observers see a much bigger -- and more accessible -- picture.

In fact, many feel that education is on the cusp of a major paradigm shift. Cloud applications, e-books, video conferencing and other such tools represent the dawn of a new era, all powered by the emerging Education Technology industry. "College is not affordable without crushing debt; K-12 is not serving us well," says technology investor Mitchell Kapor. Kapor knows a thing or two about the bleeding edge of technology, having been involved in the successful launch of ventures ranging from Lotus 1-2-3 software in the 1980s to Second Life in the 2000s. "By having computers do what they are good at – individualized fashion; teachers can actually uplevel, be coaches, help do the kind of things that only people can do using technology. I'm a big 'blended learning' fan."

Classroom technology has evolved greatly in the past two decades. In the 1990s, computers were used for highly specified purposes and basic communication. In the 2000s, online distribution of course materials and supplementary training materials emerged. Today, Education Technology leaders project a movement away from the old textbook/lecture model and a greater focus on dynamic learning. "What we are beginning to see is a huge shift in attitudes to education technology, which includes the openness of teachers and school administrators to embrace technology as well as the investment world seeing the value and profitability of EdTech," says Liam Don, co-founder of ClassDojo.

That openness breaks down many of the previous hurdles experienced by innovative startups. Just a few years ago, the education industry was mired in the slow traditions held by a few major companies. Today, new methods for teaching and learning are being created by the hungry entrepreneurial minds behind Education Technology start-ups.

As teachers and administrators open up to the idea of new teaching methods and lessons through technology, bureaucratic roadblocks are being streamlined -- sometimes because budget cuts demand creative solutions, sometimes because technology allows new ideas into the traditional teaching model, and sometimes because parents want better ways to supplement a child's education. "With the current model, if you want to sell a product to a school it can take at least a year to go through the cycle, because of how school budgets...the good news is that new models are being developed to address and work around these issues.," says Don. "Additionally, as organizations like Khan Academy have made clear, there is a demand for independent learning outside the traditional classroom setting. Technology is the driver behind this, and this 'individualized' approach to education will only continue to expand and grow in the coming years."

Education Technology companies are working to satisfy all three key targets: administrators (who set budgets), teachers (who create curriculum), and students (who ultimately use the product). Some innovations target one group more than the other. In the case of digital textbooks, all three benefit. "The advent of the Ebook can revolutionize textbook accessibility," says Osman Rashid, CEO/Co-Founder of Kno, Inc. "Digital textbooks minimize cost and streamline distribution. A tablet can carry hundreds of textbooks while bringing in smart features -- and it won't weigh down a student's backpack."

Digital textbooks provide the foundation, but what does the future hold for Education Technology? For starters, imagine WiFi in every classroom to power those tablets. "At a minimum, tablets will be adopted as a digital book," says Zack Schuler, Founder & CEO of Cal Net Technology Group. "In some schools, higher-end tablets will take an all-inclusive role as a PC, digital book, communication device, and collaboration tool. In the middle, tablets like the iPad will play a key role in digital books, videos, and learning apps."

Tablets and WiFi can come together in the classroom through cloud-based applications, supplementary materials, even virtual field trips. All of this can crunch sage statistics for teachers, creating student-by-student metadata to provide an overview of what's working, what isn't, and how to create more effective lessons.

The focus on curriculum and lessons presents the core of Education Technology. However, a bigger picture exists, one that helps to answer the age-old parent question of "What do you want to be when you grow up?" One of Education Technology's biggest trends stems from this very idea, as start-ups are investing in platforms to help students explore career aspirations and achieve critical milestones on the path there. In addition, the journey to that goal is easier than ever before -- as online courses offer more robust opportunities, a greater selection of degree choices exists for students of all ages, backgrounds, and budgets while digital course materials enable access outside of the traditional classroom.

Greater access, more-focused materials, and innovative lessons; it's all part of the emerging Education Technology industry -- an industry that Mitchell Kapor predicts will be in the "billions and billions" of revenue dollars. Of course, tablets, WiFi, and apps are a means to an end, but there's one thing that Education Technology can't do: sorry parents, you'll still have to figure out a way to motivate your kids to do their homework.

Ahmed Siddiqui, B.S., MBA grew up in Minnesota, graduated from the University of Minnesota and completed his MBA at Babson College. He coordinates Startup Weekends in the San Francisco Bay Area. He is also founder of Go Go Mongo! at GoGoMongo.com, a game company that inspires kids to eat healthier. He can be reached through twitter: @siddiquiahmed

Listen to this chapter at HowToLearn.com/amazing-grades-audio

Teaching Strategies for Transitioning in a Multilingual Educational Environment

Currently the country of Kazakhstan, once part of the former USSR, is the only nation of the former union, thus far, to create special schools for the gifted and talented student population.

These schools select and cater to the development of the nation's future intellectual capital. To this end, the Nazarbayev Intellectual Schools (NIS), are implementing international 'Best Practices,' along with experienced international English-speaking teachers, to ramp up student academic achievement levels and increase the number of students entering Nazarbayev University. I write this chapter to share our experiences which will hopefully enrich yours.

Kazakhstan is unique in its attempts to transition from a bi-lingual teaching and learning environment, to English as First Language. A major goal of the reform is to substantially increase the number of students who are able to attend Nazarbayev University, over previous years, where the language of instruction is in English. The six (6) international teachers at NIS Semey are from the United States, England and Canada.

At the beginning of the year, diagnostic tests were conducted to determine the linguistic ability, learning styles and math and science abilities of the students, so the proper strategies could be selected and applied by the team for all encompassing school support. Some of the most heavily employed strategies included:

Individual student and group support
EFL for IELTS
ESP concept learning (biology, chemistry and math)
Professional Development Workshops for NIS and local teachers, as well as the school management team
Differentiated with emphasis on tasks and outcomes
Modeling Good Teaching Practices
English speaking clubs (topic-driven, e.g. Business Purposes)
Web Design Club
Writing competitions
Plays (Pygmalion)
African Week and Women's Day (International dimension)
Local language dimension with emphasis to other curriculum areas
Project Based Learning
Genotype and phenotype (local dimension)
Textual math and application of statistics to explain select terminology (median, mean, range, etc.)
ESL strategies (subject specific, e.g. lab report writing)
Application of Bloom's Taxonomy (especially evaluating and creating categories)
Lesson Planning and Team-teaching in the higher grades (Kazakh/English, Russian/English, ESL English)
Cooperative Learning Techniques (peer teaching, Jeopardy subject competitions)
Critical Th inking (as a separate subject as well as subject-specific application of principles)
Olympiad preparation (Competitions),
Test-taking skills (online and paper, Study skills and Time Management skills)
Graphic Organizers and Concept Maps
SET and SAT Preparation
Future Scientists Club
Recycle Club
Chess Club
French Club

The international team carefully observed and noted the needs of both students and teachers, against the goals of the reform, and in agreement with the school's administrative staff and parents, employed best practice strategies deemed appropriate for this cultural and educational milieu and whose effectiveness could be measured and monitored. Careful monitoring and analysis of student achievement indicated when a change in a particular or several strategies may be needed. At several times during the year, the frequency of individual and group language practice increased, both in time and frequency. Memorization of vocabulary as a strategy was not emphasized, but rather understanding vocabulary in associative and demonstrative contexts, as most of the students are visual learners.

The team teaching strategy was heavily employed in all eight senior classes (half Kazakh and half Russian speaking), where the local teachers initially delivered the major concepts and ideas in the native language of the students. This was followed by high-ordered thinking questions and application activities from the international teachers. Team-teaching, as a pedagogical practice, is well documented in educational literature as an effective teaching strategy, especially for older students, transitioning to another language of instruction. Additionally, this strategy afforded the local teachers to more readily acquire greater contextual English terminology and observe a different teaching style. Also, it allowed the international teachers to observe local teacher practices and incorporate some of the local practices into their teaching style, and as a bonus, acquire Kazakh and Russian scientific terminology.

Two examples of tracking student progress against the strategies employed are shown below. This year, 2011-2012, 100% percent of the students who took the SET biology exam passed. The January, 2012 baseline results demonstrated that the pedagogical strategies being employed were working, as the students were within 5 points of the passing SET grade. By March 2012, the class average was well above the passing SET grade by more than 20 points. The SET results, especially in biology, demonstrated that the strategies employed, worked effectively for this group of students.

Table 1

Grade 11 Senior Class Biology Baseline Exams NIS, Semey, Kazakhstan	
Month/Yr.	Class Average
September 2011	28
January 2012	40
March 2012	66
SET Passing grade:	43

Table 2

Grade 11 Senior Class IELTS Baseline Exams NIS, Semey, Kazakhstan	
Month/Yr.	Class Average
September 2011	3.0
December 2011	5.5
January 2012	6.0
April 2012	6.3

Graph 1 of Table Data 1

Another measure of gauging the effect of having an English-speaking international teaching team in a school is to measure how rapidly students improve their English ability in the four IELTS categories of reading, writing, speaking and listening, against the baseline. The data in table 2 shows a 2.5 average gain (composite score) within the first three months of school. The next three baselines showed a less rapid rise in score, but an increase nonetheless. Students will continue taking IELTS exams to measure the improvement in their mastery of English and achieve the scores they desire, past the required passing score of 5.5. Several students are now preparing to take the SAT exams, which offer another level of academic challenge and rigor in English.

Appendix
Additional strategies employed when appropriate:

Word Banks, Self-assessments, Projects
Brain Teasers Summarizing, and Note-taking Summaries,
Exit Slips Visual Aids Scaffolding,
Ticket out the Door Modeling Sequencing,
Gaps Mnemonics Transparencies,
Jumbled Summaries Read Aloud Word Associates,
Listing Analogy Film Clips,
Matching Acronyms Pairs Worksheets,
Pop Quiz Cause-and-Effect Clustering, and
Hands-on Read Aloud Collaborative Learning

Terms/Meanings

SET – Subject Entrance Test
SAT – Scholastic Aptitude Test
ESP – English for Specific Purposes
ESL – English as a Second Language
EFL – English as a First Language
EFL – English as a First Language

Loniece Wesbee Ningo is a biology teacher in the Nazarbayev Intellectual School in Semey, Kazakhstan in Central Asia. She also works on the chemistry curriculum for the Nazarbayev Intellectual Schools. You may connect with her on education.skype.com

Listen to this chapter at HowToLearn.com/amazing-grades-audio

31 Tips to Easily Integrate English Language Learners into your Classroom

As a teacher's diversity coach and author, I want to provide you some very specific tips to help integrate your English Language Learners (ELL) into your classroom. You want to engage your ELL's so they are constantly on task even if they don't know a lot of English. How can you do this while having you and your students still enjoy every lesson? These tips are excerpted from my booklet listed at the bottom of this chapter. Each suggestion provides key advice to help you confidently teach your English language learners in any learning context.

Integrating English Language Learners

1. Create simple systems like a "buddy system" where an ELL is paired with a native English speaking student. This eases isolation and helps an English language learner adjust to his/her new classroom.
2. Use pair and trio work where one child speaks the English language learner's mother tongue and is more proficient in English. Pair and small group work helps ELLs feel more at ease.
3. Use the same reading text for the class while adapting some of the activities and providing more direct guided instruction. This allows individual ELLs to progress according to their ability.
4. Create a classroom community where ELLs interact with native English speakers. Do this by using a variety of get-to-know-you tasks.
5. Teach theme units around an ELL's country or national food. Students can prepare the national food or learn the targeted vocabulary. This creates a classroom community.
6. Do things that get the ELLs to respond together. These can be pointing to things, raising hands or fingers, or answering in chorus, moving their bodies, checking off items, or writing.

7. Build a good relationship with diverse families and students by reading and understanding multicultural literature. You can teach the values of tolerance and diversity through multicultural books.
8. Create a sense of belonging by reading multicultural literature. With the increasing number of English language learners in schools, you need plenty of authentic fiction and non-fiction that caters to student diversity.
9. Have ELLs keep a reading diary where they are encouraged to write in their mother tongue or use pictures and a few words. Their entries can connect their feelings to the process of reading. They can also write about the characters, setting, or plot.
10. Provide opportunities for ELLs to compare and contrast themselves using a Venn-Diagram. Display the diagrams and have students report to another pair what they learned.
11. Give instructional support for ELLs to thrive within their educational setting. ELLs feel more connected with what is going on in the classroom when you give them more word-based skills and activities.

tinyurl.com/76uudck

Teaching Vocabulary

12. Motivate ELLs to learn new words. Use a variety of exercises, strategies, and activities to supplement reading and vocabulary lessons.
13. Start the first stage of vocabulary teaching by having ELLs notice the words. Flashcards are ideal for introducing word families and for pointing out capital and small letters, consonants, and other sound blends.
14. Give ELLs an opportunity to notice new words visually using flashcards and pictures. Noticing new words is the first stage in vocabulary acquisition.
15. Offer ELLs the chance to recognize new words using true/false type activities, word categorization, matching, multiple choice, listening activities, and games such as Bingo. ELLs can produce new words when they have practiced them at least 7 times.
16. Cater to ELLs in advanced vocabulary learning stages by providing them with activities focused on producing new words either in writing or orally. Such activities include dictations, answering

questions, guessing games like "I'm thinking of," picture description, and miming.

17. Use a large number of photos or realia and hand movements and gestures to pre-teach images. Visual methods are important for supporting meaning and generating interest.

18. Build charts with daily words. Have children sort words by pattern and meaning. Create word walls and other word support in rooms so ELLs can refer to them as often as necessary.

19. Use texts with familiar vocabulary. Developing fluency involves practice with easy texts in which all the words are familiar.

20. Work with students on common vocabulary. Pull small groups for word level instruction as other students read their books silently. This is one way to bridge the gap between word and text level skills.

21. Support students in discipline- specific vocabulary by creating charts or creating notebooks with targeted words. Photos can also be used. This is one way to expand their English knowledge.

22. Pre-teach 5-7 new words for any lesson. Too many new vocabulary items de-focus ELLs and defeat the lesson's purpose.

23. Look at the textbook and develop an easy-to-stick -with oral syllabus when teaching unknown vocabulary to young ESL learners. Start by writing an oral syllabus. Focus on a time framework to teach these new words. Teach young ELL 6-8 new words a day.

Oral Instruction and Activities

24. Reinforce sound-letter correspondences in decoding and reinforcing vocabulary by including oral instruction in every day lessons. Oral instruction bridges word and text based skills. That is the main obstacle when preparing ELLs to read.

25. Use an appealing form of oral instruction like chants, songs, and dialogues to reinforce sound patterns and blends, then later dialogues. Chants are a fun and musically effective way of introducing language. Provide ELLs with a diverse oral repertoire to hear English orally, using read-alouds, songs, spoken texts and narratives, interviews, and dialogues.

26. Connect both oral and written forms in instruction. Engage students in constructed response where they are expected to write answers or solve and explain problems.

27. Cover part of the word and/or sentence and/or provide just one syllable and/or sound as a trigger for students. This reinforces the sound awareness and provides practice for ELLs to produce the word, sound, or sentence.

28. Have students make a list of their favorite sentences and/or words (or both). They can then label pictures before writing sentences that accompany their drawings. Using pictures is an ideal way to expressive communication.

29. Have ELLs do a shared repeated reading where each student gets one list of words and/or sentences and the other students get an entirely different list. In turns, each one says the words while the other numbers the words/sentence. They then must relay the words/sentences in order while the other checks for accuracy.

30. Introduce communicative methodology techniques that are both fun and appealing. Have each student number a set of pictures and/or match the sentences or words to a picture. He/she can tell his/her version of the story with his/her partner and then share with another pair. You can then gather all the responses on the board and provide the class with the "right" story version.

31. Provide whole group responses instead of calling on individual students as all other students lose focus. One effective way to do this is to partner children where each child has a letter or number (1 & 2 or A & B). Ask partner A to share with B or the reverse. Partnering allows children numerous opportunities to practice.

Dorit Sasson, M.A., is the founder of DoritSasson.com and known as The Teacher's Diversity Coach. She is a veteran ESL educator, teacher-trainer and author. She also helps gives teachers, students and other professionals voice to their stories. You can read more at GivingAVoiceToTheVoicelessBook.com. Excerpts in this chapter are from Sasson's booklet, "Yes! You Can Teach K-12 English Language Learners Successfully."

Listen to this chapter at HowToLearn.com/amazing-grades-audio

Cultural Matters in the Classroom

Teachers face an enormous range of diversity in their work with students, and they must understand and deliberately address the complex range of diversity in their classrooms in order for them to be successful teachers of all learners.

Culture is at the heart of diversity. Our schools are increasingly places where students are multiracial, multiethnic, multilingual, and multicultural. Students have various religious backgrounds, home structures, and they possess a range of cognitive, social, behavioral, and emotional needs. Teachers must be prepared to address these needs; yet, they are often not.

When teachers do not understand the cultural background of students, it can be difficult for learning to take place in the classroom. Unfortunately, students are often the scapegoats for most of the problems associated with schools when teachers, administrators, and counselors also contribute to these same issues. Some of the issues in schools are direct results of cultural realities that emerge between teachers and students.

Individuals and groups of people operate in and through cultural frames of reference in particular social contexts. Our beliefs, ideologies, ways of knowing, preferences, and practices are shaped and guided by culture. However, we have learned through our research and our practices that White teachers, who make up the vast majority of the teaching force, sometimes do not believe and fully understand that they have a culture or that their worldview and practices are culturally grounded, guided, and facilitated.

They may struggle to understand that they too, like people of color, are cultural beings and that their conceptions, decisions, and actions are culturally shaped and mediated. They sometimes classify others as "cultural beings" and sometimes do not recognize the salience and centrality of their own culture and how it is woven through their work with students.

Culture is not a static concept "for conveniently sorting people according to expected values, beliefs, and behaviors" (Dyson & Genishi, 1994, p.3). Rather, culture is ever-changing and ever-evolving, and the work of teachers and others in schools is deeply guided by culture and the places where students learn (Milner, 2010).

We are cultural beings and workers. Accordingly, we must engage our work in ways that allow us to understand how students experience the world both inside and outside of school. Culture encompasses various other concepts that relate to its central meaning. For instance, culture may include individual or group identity markers such as class, socio-economic status, gender, race, sexual orientation and language. Thus, we invite teachers and other readers of this chapter to think about and to deconstruct the following definition of our conceptualization of culture: the implicit and explicit characteristics of a person or group of people--characteristics developed through historic, socio-cultural backgrounds, current experiences, knowledge, disposition, skills, and ways of understanding. These characteristics and ways of being are informed by race, ethnicity, history, heritage, customs, rituals, values, symbols, language, identity, class, region/geography, resources, gender and sexual orientation.

It is important to note that we do not mean to imply that culture is synonymous with race although race influences people and groups of people's cultural experiences. However, culture is much more dynamic in terms of the multiplicity of guiding factors. Still, race is an important dimension of culture. Because they sometimes do not necessarily see themselves as cultural beings and because they may not believe they are governed by a culture, teachers may see themselves as the norm and others as diverse. This way of thinking about students is problematic because normality is socially constructed.

Thus, it is important to note that teachers themselves are cultural beings as well and although they have power, students have a right to their own cultural beliefs systems (as long as their cultural practices do not harm themselves or others). Indeed, teachers have their own belief systems that are shaped by their race, ethnicity, socio-economic status, geography, and so forth. Our major point is that these cultural characteristics are sometimes inconsistent with those of students. And students typically suffer in these situations because teachers have the power to make decisions about student learning. When there are cultural disconnections between teachers and students, students typically suffer.

Reflecting on several important questions can prove useful to teachers on a school and classroom level in meeting the needs of students:

★ What cultural ways of knowing do students and teachers bring into the classroom, which are consistent and inconsistent?

★ In what ways do cultural inconsistencies between teachers and students enable or stifle learning opportunities in the classroom?

★ How do students' identities, their representation of that identity and their perceptions of that representation influence teaching and learning?

★ What are the links between and among the culture of students and teachers and the curriculum that should be taught in schools?

In conclusion, we hope teachers (and others in our schools) will think seriously about the role and influence of culture in teaching and learning. Thinking seriously about culture is not a trivial matter because students' learning opportunities and their futures are intricately tied to teachers' abilities to understand and respond to students' cultural identities. Thus, we invite and encourage teachers to:

★ Define their own culture.
★ Invite students to define their culture through various assignments in schools.
★ Consider the connections and disconnections between teachers' and students' cultures.
★ Develop bridges between inconsistencies that emerge between teachers and students.
★ Communicate with others from different "cultural" groups in order to deepen knowledge and understanding about various groups of people.
★ Search for deep meaning even if it contradicts teachers' own cultural ways of knowing and experiencing the world.
★ Avoid deficit thinking about other cultural groups—consider what students actually possess and bring into the learning environment rather than what they do not.

Culture and diversity do matter in learning, and our work should reflect this reality.

H. Richard Milner IV, PhD is an Associate Professor of Education at Vanderbilt University and the author of *Start Where You Are, but Don't Stay There: Understanding Diversity, Opportunity Gaps, and Teaching in Today's Classrooms* (Harvard Education Press). Elizabeth Self, M.Ed. and Alvin Pearman, M.Ed., doctoral students at Vanderbilt University, co-wrote this chapter. References Dyson, A.H. & Genishi, C. (1994). *The Need for Story: Cultural Diversity in Classroom and Community.* Boston: Harvard University Press. Milner, H.R. (2010). *Start Where You Are But Don't Stay There: Understanding Diversity, Opportunity Gaps, and Teaching in Today's Classrooms.* Cambridge, MA: Harvard Education Press.

Listen to this chapter at HowToLearn.com/amazing-grades-audio

A Letter from the Principal
- How Home Centered Parental Involvement
Creates Student Success

Parental involvement is an important topic of discussion because it directly relates to the academic and social success of their children. While some people define parental involvement as parents helping out at school, chaperoning school events, and attending conferences about their child's progress there is an alternative perspective.

From my point of view, I realize that 21st century parents work long hours to make ends meet or in many instances, are very involved taking care of everything on the home front as a stay at home Mom or Dad. Therefore, I would posit, with compassion, that parental involvement center on what the parents do at home with their children in order to add value to their academic and social development. Here is an Interactive Process Design (IPD) that parents may use as a guide.

When the IPD is implemented at school it is Protection of the Learning Environment; when IPD is applied in the home it is Parallel Supervision.

The four components of IPD are Boundaries and Academic Expectations Conversations, Support and Monitor Interactions, Acknowledge and Recognize/ Consistent and Persistent Consequences Interventions, and Activation of the Feedback Loop.

In my experience, parents who embrace the concepts that drive the Interactive Process Design are those most pleased with their child's success. The focus here is on parallel supervision; what the parents can do at home to nurture their child's academic and social success at school.

Academic and Behavioral Expectations

At home, parents can have multiple conversations about the academic and behavioral expectations upon which the parents and children can agree. These conversations begin several weeks before school starts and continue at least once a week through the summer vacation or year round school models.

It is important that your children have input so that they have buy-in to the agreement. The academic agreement is simply related to terms of a grade and an attitude.

For example, no grade lower than a B is acceptable and the maximum effort is expected on all assignments. Rather than having rules that are too rigid, a comprehensive flavor makes more sense. For instance, instead of saying no profanity, no hitting others, and no name calling just simply say, "Treat everyone with dignity and respect."

The three to five agreements are written as a contract that both parents and children sign; and the contract is reviewed weekly and monthly, as well as during the summer.

Support and Monitor

Once the academic and behavioral expectations are set, the parents and children determine how the parents will Support and Monitor the children so they can be successful and live up to the academic and behavioral expectations. The parents and children will agree on a study time of 10 minutes per grade level:

K	1st	2nd	3rd	4th	5th	6th	7th	8th	9th	10th	11th	12th
10	20	30	40	50	60	70	80	90	100	110	120	130

During the study period the parents and child agree that there are no interruptions, phone calls, texting, social or cyber media connections, and no visitors. Study time takes place in a common area where parents can see the child. This study time must be done four days a week, perhaps Sunday, Monday, Tuesday, and

Wednesday evenings. Thursday, Friday, and Saturday evenings are used as make-up nights if one of the four study days is missed for some reason.

The parent and the child agree that anytime the grade expectation drops to below B – the parent will contact the school by phone or email once a week to check on the student's progress. The Parent agrees to attend all school scheduled conferences and the parent and child agree on three to five ways the parent can support and monitor the student during the school year.

The parent and child also need conversations concerning the types of **acknowledgments, recognitions, and accolades** that the child will appreciate when compliance is met each week.

Compliance should not involve money or gifts. Parents should **encourage their children to get involved with a school sponsored activity** such as the band, chorus, clubs, sports, or performance groups. Parents should talk with their children about **the consequences** when the expectations are not met. They agree that consequences will occur with persistence and consistency. Also, the penalties must escalate so that each time there is a breach of the contract the consequence becomes more cumbersome for the child.

Parent and child agree that the **feedback loop will be activated** when interventions occur; everyone that needs to know will be contacted so that complete transparency exists. Each teacher and caregiver should be advised when one caregiver introduces an intervention. Activation of the feedback loop is a must; this should be done to ensure there are no communication breakdowns and the child is less likely to fall through the cracks.

In general, the child needs to know that the parents are engaged in Parallel Supervision with the adults at school. The child needs to see themselves as not only representing themselves but that they are representing their family, their community, and their school. Consequently the adults expect that the child will adhere to:

Four Steps of Success:

1. Be responsible and reliable
- ★ Arrive on time and prepared
- ★ Work thoroughly and smart and do something extra

2. Carry yourself in a dignified manner
- ★ Be clean and neat and maintain consistency of purpose
- ★ Master and demonstrate a demeanor that is highly regarded in the mainstream environment

3. Treat everyone with dignity and respect
- ★ Demonstrate a cooperative and collaborative spirit
- ★ Honor and support what is good and right

4. Mentor someone younger

Be a positive role model and mentor for a younger person and tutor a younger person. Home centered parental involvement enriches children and helps them respond with maturity to their experiences. The adults in a child's life needs to convince children that they are in control of their own success and that they should leave a place better than it was before they arrived. When parents follow these common sense rules good things happen for their children and this is what we all really want anyway.

Ed Harris, Ph.D, author of *Shattering Low Expectations*, has been the principal of four high schools and is currently assistant principal at of at Claymont Elementary School in the Brandywine School District in Wilmington Delaware. He has won numerous awards including Principal of the Year and served as an adjunct professor at Maryville University in Missouri. His mission is to help schools improve effectiveness and increase student learning and therefore develop a comprehensive school improvement system called Collaborative School Transformation, which contains the QUO Process, Shepherding and Professional Development.

To listen to this chapter at HowToLearn.com/amazing-grades-audio

Three Techniques to Help Your Child Build a Faster, Better Brain

Information and ideas are the tools we use to craft success in school, at work and in life. The brawn that allows us to wield these tools, however, comes from the brain's underlying cognitive skills. Even one weak skill can keep the brain from grasping and applying information well no matter how many times lessons are explained! In fact, weak cognitive skills are the cause of 80% of all learning struggles.

The best way to help your child get better grades—and experience greater success in life—is to strengthen the cognitive skills that are absolutely crucial for processing information taught in the classroom and beyond. Cognitive skills can be improved thanks to "neuroplasticity," which is the brain's unique ability to physically change and grow at any age. This is great news for students, career adults, busy moms & dads, senior adults, as well as anyone impacted by autism, ADHD or dyslexia or even a traumatic brain injury.

If your child is struggling, stronger cognitive skills *will* help. For a faster, stronger brain, observe the following techniques to: 1) prevent cognitive loss; 2) maintain mental agility; and 3) create "mental sweat" to strengthen cognitive skills and improve mental performance in every area of life:

Prevent cognitive loss with a healthy lifestyle

tinyurl.com/c9ugx83

A healthy lifestyle prevents cognitive loss due to poor health, and can delay age-related cognitive decline, too. Eating colorful vegetables, for example, combats oxidative stress on the brain. Drinking enough water staves off mental fatigue. Regular exercise lowers the risk of dementia as much as 38%. And getting good sleep for the night moves information from short to long-term memory (good news for students who cram the night before exams!)

Maintain agility with regular mental activity

Engaging in challenging mental activities is another way to improve mental agility and put off age-related decline. For an agile brain, encourage your son or daughter to fall in love with learning. (Learning a second language, for example, can delay the onset of dementia as much as five years!) Crossword puzzles, Sudoku, and memory games help, too. So do brain-improvement software, websites & video games. And while there's little research suggesting these particular activities translate into improved performance at work or school, staying mentally active overall continues to be linked with staying sharp at every age.

Build a faster, more efficient brain with mental sweat

Preventing loss and maintaining agility are good, but sometimes what's *really* needed are dramatic, measurable improvements in the way the brain functions. I see this need quite often with families of struggling students, with children or adults diagnosed with dyslexia, autism or ADHD, and with stroke and TBI victims.

Very intense, targeted mental exercises (also known as one-on-one brain training) can create this kind of dramatic change by stimulating the brain to reorganize neural pathways to handle information more efficiently. The exercises also reinforce those pathways for hardwired, permanent changes. If Sudoku, crossword puzzles and brain-improvement games are like taking a brisk walk, what I'm talking about is more like hiring Jillian Michaels to take you from "dough boy" to "hard body." These exercises are intense enough to create what I call "mental sweat," are done one-on-one with a personal coach, and the results are extreme and life changing. In fact, they are documented to raise IQ, on average, by 15 to 20 points.

Best of all, they translate into real life improvements in how people perform in school, at work, in life—even on the athletic field or behind the wheel of a car. In considering brain training for yourself or your child, look for five key elements that must be present for dramatic, measurable results:

1. Serious brain training for results can't be taught in a classroom or simulated on a screen. It is a skill that must be physically practiced and **drilled**, like learning to play tennis or the piano.

2. Serious brain training for results creates intensity. Just as building muscle requires high impact and concentrated repetitions, building neural connections requires the same intensity.

3. Serious brain training for results must be done in a particular sequence. Certain sequences of exercises work better than others at forcing the brain to recruit nearby neurons to handle complex tasks, the key to making the brain fitter, faster and smarter.

4. Serious brain training for results incorporates loading. A form of multitasking, loading stimulates the brain to automate familiar tasks so it can focus on newer tasks, making these skills permanent.

5. Serious brain training for results involves instant feedback. When brain training contains all the above elements, it creates the perfect environment for maximum, permanent changes in your brain, so feedback from a brain training specialist is crucial to keep you on the right track.

Working one-on-one with a brain training specialist is the most effective way of getting this kind of intense mental workout. Trainers also provide the experience and accountability necessary for maximum results in the shortest amount of time. These advantages are the key to turning good intentions and high hopes into life changing improvements. Better grades are just the beginning. This is because a better brain doesn't just make school easier, it makes *life* easier.

Ken Gibson, O.D. is the founder of the LearningRx Brain Training Franchise system (learningrx.com) and the author of two books: *Unlock the Einstein Inside: Applying the New Brain Science to Wake Up the Smart in Your Child*, and *The Purpose Directed Business: An Insider's Look in the Values, Strategies and 15 Profitability Keys of Small Business*. LearningRx is the premier one-on-one brain training company in the world, offering serious brain training with life changing results to struggling students, high achieving students, career adults, busy moms and dads, senior adults —plus anyone impacted by autism, ADHD, dyslexia, a stroke or traumatic brain injury. Get a FREE download of the book *Unlock the Einstein* Inside at learningrx.com

Listen to this chapter at: www.learningrx.com/amazinggrades 🔊

A Parent's Formula for Your Child's Success: Success = Engagement

Parents can and do make a difference in the education of their child. When parents and families are engaged in the educational process, everyone benefits –students, teachers, parents and the school.

Research confirms that, regardless of the economic, racial, or cultural background of the family, when parents become partners in their child's education, the results not only include improved student achievement, school attendance, reduced dropout rates, but there tends to be a decrease in antisocial behaviors.

tinyurl.com/848nsbk

Children learn best when significant adults in their lives work together to encourage and support them. Engagement involves teachers and parents actively creating learning environments that foster students' desire to be involved in their work regardless of challenges they encounter and to do so with pride and passion.

This "ENGAGEMENT" formula includes information, strategies, and resources that will help parents as they help their child strive for success. Each component of the formula is interconnected and should be addressed in order to ensure success for your child.

"ENGAGEMENT" Formula	Key Components	Descriptions/ Example/Resources
E	Expectations/Engagement	★ Set high expectations for your child, school, self (parents).
		★ Communicate expectations for academics, behavior and effort to school officials at the onset of the year.
		★ Put in writing to the teacher and keep a copy -Ask to be informed if either drops.
		★ Establish specific goals and discuss them with your child including an emphasis on the effort put forth when completing assigned tasks.
		★ Ensure your child understands the consequences for not meeting expectations, hold your child accountable for his/her actions.
		★ Commit to active involvement in your child's school including PTA meetings, booster club, field trips, conferences, field day, volunteering, classroom speaker and other school activities.
		★ Read and review with your child all information (student handbooks, newsletters, other communications).
N	Nurturing of: Academic Social Emotional Physical	★ Learn the difference between IQ and EQ and how they impact your child's success.
		★ IQ - A number that shows the relative intelligence of a person.

★ EQ - A measure of one's emotional intelligence.

★ EQ skills help children be able to effectively communicate; interact within teams; have efficiency in organizational skills and in making sound decisions.

★ Encourage participation in extra-curricular activities and friendship building.

★ Monitor weight to ensure your child doesn't fall in the dangers of obesity and its side effects – a routine exercise program is important.

★ Be sure your child gets plenty of rest.

★ Utilize appropriate websites for resources to enhance academic skills.

G

Guidance in
Study/Homework area
Organizational and Study skills

Homework/Study Heaven

★ Focus, effort and consistency are keys to success in completing homework assignments

★ Identify a place and specific time for homework/study. Routines are critical.

★ Homework/study area should be well lighted, free of clutter, distractions and have supplies needed to complete the assignment.

★ Breaks and healthy snacks enhance the homework/study process.

★ Invest in having your child take a learning styles inventory to determine how he/she learns best.

Organization and Study Skills

★ Success and strong organizational and study skills go hand-n-hand.

★ Important skills to learn include: Cornell Note Taking, learning maps, Costa's Levels of Questioning, SQ5R Method, KWL, learning maps and graphic organizers.

★ Encourage reflective writing and using writing as a learning tool. Writing enhances reading abilities, aids in critical thinking, contributes to self-knowledge and helps explain and order a child's experiences.

★ Inquire if an AVID program is available and request that your child be considered.

★ AVID (Advancement Via Individual Determination) is a college readiness system for elementary through postsecondary.

★ Emphasize your goal is to create every opportunity to ensure he/she is prepared to go to college whether they choose to go or not!

A   Attitude and Motivation

★ "Attitude is the latitude to Success"
★ Children's beliefs and attitudes have a significant effect on their success or failure in school.
★ Research indicates a clear connection between effort and achievement – If your child believes he can it will become a reality!
★ Reinforce effort using graphs and charts - this helps to make the connection between effort and improvement.
★ Create an attitude and opportunities to make learning a lifetime experience such as vacations to historical places, keeping journals during vacation trips.

G   Gaining and Communicating Information
Curriculum
Assessment Program

★ Know your child's grade level state and district curriculum standards.
★ Determine when and how student progress is reported.
★ Find out grade levels, times and passing standards for state mandated test.
★ Ask teachers what you can do to support and prepare your child for the test.

E   Embracing Diversity
Ethnic
Cultural
Learning differences
Gender

★ Proud to be me!
★ Have child tell at least one thing weekly describing why he/she is proud to be who they are.
★ The school and classroom should reflect the diversity of all students via literature, pictures, etc.
★ Ask teachers, principal or librarian if you can provide materials if they aren't available.
★ Determine services available for learning differences and second language learners (gifted, special education, Bilingual/ELL).

M   Monitor and Management
Time
Assignments
Behavior
Effort

★ Establish ways to monitor and manage academic, behavioral and effort including self-monitoring.
★ Create a routine of asking your child to tell at least one thing learned at school each day.
★ Caution: don't allow them to tell you what they did… but what they learned (example: I learned how to multiply integers).
★ Have child make a daily "To Do" lists -- check tasks off each day.
★ Post classroom rules, school calendar and school communication in a special location in the home.
★ Use timers and charts to customized monitoring and management system.

E

Environment
Home
Classroom
School

★ Make home a safe haven where your child is comfortable sharing successes and failures.
★ Set priorities and boundaries related to Internet access, schoolwork, recreation, use of correct language and respect for self and others.
★ Frequent communication and visits to the classroom and school will help parents determine if school is a safe haven – free from bullying tactics.
★ Emphasize that education is valued and related to the real world.

N

Nutrition

★ A healthy lifestyle provides energy needed to perform at high levels.
★ Ensure your child eats healthy meals/snacks.

T

Test Taking Strategies

★ Despite how hard students may study for tests, it will be useless unless they know something about the type of test and how to approach taking tests.
★ Different types of test require different types of strategies.
★ Use websites and books to provide support.

tinyurl.com/876sqp2

Marva T. Dixon, Ed.D. is the author of *The Power of the 5 Ps – What Every Educator Needs to Know.* She is an educational consultant, former principal, and former Executive Director of Innovation and Support from Grand Prairie ISD. She also has a book website at tinyurl.com/858vwp9 and consulting firm website at DrMarvaTDixon.com

Listen to this chapter at HowToLearn.com/amazing-grades-audio

Don't Let Your Child Be Mistakenly Labeled for ADHD

So many conditions can look just like attention deficit hyperactivity disorder (ADHD) that it causes confusion in the diagnosis. Therefore, it is not surprising that so many people are misdiagnosed with ADHD!

Often, parents, teachers and doctors believe diagnosing ADHD in a child with a behavior problem is as simple as 1-2-3 or A-B-C. Unfortunately, this is not the case. Unlike medical problems such as diabetes mellitus, pneumonia, or a heart attack, there are no tests that can conclusively nail down the diagnosis. That's right, there aren't any blood tests, brain scans, genetic tests or even psychological tests that can tell a parent or a doctor that a child definitely has ADHD, or for that matter, doesn't have ADHD.

tinyurl.com/7a87laf

In fact, ADHD is best diagnosed by first excluding more than 75 current medical, social, environmental, and psychological conditions that can mimic ADHD and cause mis-diagnosis of ADHD. Then, once those medical "zebras" have been ruled-out, the diagnosis of ADHD is made by observation and accurate reporting of behaviors that are consistent with ADHD as outlined by the American Psychiatric Association (APA) DSM-IV guidelines.

You can learn more about each of these ADHD zebras at MistakenforADHD.com/Zebras. As you can see, the list is long and includes things most parents and teachers don't think about as causing a child's behavior problems, failing grades, or social problems. As many children will only show mild symptoms of ADHD we must keep watchful eyes, open minds and question whether learning-social-behavior problems could best be explained by something other than ADHD.

A few of the more than 75 things that can cause ADHD misdiagnosis include:

★ Hypothyroidism
★ Obstructive sleep apnea
★ Diabetes Mellitus
★ Pesticide poisoning
★ Lead poisoning
★ Divorce
★ Bullying
★ Teacher-student mismatch

★ Bipolar disorder
★ Generalized anxiety disorder
★ Depression
★ Asperger Syndrome
★ Sensory processing disorders
★ Learning style differences
★ Perceptual problems
★ Hearing problems

The DSM-IV guidelines include observed behaviors of the core symptoms of ADHD-impulsivity, inattentiveness, and hyperactivity. Critical to this part of the diagnosis is the requirement that these behaviors:

★ Must occur in more than one setting, such as home, school, work, church, social occasions or athletic events. A behavior only seen in one setting such as the classroom and nowhere else leaves the diagnosis seriously in doubt.
★ Must cause the involved person a disability of some type - learning, getting along with others, participating, engaging in sports or social events.
★ Must not be caused by or better explained by some other physical, medical, psychological, environmental or social condition.
★ Some symptoms of ADHD (impulsivity, inattention, hyperactivity) should have been observed before age 7.
★ Must include the key symptom of ADHD-inattentiveness, inability to focus or problems remaining on task.
★ Learn more about the American Psychological Association's DSM-IV guidelines for diagnosing ADHD at ADHDbehavior.com/DSMIV.html.

As you can see, making the diagnosis of ADHD is not as simple as some would have us believe as evidenced by the fact that about ten percent of US children, ages 2 to 18 years, have been diagnosed as ADHD. You might be alarmed to discover that of those 15 million children and teens, about 25% to 40% or as many as 7 million have been wrongfully labeled with ADHD. Children misdiagnosed as ADHD often become victims of discrimination, bias and classroom bullying. Once labeled as ADHD, everyone just assumes they will fail or cause problems for the rest of their life.

We as parents, teachers, counselors, and healthcare professionals should slow down a little and avoid being so quick to slap the label of ADHD on behavior challenged children. As a result, about 7 million children won't be exposed to unnecessary ADHD drugs and often serious side effects. And even more importantly, if inaccurately diagnosed and inappropriately treated, then the real reason for a child's ADHD behavior will go undiagnosed and untreated subjecting them to failure in life.

What Can You Do To Prevent an ADHD Misdiagnosis?

If your child's teacher is the one that brought the problem to your attention, don't fall into the trap of assuming the teacher is absolutely correct. When discussing your child's behavior or learning problem with their teacher, keep an open mind, ask a lot of questions and expect precise answers. Do not equate ADHD with replies like, "He acts up in class" or "he disrupts the class." If a learning problem is suspected, gather as much information as you can about exactly what your child's learning problem is and just as importantly, what it is not. Then have your child evaluated for the type of learning problem suspected. A Learning Disability (LD) is one of the medical zebras that can cause confusion about the diagnosis of ADHD.

Watch for signs of similar behavior problems in your child outside of the classroom- at home, church, athletic events, and other social occasions. By definition, ADHD is diagnosed by observing the disabling behavior or disability in more than one setting. Ask your child what he or she thinks is causing the teacher's concern or is responsible for the behavior. Your child may be anxious, depressed or just going through a tough adjustment period or school/home transition and once treated, their behavior may return to what is normal for them.

Give your child's ADHD doctor as much information as possible about his or her behavior problem and learning difficulties on their initial doctor's visit. Failure to provide input from other family members, friends, teachers, and persons other than the parent is one of the most common reasons ADHD is so often misdiagnosed or under diagnosed.

Do not expect pills to always be the answer. Some kids with conditions that mimic ADHD may only need coaching or tutoring, while others might need treatment for childhood anxiety or depression or therapy for a medical problem such as hypothyroidism. Above all… you must be a very strong advocate for your child. Consider lifestyle changes as first line treatment for ADHD and don't unnecessarily expose him or her to drugs, many amphetamines, with serious side effects that you wouldn't take yourself.

To help with your child's first doctor visit for evaluation of ADHD, I've prepared a checklist of questions that need to be answered. You can access the checklist at ADHDBehavior.com/ADHDquestions. These are very important, as the answers will set the overall tone for your child's evaluation and successful treatment! In conclusion, it's just as important that we not miss the diagnosis of ADHD in a child who is ADHD; as it is to prevent ADHD misdiagnosis in a child who is not. Both efforts will prevent your behavior or learning problem child from suffering inappropriate treatment and ending up labeled as a failure in life.

Frank Barnhill, M.D. has a private medical practice in South Carolina and is also the author of *Mistaken for ADHD*. For more information visit MistakenforADHD.com and ADHDBehavior.com.

Listen to this chapter at adhdbehavior.com/MistakenADHDlabel/MP3

5 Best Behavior Strategies for ADHD

Attention Deficit Hyperactivity Disorder (ADHD) is greatly misunderstood and most people have a very poor impression of children diagnosed with the condition. Largely believed to be a behavioral disorder, this is mostly untrue.

Even the symptoms of hyperactivity, impulsivity, and inattention poorly describe what is happening. True, ADHD is a condition of variable attention, difficulty with tasks of executive function (i.e., time management, decision making, planning, working memory), and motivation.

Now, this doesn't mean behavior problems won't ever exist. After all, your son's difficulty with focus and attention during a classroom lecture can lead to unwanted behaviors (hyperactivity). Your daughter's excitement, during a class she actually enjoys, can lead to blurting out answers (impulsivity). Your son's lack of interest or not feeling challenged enough by the material being taught can lead to daydreaming or doodling (inattention).

So what can you do? Ultimately, your child ends up getting judged based on the behavior others see, rather than what is really happening on the inside. As a parent, you spend a great deal of your time responding to calls from school, complaints from teachers, battling to get homework done, and to get your child to listen to you sometime within the first 20 times you ask them to do something. Let's face it, your job as Mom or Dad feels incredibly difficult and stressful.

Here are five behavior strategies that will make a huge difference in the long run.

1. Work With Your Child's ADHD And Not Against It! The biggest mistake I see people make is thinking that this child is broken and needs to be fixed. In other words, most people will want to try and make your child less "ADHD." This will backfire and make life even more miserable. The key to success is to work with your child's ADHD rather than against it. It's like swimming with the current, instead of against it. You'll never cure your child's ADHD difficulties, but in working with them, your son or daughter will develop specific strategies to overcome any challenge.

2. Set Clear, Measurable Goals! As a parent, it's very easy to tell our children what we don't want them to do. But how often do we tell them, specifically, what we do want? The more clearly you can define what acceptable behavior is, the more likely you will see success in changing your child's behavior. Take reward charts for instance, instead of listing what you don't want to see, focus on what you would like to see. To go one step further, set goals and expectations that are easily measurable. Too often we make general statements that are all but impossible to measure whether or not any change has occurred. Be specific. Be clear. Set one large goal, and break it down to several short term goals that you can track.

3. Limit Multiple-Step Commands. When was the last time you gave your son or daughter a list of chores or activities to do "right now," and they actually all got finished? In most cases, we parents think our child is being defiant. However, this usually isn't the case. A child with ADHD has a difficult time with working memory. That means when you ask them (tell them) to go upstairs, pick up their clothes, put their homework in the folder and into the backpack, get their pajamas, and brush their teeth, there's a good chance they have forgotten most of those steps. I swear, it's NOT them being defiant. On the contrary, it's a difficulty with remembering all those different tasks. So rather than come to you and ask you to repeat them (and get yelled at), your son or daughter will just do what he or she remembers.

4. Offer Rewards, Not Punishment. There are different theories on behavior modification in terms of what works and what doesn't. Rather than get caught up in theory, let's focus on basic psychology for a moment. Reward good behavior by offering a treat, and offer no reward for bad behavior.

I hear from a lot of parents today that their children feel entitled to playing video games whenever they want (all day) or that it's okay to take the car to the mall, even after missing school that day. I don't buy that! For me, playing games, taking the car, and having fun is a privilege. It has to be earned. If you've been doing the latter, it will take time to work up towards the former approach. But rest assured, it will work wonders.

5. Prepare Your Child For New Situations. It's pretty well known that children with ADHD have a difficult time with transitions. Facing the unexpected can lead to anxiety and "acting out" behaviorally as a default way of getting attention, and feeling more connected. You can stop this. We know that children with ADHD benefit from structure. They benefit and thrive in situations that are familiar to them and that are predictable.

When it comes to a new situation, ease them into it as soon as you can. When setting up a job interview, take them to where they are going the night before. Give them a chance to familiarize themselves with their surroundings.

Truth be told, behavior problems are going to arise no matter what you do. The best strategy I can offer you, or anyone really, is that you need to be prepared with backup strategies when your primary strategy does (and will) fail. It's that moment we need to prepare for. How you teach your child to handle the unexpected will typically reduce the anxiety and uncertainty that leads to blurting out answers, tapping pencils and feet uncontrollably, and staring out the window.

Discovery consists of looking at the same thing as everyone else and thinking something different.
- Albert Szent-Gyorgyi

 Rory Stern, Psy.D. is a "recovering therapist," who after completing his doctorate in clinical psychology, walked away from the medical field. After seeing how children with ADHD and their parents were treated, he vowed to not let another child be treated that way on his watch. As an advocate for children across the globe, Dr. Stern's mission is to ensure that no child ends up being mislabeled, misdiagnosed, mistreated, or misunderstood. For more information visit his two websites: ADHDFamilyOnline.com and HelpYourADHDChild.com

Listen to this chapter at ADHDFamilyOnline.com/bestbehavior

How To Advocate for Your Child with Special Needs

In a previous chapter, students were advised by a special education university department chairperson about how to advocate for themselves if they have special needs. This chapter is specifically for parents to help as you advocate for your child with special needs who is either in high school or college.

Some of this may sound very basic, but in the world of Special Education, knowledge of your rights and what is available for your child is crucial for your child's success. All too often parents may feel too intimidated to ask questions or show that they don't understand something. If you want your child to get better grades, start with the basics and arm yourself with your rights. Parents know their children best, and are their child's best advocate.

idea.ed.gov

★ For children who have special education needs (k-12) most information is found under the IDEA Act at Idea.ed.gov. You need to know that your child has many rights and this is one place to find out what they are. Look up your state's special education regulations as well. Know your procedural safeguards. This is the best way to start to become informed of what you and your child are entitled to.

★ If your child is 18 or over, you will want to look at the ADA – Americans with Disabilities Act at Ada.gov as the information varies for adults. You will also want more information on what is known as a 504 plan. Visit this site for more: wrightslaw.com/info/sec504.index.htm

★ If you don't understand your regulations or procedural safeguards, call your state's special education department and have someone explain them to you.

★ Know and understand your child's strengths and needs. These are determined through an evaluation by the district and/or a private school Psychologist. The student's identified needs are what drive the IEP goals, specially designed instruction, and related services such as speech therapy or time with a reading or math specialist.

★ If you don't understand your child's evaluation, make sure it is explained to you in a way that you understand. You are an equal member of the IEP team, and need to have "informed consent" when making decisions on what goals or services your child needs. These meetings can be long and confusing with the 'experts' weighing in on your child.

★ After understanding your child's evaluation, if you do not agree with some or all of it, you have the right to ask for an Independent Educational Evaluation at public expense. This is called an IEE, and it means you get to choose a private evaluator that the school district would have to pay for. Further explanation on how to obtain an IEE should be in your procedural safeguards.

★ Know what reading/math programs are being used. Make sure that they address the areas of need your child has. Just because your district is using a reading/math program, it might not be the one that is right for your child. You can ask for a different research-based program if the one they have is not appropriate.

★ Keep track of progress reports, and ask for the progress monitoring data used to track your child's goals. Make sure it is reported to you in a way you understand. Make sure you get progress reports at least three to four times a school year.

★ School districts can provide your child with a tutor or time with a reading or math specialist if appropriate to meet your child's needs. This time can and should be written into the IEP.

Make certain that your child's IEP is written with names of people responsible for implementing each section and full accountability for all people listed on the IEP.

★ If your child is found to be eligible for extended school year services, these services should be as individualized as the regular school year program. Your child should not just go to the district's ESY program because "that's all they have". If it does not meet your child's needs, then a different program needs to be put in place. Again, this could be private tutoring or working with a reading/math specialist.

★ Transition planning is extremely important. This is what is going to give your child the skills to be independent beyond high school. Transition goals should be outcome based not just going to the guidance counselor once a year to look at colleges. Make sure the classes your child is taking match the entrance requirements for the major they are exploring.

★ Know what age your child will start being invited to the IEP meetings. It is extremely important that the IEP team hears from the student what does and does not work for them. Your child should tell the team what concerns they have and what their plans are for their future. If they don't want to go to the meeting, have them write something to be read at the IEP meeting.

★ For students with a Section 504 plan the same tips apply.

★ Section 504 plans can contain measurable goals, objectives, and related services - not just accommodations.

★ For any student going into a 2 or 4 year college/university program, you will need to have a full re-evaluation within a year of starting the program. Once the student gets into college, it's all on the student to get the accommodations they need to be successful.

★ All colleges/universities that accept federal funding must address the needs of students with disabilities under Section 504.

★ Go to the college/university disability office, make an appointment and show them the current evaluation. Some accommodations requests must be made directly to the professor. Keep in mind that under Section 504 the school only has to make "reasonable" accommodations.

There are many more resources available for you online and if you need additional help to insure your child has the services they need I suggest consulting a special education advocate.

Becca Devine is Special Educational Advocate and the parent of a child with autism. She works with families throughout Pennsylvania, New Jersey, and Delaware. Devine is currently the Vice President of the Pennsylvania Education for All, Inc., on the board of PA-TASH (tash.org) and the chair of their Education Committee. For more information see: http://sites.google.com/site/teaminclusionadvocacy/

Listen to this chapter at HowToLearn.com/amazing-grades-audio

Why Grades are Important to Homeschoolers

Why Grades Really Matter

The obvious reason grades matter is because you need good grades in order to get into college or graduate school. But there is another, more important reason that good grades matter. Becoming an "A" student changes you, and you are a different person as an "A" student than you are as a "C" student. You grow along the way.

In order for you to get that "A", you will probably have to overcome some hurdles and challenges. You will have to develop will-power and self-discipline. Instead of partying with your friends, you may find yourself staying in and studying. Instead of sleeping in on the weekends, you may find yourself getting up early so that you can study before you go to work. You may also find yourself asking for help or working with a study group. Most mostly, you will have to manage your time better, because earning "A's", for most people, takes more time. If you were aiming for a "C" grade, you might not have to make these choices. But once you decide you want that "A", you are "raising the bar" for yourself and bringing your ga me to a higher level.

The beauty of earning "A's", is that once you know how to earn an "A" and excel in one area of your life, you can do it in other areas of your life. Because of those "A's", you will have the confidence in yourself and your time management skills to let you do well in whatever area you choose, whether that be ballet, sports, writing, music or anything else. You will be thinking and acting like an "A" student.

Homeschoolers Make The Grade

A study published in the *Journal of College Admission* concluded that homeschool students enjoy higher ACT scores, better grades, and higher graduation rates, compared to other college students. Homeschool students also earn more college credits (14.7) prior to their freshman year than other students (6.0). And, college freshman who were homeschooled finish their first year in college with a higher grade point average -- a 3.37 GPA compared to a 3.08 GPA. They are also more likely to graduate from college -- a 66.7% graduation rate compared to 57.5% for other students.

A former Dean of Admissions for Stanford University described homeschooled students as having "academic vitality" -- a love of learning that makes them highly motivated, self-directed, life-long learners.

Make These Study Techniques A Habit

If you are a homeschool student, it is up to you to take advantage of the educational opportunity you have been given. Take charge of your education. You have the chance to learn at your own pace, learn in the way that works best for you, and master each subject as you go, instead of just racing ahead in order to keep up with the class. Here are some popular study techniques that homeschoolers use. If you make these a part of your daily study habits, you will have no problem getting good grades, because you will thoroughly understand the material.

Tip #1: Do not go on, until you have mastered the material

Make sure you understand the material you are working on, before you go on to the next level. If this means reading a chapter and doing the exercises twice, do it. This will result in you mastering the material as you go along and you will be well prepared for any essays or tests that come later. If you are in the chemistry lab and suddenly everything seems overwhelming, go back to where you were able to understand the material. Most likely, you have taken too big of a step and "bitten off more than you can chew", so now you just need to go back and start again, this time taking "smaller bites."

Tip #2: Look up words you don't know

Whenever you are reading and come across a word you don't know, stop and look it up. It's time-consuming, especially when you first start doing it, but it's worth the effort. An interesting study showed that if you do not stop to look up a word you don't understand, the pages that come after it might as well be blank, because your brain is not able to take in the information. Experiment for yourself. If you are studying and suddenly find yourself "not getting it," go back and see if there were any words you didn't understand. Then take the time to look those words up and you will find that you are now able to understand the material going forward.

Tip #3: Make it tangible

If you find that you are not able to understand something, it often helps if you can draw it out. For example, if you are studying history and it all seems like a big blur, draw it out on paper, showing how one event or person led to another. If you don't have paper handy, you can use pennies. Just anything to get the information out of your head and turned into something you can see and touch. You'll be amazed how well this works.

Tip #4: First things first

"First things first", sounds grandmotherly, but it's actually a good rule. If you put off studying until later in the day, odds are you will get too busy or become too tired to get it done. But if you get your studying done early in the day, it will be done and you won't have to worry or stress about it. If you study first thing every day, it will become a habit and you will do it automatically, without having to think about it.

The Bottom Line

The bottom line is that grades matter because you want to think of yourself as a powerful "A" student. This will give you the confidence to dream big and set challenging goals for yourself, because you will know in your heart that you have the staying power to achieve them.

I still say the only education worth anything is self-education.
- Robert Frost

Rebecca Kochenderfer, M.A., is Senior Editor and Co-Founder of Homeschool.com, the #1 homeschooling site on the Internet, with over two million visitors a year. She is also the author of two popular homeschooling books: *Homeschooling and Loving It* and *Homeschooling For Success.*

Listen to this chapter at HowToLearn.com/amazing-grades-audio

Are You Prepared for Learning and Work? Assessing 21st Century Skills

Change is omnipresent in today's world. Knowledge is growing exponentially as technology continually transforms the way we live and work. From local to state and national perspectives, global markets and forces are transcendent.

Stunning scientific and engineering advances have brought with them vexing social, political, and economic dilemmas. Individually and collectively, citizens in a democracy need to be able to respond to these changing conditions, make informed decisions, and take action to solve current and future challenges.

It would seem to go without saying that students of today must be prepared to take hold of life's demands and thrive in tomorrow's world.

The changing nature of the workplace is a prime case in point. The routine jobs of yesterday are being replaced by technology and/or shipped off shore. In their place, job categories that require knowledge management, abstract reasoning, and personal services seem to be growing. These jobs involve skills that cannot easily be automated, such as adaptive problem solving, critical thinking, complex decision making, ethical reasoning, and innovation.

Technology cannot be programmed to serve as supervisors or to perform tasks that rely on effective human interactions. It cannot easily be trained to negotiate, persuade, or perceptively handle person-to-person interactions. It cannot teach a classroom of students, treat the sick, care for the elderly, wait on tables, or provide other such services. These are all tasks for humans.

Effectiveness in the workforce also requires the ability to work autonomously, be self-motivating and self-monitoring, and engage in lifelong learning. Individuals must be able to adapt to new work environments, communicate using a variety of mediums, and interact effectively with others from diverse cultures. Increasingly, workers must be able to work remotely in virtual teams.

This broad set of cognitive and affective capabilities that undergirds success today often is referred to as "21st century skills." Numerous reports from higher education, the business community, and labor market researchers alike argue that such skills are valued by employers, critical for success in higher education, and underrepresented in today's high school graduates. [end of article reprinted with permission]

Editor's note: As the article above continues into a full book called *Assessing 21st Century Skills*, (see reprint quote below), we consider what it will take to ensure that you, the student, know 'how to learn; and get better grades, and have the cognitive, interpersonal and intrapersonal skills you need to succeed in this century.

Do you feel prepared in all these areas? If not, what steps do you believe you can take to add these skills to those you already have?

Cognitive skills involve critical thinking, systems thinking and solving problems in a unique way; **interpersonal skills** require that you can work with a team, deal with diversity, communicate in complex ways and are culturally sensitive; **interpersonal skills** development means that you can manage your time well, adapt to change, have good executive functioning skills, and can regulate yourself.

Throughout *Amazing Grades*, there are chapters addressing each of these skills as they relate to getting better grades in school. Getting higher grades is a representation of each of the skills you use the rest of your life in school, work, home, community, country and the world.

We hope we have done our best to provide you as many opportunities as possible to attain these skills.

Everyone here has the sense that right now is one of those moments when we are influencing the future.

- Steve Jobs

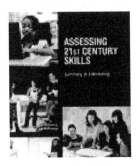

Reprinted with permission from the National Academies Press, Copyright [2011], National Academy of Sciences. Reprinted from *Assessing 21st Century Skills: Summary of A Workshop* by Judith Anderson Koenig, Rapporteur; National Research Council; Board on Testing and Assessment (BOTA); and Behavioral and Social Sciences and Education (DBASSE) organizations (Quote added).

Listen to this chapter at HowToLearn.com/amazing-grades-audio

A

accommodations xii, 127, 129, 131-2, 144, 202

acronyms 85-6, 184

acrostics 85-6

ADHD (attention deficit hyper-activity disorder) vii, ix, xii, 71-2, 127-8, 136, 139-40, 144, 147-8, 149-50, 191-2, 197-8, 199-200

ADHD, diagnosis of 149-50,197-8

advocate vii, ix, 47, 52, 131-2, 141, 163, 172, 198, 200, 201-2

algebra iii, vii, 42, 77-8, 79-80, 89, 105

alpha state 41-2

anti-stress 7-8

anxiety vii, viii, 21, 28, 37, 43, 59-60, 149, 157-8, 161-2, 165-6, 197-8, 200

Arduini, Douglas 124

Armendaris, Francesca 158

Asperger's vii, xii, 141-2

associations 24, 43, 86, 102, 111, 155

attention deficit hyperactivity disorder see ADHD

attitude vii, 7-8, 30, 47, 63, 76, 93, 163, 165, 171, 177-8, 181, 189, 195

auditory learners xi, 56, 101

autism 27-8, 142, 143, 191-2, 202

Azad, Kalid 84

B

balance vii, 7, 22, 27, 43-4, 46, 77-8, 150

Ball, Amanda 4

Barnhill, Frank 198

Beadle, Phil 660

Beale, Abby Marks 116

behavior ix, 16, 24, 29, 46, 107, 139-40, 146, 147, 149-50, 152, 159-60, 163, 165-6, 173, 193, 195, 197-8, 199-200

child's 197-8, 199

behavior problems 173, 197-8, 199-200

behavioral optometrists 35-6

beliefs 63, 91, 160, 163, 166, 187, 195

Berg, Howard Stephen 126

better grades iii, vii, viii, x, xi, xii, 3, 11, 16, 17-8, 19-20, 21, 23, 37, 41-2, 50, 72, 73-4, 87-8, 94, 99, 101-2, 103-4,121-2, 133-4, 141-2, 147-8, 173, 191-2, 201, 203, 205, 207

better study skills 113-4

bilingual 195

biology viii, 85-6, 88, 90, 107, 177, 183-4

Boniface, Carl 8

Borenson, Henry 78

brain vii, viii, ix, xi, xii, 7, 11,13-4, 17-8, 19-20, 21-2, 23-4, 27-8, 29, 37-8, 41-2, 43-4, 46, 51, 53-4, 55-6, 59, 64, 65-6, 72, 75, 83, 95-6, 98, 102, 105, 111, 114, 115, 117, 125-6, 134, 135-6, 145-6, 147-8, 161, 184, 191-2, 197, 204

better ix, 147, 191-2

child's 147

human 13, 111, 117

brain cells 14, 23-4

brain development 21

brain for better grades viii, 147-8

brain functions 23, 54, 191

Brain Gym 43, 46

brain health, optimal 14, 147

Brain Healthy Foods Relate To Higher Test Scores vii, 13-4

brain injury, traumatic 191-2,

Brain Matters That Make A Difference In Your Grades vii, 23-4

Brain To Boost Your Grades vii, 43-4, 46

brain training 191-2

brain waves 41

brainstorm 59, 92, 120, 124

brainstorming 83, 123, 129

breakfast xii, 13, 17-8, 23, 58, 59, 142

Brewer, Jan 178

bullies viii, 152, 153-4

bullying viii, 16, 151-2, 153-4, 165, 171, 196, 197-8

bullying behavior 152

C

calculators 79

calculus iii, viii, 75, 79-80, 83-4, 105, 181

Camacho, Cristina 100

Cantarella, Marcia 62

carbohydrates, complex 13, 23

Carder, Barbara ii, 40

cards 62, 67-8, 85, 87, 89-90, 94, 125-6, 137-8, 155

flash 58, 67, 75, 85, 109-10, 185

Carreker, Suzanne 108

Cerullo, Claudio 152

Chambless, Kendra 102

Chessen, Eric 28

Clark, Patricia 42

CLEP viii, 125-6

Clifton, Alison 176

cognitive skills 191, 205

college iii, vii, viii, 27, 31-2, 33-4, 40, 48, 51, 57, 61-2, 63-4, 71, 99-100, 101, 104, 105-6, 109, 115-16, 118, 119, 125-6, 129-30, 131-2, 143-4, 157-8, 177, 179, 181, 195, 201-2, 203

right vii, 31-2

college courses 118

college permission 132

college students 104, 115, 203

community colleges 31-2, 33

comprehension viii, xi, 35, 43-4, 45-6, 62, 71-2, 86, 97-1, 107, 111, 113-4, 123, 125, 207

reading 44, 45-6, 71, 11, 113-4

computers 27, 75, 130, 145, 181

concentration xii, 3, 7, 13, 23-4, 43, 46, 55, 115-16, 147, 161, 207

confidence 5-6, 29, 53-4, 58, 71, 123, 130, 157, 159, 164, 167, 171, 173-4, 203-4

Conway, Barbara 108

creative visualization vii, 41-2

creativity xiii, 21, 24, 27-8, 45, 55-6, 67, 169

Crowder, Deborah 66

cultural beings 187

cultural matters ix, 187-8

culture 37, 155, 157, 165, 171, 187-8, 205

curiosity 26, 43, 63, 99, 169, 175

curriculum 1-2, 72, 137, 165, 173, 179, 182, 183, 188, 195

D

Dennison, Paul and Gail 46

DePorter, Bobbi 64

depression 161-2, 197-8

Devine, Becca 202

DHA 14, 147-8

diagnosis 140, 149-50, 161, 197-8

diagrams 62, 109, 121, 165, 179, 185

disability 127-8, 129-30, 131-2, 197-8, 202

Disabled Student Services (DSS) 131-2

disorders 127, 140, 147, 149, 197

diversity 185, 187-8, 195, 205

Dixon, Marva T. 196

Dorsey, Megan 144

Downs, Chalon 90

dysgraphia xii, 127-8, 130

dyslexia viii, xii, 133-4, 139, 191

E

eating xii, 13, 17, 23, 28, 148, 156, 161, 191

education viii, ix, xi, xii, xiii, 1-2, 4, 7, 28, 31, 33, 58, 71, 102, 109, 131, 137-8, 144, 146, 148, 152, 157, 159, 167, 175-6, 177-8, 179, 181-2, 193, 195-6, 201-2, 203, 205

child's 181, 193

education technology ix, 181-2

effective goals 47-8

effort 9, 15, 19, 29, 47, 51, 54, 64, 73, 80, 91, 100, 134, 143, 151, 164, 165, 167, 175, 189, 193-4, 195, 204

best 64

ELLs (English Language Learners) viii, ix, 157-8, 185-6

emotions vii, 1, 11-12, 65, 119

negative 11-12

employers 71, 205

engagement ix, 1, 54, 163, 193-4, 196

English viii, ix, 82, 84, 95, 105, 111, 113, 141, 144, 155-6, 157-8, 179, 183-4, 185-6

English class 111, 141, 157

English language viii, ix, 105, 155-6, 157-8, 185-6

English Language Learners see ELLs

EQ 165, 194

equations 52, 75, 77-8, 82, 84, 90, 166

abstract 77-8

algebraic 77

essay viii, x, 43, 57, 59, 94, 99-100, 105, 117-18, 129, 157, 203

evaluation, child's 198, 201

exams iii, vii, xii, 15-16, 23, 47-8, 49-50, 51, 57, 59-60, 61, 87-8, 94, 126, 184, 191

exercises 7-8, 21, 24, 56, 74, 95, 119-20, 176, 185, 191-2, 203

expectations 40, 49, 57, 122, 144, 151, 159, 171-2, 189-90, 193, 199

behavioral 189

eye-hand coordination problems 35

Eye-Q Reading Inventory xi, xiii, 207

eyes iii, 4, 5-6, 15-16, 21, 24, 35-6, 42, 44, 45, 58, 93, 115, 122, 125, 134, 145, 197

mind's 134

F

failures 9, 163-4, 196

fats viii, 13-14, 18, 23, 147-8

Fay, Kayla 136

fear 3, 39, 158, 159, 162, 166

feedback loop 189-90

feelings 4, 6, 9, 11, 15, 24, 145-6, 161-2, 185

finish college viii, 125-6

fish oil supplements 147-8

fitness vii, 7, 27-8

fitness programs 27-8

foods vii, 13-14, 17-18, 23, 74

formula ix, 7, 42, 55, 79-80, 81-2, 83, 85, 111, 117, 125, 148, 193-4, 195-6

Forwood, Albert 22

functions 20, 23, 31, 54, 74, 79, 145, 191

graphs of 79

G

games viii, 24, 58, 102, 123-4, 138, 153, 155, 179, 185-6, 191, 199-200

getting good grades 61, 141, 205

Gibson, Ken 192

Glaeser, Barbara 132

Glavac, Marjan 168

glucose 13, 23

goal-setting 47-8, 167

goals vii, ix, x, 9-10, 28, 31, 33-4, 39, 46, 47-8, 57, 65, 73-4, 123, 144, 163-4, 167, 171-2, 183, 193, 199, 201-2, 204

ineffective 47-8

long-term 73, 171

set 47, 123, 167, 171, 199

weak 47

Goldstein, Elisha 38

Google viii, 1, 21, 95, 103-4, 126, 154, 202

GPA 32, 40, 48, 61, 71, 73, 86, 203

grades ii, iii, iv, v, vi, vii, viii, ix, x, xi, xii, xiii, 2, 3-4, 11, 14, 16, 17-8, 19-20, 21, 23-4, 27, 31, 35, 37, 39, 41-2, 43-4, 46, 47-8, 53, 61-2, 63, 65-6, 67-8, 71-2, 73-4, 75, 80, 87-8, 90, 94, 99, 101-2, 103-4, 105, 109, 111, 121-2, 123, 130, 133-4, 141-2, 143, 145-6, 147-8, 149, 151, 153, 158, 159-60, 167, 173, 177, 183, 191-2, 197, 201, 203-4, 205, 207

best iii, vii, viii, x, xi, xii, 3, 11, 16, 17-8, 19-20, 21, 23, 37, 41-2, 73-4, 87-8, 94, 99, 101-2, 103-4, 121-2, 133-4, 141-2, 147-8, 173, 191-2, 201, 203, 205, 207

excellent xiii, 47

good iii, vii, x, xi, xii, xiii, 3-4, 27, 39, 61-2, 141, 149, 153, 159-60, 177, 203

grades faster v, vii, xi, 41, 47-8, 207

grammar 128

graphic organizers 94, 113, 183, 194

graphs 79, 88, 121, 127-8, 179, 195

Guffanti, Stephen 150

Gupta, Ujjwal 58

H

habits xii, xiii, 2, 13, 28, 67, 203

hands x, 21, 24, 45, 85, 102, 109, 115, 161, 170, 173, 181, 184, 185

happiness vii, 29-30, 161

Harris, Ed 190

Harter, Angela 110

high school viii, 27, 51, 67, 71, 99-100, 105, 117-8, 129, 131-2, 150, 157, 167, 175, 177, 201-2, 205

high school and college viii, 51, 99-100, 129

high school life 117-8

high school students 27, 118, 175

higher education xiii, 7, 33, 157, 205

history viii, 1, 33, 42, 82, 93-4, 97, 109, 111, 121-2, 123-4, 140, 162, 187, 204

Hodgdon, Linda 142

Holland, Donnie 10

Homeschool ix, 203

homeschool students 203

Homeschoolers ix, 203-4

homework 25, 64, 67, 72, 73, 80, 99, 119, 123, 135-6, 141-2, 163, 182, 194, 199

Hornick, Lisa M. 92

HowToLearn.com v, vi, xi, xii, 207

hyperactivity 147, 197, 199

I

identity 187-8

improve comprehension 113-4, 207

impulsivity 197, 199

inattention 35, 197, 199

involvement, parental 189-90

J

Jones, Ellen 172

Jordan, Michael 6

K

Kamal, Rick 74

Kamal, Teena 112

Kastner, Robin J. 162

Kelman, Jennifer 16

keywords 49, 55, 87-8, 103
kinesthetic learners viii, 109-10
Kirkland, Nneka 80
Klein, Erin 68
Kochenderfer, Rebecca 204
Koenig, Judith Anderson 206
Konstenius, Stephen A. 14
Krajnjan, Steven 174
Kruger, Susan 72
Kuhn, Robert 122

L

language ii, viii, ix, xii, 11, 15, 43,
45, 95-6, 99, 105, 131,139-40, 147,
155-6, 157-8, 163, 165-6, 173,
183-4, 185-6, 187, 191, 195-6
language learning viii, 95-6
laugh vii, 19-20, 153
laughter 20, 179
LD see Learning Disability
learning differences viii, x, xi,
127-8, 129-30, 131-2, 133, 135,
137, 139, 141, 143-4, 195
learning disabilities 71-2
Learning Disability (LD) 127,
130, 131, 198
learning environments 102, 172, 193
learning history 121
learning problems 35, 145
learning styles xii, 57, 109, 177,
183, 194, 207
life skills ii, vii, x, xii, xiii, 1, 3, 5,
7, 9, 11, 13, 15, 17, 19, 21, 23,
25, 27, 29, 31, 33
lifestyle, healthy 191, 196
lifetime earnings 57
listening xi, xii, 43-4, 45, 51-2, 56, 63,
71, 80, 96, 101, 105, 109, 114, 121,
155-6, 107, 171, 177-8, 184, 185

M

Mali, Taylor 25-6
Marshall, Keri 148
mastery ix, 51, 177-8, 184
mastery learning 177-8
math iii, viii, x, 1-2, 13, 30, 48, 52,
55, 57, 62, 69, 73, 77, 79-80, 81-2,
84, 89, 105, 110, 118, 123-4, 126,
127-8, 141, 144, 183, 201-2
math specialist 201-2
mathematics 33, 79-80
Mavredakis, John Patrick 130
McLeod, Maire 138
meaning xi, 34, 72, 76, 77-8, 82,

85, 93, 107, 110, 125, 133, 145,
155-6, 184, 186, 187-8
unit of 107
medication 144, 147, 149-50, 161-2
Meek, J. Collins 134
Memler, Jeff 94
memorize 1, 42, 49, 51-2, 55, 65,
75, 86, 95, 111, 117
memorizing 41, 49, 55, 58, 76,
111-2, 113, 123, 125, 157
memory vii, x, xi, 13, 21, 23-4, 38,
43, 51-2, 53-4, 55-6, 59, 63-4, 72,
75-6, 85, 89, 110, 111-2, 116, 120,
126, 147-8, 161, 191, 199, 207
photographic 53-4
mental pictures 75-6, 111
metaphors 75-6
Milner, Richard 188
mind xi, xiii, 2, 3, 5-6, 15, 21-2,
26, 27, 29, 37-8, 41-2, 47-8, 52,
53-4, 56, 58, 59, 63, 71, 73, 80,
87, 91-2, 97, 111-2, 114, 115, 119,
122, 125, 129, 133-4, 143, 155,
159, 173, 175-6, 197, 198, 202
open 91, 119, 155, 198
state of 5
mind maps 87
mindfulness 38
Mohd, Suria 18
money 9, 30, 34, 39, 83, 111, 149, 190
morphemes 107-8
motivation vii, 2, 9-10, 25, 28, 39-
40, 50, 64, 65, 71, 75, 89, 123, 127,
146, 161-2, 163, 175, 195, 199
Mouchmouchian, Koko 32
music vii, 24, 51-2, 63, 68, 72,
96, 112, 137, 176, 179, 203, 207
classical 51

N

neurons 14, 23, 28, 65, 192
Ningo, Loniece Wesbee 184
Nordic Naturals 148

O

ODD (Oppositional Defiant
Disorder) vii, xii, 139-40
office hours vii, 25-6
Olson, Steve 34
Olyai, Tina 160
omega viii, 14, 18, 23, 147-8
omega-3s 18, 147-8
OEP 36
Optometric Education Program

Foundation xi, 36
O'Regan, Fin 140
outline 3, 109, 116, 118, 135
oxygen 13, 19-20, 23-4

P

Panzo, Shannon 54
parents iii, vii, ix, x, 2, 15-6, 27-8,
30, 33, 35, 40, 48, 53, 61, 74, 114,
131-2, 139, 141, 145-6, 149-50,
151-2, 153-4, 159-60, 166, 167,
173, 181-2, 183, 189-90, 191, 193,
195-6, 197-8, 199-200, 201, 203
Parent's Formula ix, 193-4, 196
passion 150, 159, 169, 175, 193
pathways 32, 65-6, 191
Pavliv, Gregory 52
peer group 16, 159
peer pressure viii, 159-60
peers 40, 65-6, 67, 80, 129, 139-
40, 148, 151, 153-4, 159-60
Philomena, Sister Maria 98
phone, smart vii, x, 43, 65, 96,
123, 142
phonemes 137-8
picture map vii, 49-50
pictures xi, 4, 41, 49, 59, 62, 63, 72,
75-6, 85, 87, 97, 109, 111, 113-4,
121, 133, 135, 155, 185-6, 195
making 114
playing games 24, 123, 200
playlist 51-2
Plevin, Rob 170
Post-Traumatic Stress Disorder
(PTSD) 162
precalculus viii, 79-80
presentations 79, 176, 179
pretest 177
protein 13-14, 23
Puri, Amita 180

Q

Questions vi, 1, 25, 31, 54, 55-6, 59,
65-6, 75-6, 80, 86, 87-8, 97-8, 100,
105-6, 110, 113, 121, 123, 125, 132,
135,138, 139-40, 141, 143-4, 149,
158, 159, 164, 165, 169-70, 171,
174, 175, 183, 186, 188, 198, 201
exam 87, 175
good 2, 25-6

R

Reading, Mike 104
recall iii, xi, 13, 19-20, 24, 37, 46, 56,

59, 71, 85-6, 111-12, 126, 141, 177
Reifman, Steve 30
relax 5, 21, 24, 41-2, 43, 45, 54, 90, 105, 115, 134
Remick, Kristy xi, 146
resiliency 171-2
retention 1, 13, 52-2, 111, 114
review 39, 56, 58, 59, 62, 63-4, 72, 87, 94, 105-6, 116, 120, 121, 135, 140, 141, 148, 193
rewards vii, 9-10, 169, 199
rights vi, 93, 131, 165, 201
Rose, Colin 2

S

Sanders, Susan M. 120
Saparov, Philip 118
Sarris, Jim 96
Sasson, Dorit 186
SAT iii, vii, viii, 57-8, 84, 97, 105-6, 110, 122, 143-4, 183-4
scan tags 40, 43
second language viii, 155-6, 157-8, 184, 191, 195,
Seifert, Kathy 153-4
self-advocate 131
self-esteem vii, 15-6, 146
short-term goals 73
Siddiqui, Ahmed 182
Sirvent, Ralph ii, 70
Smith, James 56
Smith, Lorraine 88
Smith-Walters, Cindi 86
social studies 94, 121-2
speaker, native 95-6
special education 102, 122, 123, 131-2, 144, 146, 195, 201-2
special education teacher 122, 131
special factors viii, x, 145, 147, 149, 151, 153, 155, 157, 161
Special Section for Parents ix, 191, 193, 195, 197, 199, 201, 203
Special Section for Teachers ix, 165, 167, 169, 171, 173, 175, 177, 179, 181, 183, 185, 187
Sriram, Meenakshi 156
standardized test scores 143
Stern, Rory 200
Stewart, Beverly 106
stop bullying 151, 154
strategies iii, iv, vii, viii, ix, x, xi, xii, xiii, 1-2, 9, 30, 31, 40, 52, 55, 63-4, 69, 71-2, 73-4, 77, 79-80, 81, 83, 85, 87-8, 89, 91, 93-4, 95, 97, 99,

101, 103, 105, 107, 109-10, 111-12, 113, 115-16, 117, 119, 121, 123, 125, 134, 137-8, 140, 142,143-4, 147, 151, 159, 163, 165, 173, 183-4, 185, 192, 193, 196, 199-200
stress vii, xi, xii, 2, 7-8, 13, 19-20, 21, 24, 28, 37-8, 42, 43, 46, 54, 60, 74, 90, 105-6, 123, 127, 129-30, 139, 149, 155, 161-2, 165, 199, 203, 207
sources of 74
Study Skills vii, x, 35, 37, 39, 41, 43, 45-6, 47, 49, 51, 53, 56, 61, 63, 67, 69, 71-2, 73, 75, 87, 113-4, 122, 183, 194
study skills and time management skills 183
study skills class 71
study skills strategies 87
success ii, ix, x, xi, xii, 2, 4, 9, 11, 13, 16, 18, 27-8, 34, 40, 41, 47-8, 54, 57, 59, 63, 72, 73-4, 77-8, 80, 90, 94, 97, 111, 114, 116, 118, 130, 131, 134, 137, 143, 150, 161, 163-4, 165, 167, 171-2, 173, 189-90, 191, 193-4, 195-6, 199, 201, 204, 205
academic x, 13, 73, 111, 118, 171
child's ix, 189, 193-4, 196, 201
social 189

T

table, periodic 42, 89, 111
tablets vii, 67-8, 123, 182
Tan, Xavier 50
target language 95-6
Taufik, Hyder 48
teachers iii, vii, ix, x, xiii, 1-2, 3, 15-16, 17, 19, 25-6, 33, 35, 51-2, 59, 64, 76, 94, 100, 102, 103-4, 111, 114, 130, 131-2, 139, 141-2, 145-6, 152, 154, 155, 158, 159, 163, 165, 167-8, 169-70, 171-2, 173-4, 175, 177-8, 179-80, 181-2,183-4, 185-6, 187-8, 189, 193, 195, 197-8, 199
good 25, 163
international 183-4
local 183-4
technology vii, viii, ix, x, 30, 33, 65-6, 67-8, 71, 101-2, 121, 173, 175, 179, 181-2, 205
term memory, long 24, 53-4, 64, 72, 85, 191
Terry, Bonnie 114
test vii, xi, 13-14, 19, 25-6, 31, 37-8, 41, 43, 46, 52, 53-4, 57-8, 62, 64, 65, 69, 71, 73,

75, 80, 86, 97-8, 105-6, 109-10, 111-12, 113, 121, 123, 129, 131, 134, 135-6, 143-4, 145-6, 147-8, 159, 178, 179, 183-4, 195-6
test-taking xi, 43, 46, 54, 64, 129, 144, 183, 196
textbooks 76, 80, 84, 93-4, 109, 113, 179, 181-2
digital 182
thesis 117-18
thesis statement 117-18
Thompson, Julia 164
time management 49-50, 71, 73, 183, 199, 203
time management skills 73, 183, 203

U

understanding diversity 188

V

values 16, 64, 77-8, 79, 159-60, 185, 187, 192
cube 7
Vass, Andy 166
vision viii, xi, 35-6, 46, 76, 145-6, 152
vision problems 35-6, 146
vision skills 145-6
visual learners ix, 99, 183
visual problems 35-6
visual representations 78, 79
visual skills vii, xi, xiii, 35-6, 145-6
visualize 1, 15, 24, 35-6, 42, 44, 76, 111-12, 135
visualizing 24, 41-2, 111, 114
Vizard, Dave 24
vocabulary vii, 58, 80, 85, 87, 96, 98, 99, 105, 107-8, 110, 120, 125, 138, 144, 147, 157, 183, 185-6

W

Watson, Judy 20
Woodworth, James 6
word problems 77-8
words/sentences 186
writing classes 157
Wyman, Pat v, vi, xiii

Y

Young, Scott 76

Z

Zainuddin, Zeal 12

Helpful Resources for Amazing Grades!

Free ★ **Learning Styles Quiz**

This Learning Styles Quiz tells you how you learn best so you can learn in your preferred style. It helps you get better grades faster as well as how to adjust your learning materials to you!

Take the Learning Styles Quiz now at HowToLearn.com

Free ★ **Eye-Q Reading Inventory™**

This reading inventory shows you exactly how you are seeing the printed page when you read, what you do that may make you tired, lose your place or forget what you read. The inventory helps everyone understand what they may need to do to speed up their reading and improve comprehension for better grades. Great for students and adults.

Take the Eye-Q Reading Inventory™ today at tinyurl.com/czefhzo

★ **Music and Learning**

The Mozart Effect music is well-known to help improve concentration, focus, and memory as you learn. We use these CD's every day in our office!

Take a look at the Mozart Effect now at tinyurl.com/c3j3fl7

★ **Colored Overlays**

Reading specialists and many eye doctors have long recommended placing colored overlays (tinted plastic sheets to cover the entire printed page) on your book or over your computer screen to reduce visual stress when reading. Studies show they have increased reading levels by more than a year in just one week!

See the Colored Overlays now at tinyurl.com/7u36pvk